In Search of the

Baby Boomer

Generation

By Rick Bava

Published by Motivational Press, Inc.
1777 Aurora Road
Melbourne, Florida, 32935
www.MotivationalPress.com

Manufactured in the United States of America.

ISBN: 978-1-62865-201-7

Contents

This book is dedicated to Lisa Marie

Foreword

By Dr. David M. Boush, Ph.D.

In Search of the Baby Boomer Generation is part pop culture history and part autobiography, with maybe a little something from Dr. Phil thrown in. Although there are elements of nostalgia in Rick Bava's "In Search of the Baby Boomer Generation," the themes that he addresses — retirement, second careers, social relationships, caring for the elderly — are top of mind for a large percentage of Baby Boomers today. If you are a Baby Boomer you are sure to identify with the issues and the events related here.

Rick and I met as students living in the Elm Drive B dorm at the University of Wisconsin in 1972, toward the beginning of his story. So I have had the pleasure of sharing some of these ideas and bearing witness to many of his experiences for over 40 years. Rick somehow passed the major milestones and rode the ups and downs sooner and more extremely than most of us, which makes him uniquely qualified to write this book. He was born at about the same time as the character Kevin Arnold (played by Fred Savage) in the television show *The Wonder Years*. Rick was in junior high school during the worst of the Vietnam War. He became the youngest tennis pro at Chicago's Lakeshore Racket Club during the 1970s tennis craze. Rick went on to a very successful corporate career, first serving as a high level manager for Commodore computers in the Northeast at the height of the PC boom, followed by directing external business for Boeing's Computer Services division and leading worldwide business development for Digital Equipment Corporation's services division. Using his established corporate experience, he later founded and served as the CEO of The Bava Group, a respected communications company.

But at the height of his success, Rick was devastated by the decline and passing of both parents and coping with all their health and personal business issues. A short time later, following the unexpected death of his oldest brother, Rick left his comfortable surroundings in Bellevue, Washington. He jumped on a train and began a personal odyssey across the country. He visited his old haunts in Boston and Chicago where he had lived and worked. In the midst of his journey, he also paid a first visit to his father's birthplace in Calabria, Italy, a place he had heard so much about growing up. Upon returning from Italy, Rick continued his journey by train. In the aftermath of the Great Recession, he spent time in some of the areas that were hardest hit by the collapse of the economy. For example, he stopped in Stockton, CA (the foreclosure capital of America at the time) and examined the recession's impact on Baby Boomers living there. While on his journey Rick also paused to mingle with wealthy Boomers in California tennis clubs, the kinds of places that he had spent younger days as a tennis pro. Travelling through Florida, his curiosity led him to stop at the Pepper Center at Florida State University, to learn more about their leading edge research on the aging process. Everywhere Rick went, his outgoing nature led him into conversations with hundreds of others, mostly Baby Boomers like himself, who shared stories and insights about their lives. What started perhaps as a search for himself grew into an intensive study of his generation and the new challenges associated with growing older. In April 2011, Rick began writing what became a successful blog about Baby Boomers and speaking publicly about issues close to their hearts, and to his.

Walking in front of a Starbucks in Palm Springs that spring evening, he never saw the driver that hit him and just kept going. Rick was in a coma for two days. When he woke up, he saw double, and pretty much everything was broken or bruised. But the story has a happy ending. We can fast forward through the physical therapy and the worry about permanent vision impairment. Rick fully recovered against the odds, and, in his late 50s met the woman of his dreams. He was the best man at my wedding in 1979 and I returned the favor in 2013.

Now, Rick has combined his unique story, and all the unique stories of those he has talked with, into this book about shared experience. I think that you will really enjoy it.

David M. Boush, is a Professor of Business at University of Oregon and Executive Director of Oregon's Executive MBA program. Dr. Boush authored the scholarly book "Deception In The Marketplace: The Psychology of Deceptive Persuasion and Consumer Self-Protection." He was previously a visiting professor at ESSEC, in Cergy-Pontoise, France, and has taught e-commerce classes in Mexico City, Buenos Aires, Santiago, and Bogota. Professor Boush's research on trust, consumer socialization, and brand equity has been published in the Journal of Consumer Research, Journal of Marketing Research, Journal of Business Research, Journal of the Academy of Marketing Sciences, Journal of Public Policy & Marketing, and the Journal of International Business Studies. Dr. Boush has played a pivotal role as a consultant to Rick Bava since 2007 on his work regarding the Baby Boomer Generation.

Acknowledgements

First and foremost, this book was written based on the inspiration I received from my wife, Dr. Lisa Wodicka. She has been a true partner with me on this book, as she is a partner in life. This book was truly a team effort in every sense.

This book received its genesis as an outgrowth of discussions with Dr. David M. Boush. This book received its vision, mission, goals, and objectives based on the consultation and friendship of Professor Boush, who I am proud to have as a best friend.

I would also like to recognize the staff at the Del Mar Library of Del Mar, California, where much of the early part of the book was written. Gretchen Schmidt was the library manager during the time that I worked on the book there and she was most helpful. Each morning during that same period, my friend Bruce Weber, a distinguished library patron, helped me talk through some of the topics covered in this book, and I will forever be grateful for those discussions.

I would also like to acknowledge Ariela Wilcox, a literary agent, who provided some initial consultation at the beginning of the book process, and Sharon Cutler and Esther Reisberg who provided some of the early editing for part of this book.

I am very grateful to the following distinguished individuals for reviewing the book and providing their commentary: Al Erisman, Susan Mallard, Howard Sholkin, Fred Raley, Al Breton, and Michael Smith, Ed Graziano, and Jim Gilmartin. Their input and sincere comments were greatly appreciated. As the final manuscript took shape, Jodi Lipson, Jennifer Perillo, and Julie Loehr provided some much appreciated feedback. Their expertise in the world of publishing was most valuable.

This book found its publisher when Wally Hauck provided a recommendation; he assured me that Motivational Press was the right avenue for "In Search of the Baby Boomer Generation." I could not agree more with Wally. Justin Sachs and the team at Motivational Press have been incredibly supportive, and I am grateful that they are my publisher.

Finally, I would like to thank the vast number of Baby Boomers who talked to me as I gathered the data that led to the writing of this book. Without all of you, there would not be a book. So, it is with great appreciation that I recognize the Baby Boomers from all across the country who lent their voices to this book.

Publisher's Perspective

By Justin Sachs – CEO Motivational Press

Rick Bava's "In Search of the Baby Boomer Generation" is a thought-provoking read about one of the most interesting generations in American history.

This book will be of great interest and value to a wide range of different audiences. The author, Rick Bava, is a thought leader for the Baby Boomer generation and primarily directs his book to these 78 million "Boomers." But this book clearly has a much wider appeal, including the vast audience from other generations who want to learn more about the Baby Boomer Generation. The children and grandchildren of Baby Boomers will enjoy reading about the generation of their parents or grandparents, much as the Baby Boomers themselves were fascinated reading about their parents' generation in Tom Brokaw's book "The Greatest Generation." Furthermore, individuals, businesses, and other organizations who provide services or resources to Baby Boomers, as well as those who market to this generation, will find that this book provides invaluable in-depth knowledge and understanding of the Baby Boomer Generation.

Motivational Press welcomes this insightful commentary on the Baby Boomer generation. We are confident that the thoughts expressed by Rick

Bava in this book will resonate with the readers. Most Baby Boomers are curious about their peers. They have an understanding that knowledge about their own lives can be enhanced by a snapshot glance at others of their demographic.

In Search of the Baby Boomer Generation will help you understand the Baby Boomer generation. It offers commentary about the topics, issues, and concerns most germane to the Baby Boomer generation. Baby Boomers will enjoy a retro feel with some looks back at the times that they have been through, in addition to a pointed look at Baby Boomers in the context of the here-and-now. The book also provides a discussion of concerns that Baby Boomers will need to pay attention to going forward, as they live out the remainder of their lives.

The concept of this book arose out of the very successful blog, "Rick Bava on the Baby Boomer Generation." The columns generated an enormous amount of interest and positive feedback, prompting Mr. Bava to write something on a larger scale to reach a wider audience. Following the introduction, the book is organized into chapters based on the topics of most interest to Baby Boomers, with the heart of each chapter consisting of a collection of Rick Bava's columns. At the beginning of each chapter is an introduction to the issues and topics discussed in the collection of columns. The introduction sets up a detailed analysis and commentary that leads into interesting stories or columns that fully explore the topic. At the conclusion of each chapter is relevant insight related to the issues discussed within the chapter. The book reaches its summation in an epilogue that sets the stage for the future of the Baby Boomer generation.

Introduction

It is a cloudy Wednesday morning in the summer of 2008. Like most Wednesdays, I sit and talk with my best friend and fellow Baby Boomer, who is now a distinguished professor at the University of Oregon. Amidst the conversation about the Presidential campaign, and discussion of family and current lifestyle, comes a revelation. I reveal to my best friend that something is lacking in my life. Perhaps it is the sadness of having lost my parents and an older brother, whom I deeply loved. This is a condition many Baby Boomers face — the loss of loved ones. Baby Boomers, so fixated on being a generation of youth, now face the grim reality that as they age, the people they care most about in life, like elderly parents, are lost or have to be cared for when Father Time begins to take hold.

In 2008, like many Baby Boomers then, and today, I was struggling with the direction of my career. Somehow all the years had caught up with me. It seems, as Baby Boomers, we have lived our lives on a treadmill, and now the workout has made us tired. It has left us searching for the meaning of life. As Baby Boomers, we want to recapture the spirit of our youth. We were, after all, whom President Kennedy was talking about when he said, "The torch has been passed to a new generation." We, more than any generation, embraced what it meant to be a Baby Boomer, long before the phrase had meaning. We are a generation that lived through the assassination of a President, the Vietnam War, and a man walking on the moon. We are a generation that lived through cultural change in society and witnessed the dawning of technology. And above all, we became the generation that represented "corporate life."

When I was in college at the University of Wisconsin in the 1970s, I could never have imagined that one day in 2008, I would be talking with that same college buddy – my best friend – about the past. For, during my college days, the world was in front of me; expectations were great and life was limitless. It seemed my bucket list (before there was a term for such a thing) was so expansive that yellow legal pads could not keep track of all the dreams. I wanted so much to experience life, to travel, and to have success. Like many Baby Boomers' experiences, my college years were rich with friendships, dorm life, and college life, which remain part of my most cherished memories. One of the objectives of this book is to tell the story of Baby Boomers through my own experiences. Further, it is to incorporate through observation, the perspectives of other Baby Boomers. It is through that thought pattern that we will get a representation of the generation.

Growing up with parents who loved me unconditionally, I was taught that education was important, that the way you carried yourself was important, and that extended family and friendships were important. My parents believed in education. Like the American people as a whole, we were once a family who came to this country, ours from the Southern part of Italy. My parents were products of what Tom Brokaw called "The Greatest Generation" – signifying that this generation had lived through the Great Depression, World War II, and moved from being city dwellers to life in suburbia. And yes, they lived through the creation of the Baby Boomer generation.

The Baby Boomer generation is defined as people born between the years 1946 and 1964. There are over 78 million Baby Boomers, with

10,000 of them retiring daily. They remain the generation with the greatest buying power, and, it can be argued, with the most influence. The Baby Boomer generation resulted from the creation of families in the post-World War II era. It represented the growth of America, where statements such as "so goes General Motors, so goes the country" defined the prosperity and strength of the United States of America.

As young Baby Boomers, many of us moved to a new house, went to a school that may have been newly built, and began taking up life in a cul-de-sac. I spent my formative years on the South side of Chicago. My grammar school, Santa Lucia, or Saint Lucy's, a Catholic parochial school, was largely built by a group of concerned citizens of the neighborhood. My parents were among this devoted group of individuals. In the fifth grade, our family took part in the Baby Boomer experiment of the times, the move to the suburbs. We moved to the North side, where the promise of a better life was realized. There, as I attended one of the great grammar schools Chicago had to offer, Queen of All Saints, the slow journey and the foundation of life began. First, there was life in Lincolnwood, Illinois amongst children of my age and stage. It is where life went from, *Ed Sullivan* to Little League baseball, to a future at Notre Dame High School. It is where life went from the Beatles to Lettermen jackets and everything in between. It was the «dawning of the age of Aquarius.»

By the time that college came, so did Title IX (giving women rights and sports equality), the draft lottery, Watergate, and the election of a Southern governor from Georgia, Jimmy Carter. Do you remember, Baby Boomers, in those times, that some said "the times, they are a-changin'"?

This book is not only about those times, but also about the times that we live in now and what comes next for Baby Boomers as we look towards our future. At this point in the introduction, you may think this book is anecdotal, and yes, there is some of that contained in this book. Maybe we can find perspective from the life and times of a fellow Baby Boomer. But you should know this is also based on the lives of hundreds of Baby Boomers.

During those summer calls in 2008, I began talking to my good friend about our generation and about observations I was making. I noticed that things were happening to us economically. I observed a consciousness related to health and wellness. It soon became apparent, for the first time that Baby Boomers were becoming concerned about the aging process. I began talking about the idea that, while having had a successful corporate career, I wanted to make a contribution to society. I began thinking about using my vast communication skills to bring meaning to our generation. With the encouragement of a good friend (and Baby Boomers, don't we need them?), I began my new journey. I have written this book based on what was learned on this journey to tell the story of the Baby Boomer Generation.

From March of 2009 through March 2011, I traveled across America, seeking out Baby Boomers, talking to them about where they have been, where they are, and where they are going in life. I talked extensively to hundreds of Baby Boomers. The sessions could be described as conversational, but always probing. I found my generation to be open, honest, and retrospective. I began talking to them about their visions for their lives and those of other Baby Boomers. I discussed with them the expectations they had for their lives, how it measured up, and what their objectives were going forward. They talked about who they were and what they were about. They spoke of hopes and dreams. They had a wonderful sense of history, of intimate memories in their lives. Many understood that they were part of a special generation. Some longed for the past and the times as they once were. Some were worried about the times that we are living in now. Some had enthusiasm for the days ahead.

In April of 2011, these interactions resulted in the beginning of my widely read blog about Baby Boomers, which later became the foundation of this book. The topics selected, the issues discussed, the commentary given, and the columns summarized are based on input from Baby Boomers in my conversations with them as I traveled across this country interviewing them. Further input was gathered in a Forum in March of

2012, where I was the guest speaker at a forum called "Baby Boomers in the 21st Century." By this time, I had spoken with hundreds Baby Boomers formally, and many more informally. There is common ground in seeking information from your peer group, listening to their attitudes, assessing their needs, and then writing about and communicating the thoughts to fellow Baby Boomers. That is the mission of this book.

Baby Boomers comprise a group that, despite the broad title, includes some very diverse situations. Many older Baby Boomers are already retired or contemplating retirement, while many younger Baby Boomers are still in the workforce, with an eye toward "The Golden Years." Some Baby Boomers have already lost parents and are grieving. Some Baby Boomers are in the process of care giving for their elderly parents. Some Baby Boomers are struggling with the right balance between their lives, travel, and grand-parenting roles, while other Baby Boomers are still struggling with the education of their children in college. Some Baby Boomers are celebrating many years of marriage, while others are products of divorce. Some Baby Boomers are thinking back to their wedding days, while a greater number than ever are single once more, still hoping to find that "one and only."

While there was so much to converse with Baby Boomers about and draw conclusions from, some topics seemed to provide a thread for our generation. It is clear that all Baby Boomers can look back to the cultural aspects of their generation and find synergism. Baby Boomers love to talk about the television of their youth. They cherish the music of their generation and will easily engage in discussions about favorite movies and sports. Baby Boomers are reading more, sending emails to family and friends, spending more time at home, and have found value in the basic pleasures of life. It is also safe to say that Baby Boomers will easily share significant stories and events that had an impact on their lives, and on the lives of all those who are defined as Baby Boomers.

This is an exploration of the Baby Boomer generation – where they have been, where they are now, and where they are going – presented by a Baby Boomer. The book is called "In Search of the Baby Boomer Generation" because that was the vision I had when I went out looking. I can say, as I write this, that I found many things that will give you a better understanding of the Baby Boomer generation.

Chapter 1

Baby Boomers in the 21st Century

On a January day in 2010, a Baby Boomer man sat with his family in the Starbucks at the center of the MGM Resort. He was in Las Vegas with his family, including two sons and two daughters. His wife was in her glory tending to her grand-children. The Baby Boomer man, originally from Indiana, now spent a considerable amount of time in his winter home of Sarasota, Florida. He rejoiced in being with his boys and talking all things Indiana basketball. That, of course, is a contact sport back in the Hoosier state. His one son was actually a Purdue Graduate, but the father was a longtime fan of former Indiana University coach, Bob Knight.

Each year, over the Christmas and New Year Holiday, this proud Baby Boomer man takes his family on a trip. Each year it is somewhere different. This year it was Las Vegas. It is hard to get the family together now, for they live in all different parts of the country. However, they make these family trips a priority, because it is the one time that the forces of togetherness are bound. He is a microcosm of Baby Boomers in the 21st century. He has the elements that a great many Baby Boomers possess. He worked hard, built a business, and his wife is still the love of his life.

They met in college, and have gone through all the stages of life together. These stages included college, marriage, children, daily routines, and now retirement.

Retired from owning an Agriculture business, this Baby Boomer man now examines his life. He thought that he would play golf for the remainder of his life, but that does not seem to be enough. He would like to make a contribution to society, perhaps have a second career. He sometimes thinks he would enjoy doing some consulting. Or maybe he could even mentor young people starting out in the business world. It is a balance that has not yet found equilibrium.

As a couple, this Indiana team, and now Floridians, know they want to travel and see a bit of the world. They want very much to do things that they missed out on earlier in life. Once upon a time, there were the pressures of paying the mortgage and attending school functions for the children. For many years of their lives, they were very involved with their parents, who were always a priority.

Now, they have become diligent about defining their "bucket list." They are making progress on what they consider to be the best places for Baby Boomers to travel to. They were good stewards of their money; they saved and invested wisely. They were prudent in their expenditures because they wanted a nest egg to be available when the time came for retirement. Their wise choice in lifestyle has now been converted into an optimal retirement. One result was the dream second home on the gulf coast of Florida. They have always loved Sarasota. They had vacationed on Long Boat Key, and then spent an extended time there shortly after retirement, all before making the decision on their second home.

There are three things that this couple is proud to have achieved. They have planned well, and thus are financially comfortable. They are grateful to have a wonderful family. And finally, they have a vision for their future. However, this Baby Boomer couple does have some issues. There is the care for elderly parents, and the decision that must be made on assisted living. While all of their children are well adjusted and beginning to raise nice families of their own, they are currently not all enjoying the same levels of success in their careers. The translation for this is that two of the children are doing very well, but the other two have struggled with job losses and require financial support.

Then there is the chasm, between the couple themselves. The female spouse loves being a grandmother; she loves to care for and feed the grandchildren, allowing her motherly instincts to pay dividends. She would feel very comfortable being the family Baby sitter. Her version of "travel," would be spending time at the homes of her children, helping raise her grandchildren. This is in direct contrast to her husband, who uses the phrase uttered by many Baby Boomers on this subject which is, "I have already raised my children."

One last piece of the puzzle, as this story unfolds is an example of Baby Boomers today in the area of health and wellness. This couple is attempting to redefine age. They may love their grandchildren, but they are not their grandparents' grandparent. This is a couple who eats right and exercises on a regular basis. While they are not chasing the fountain of youth, they are trying to be the best that they can be. They do not want to be 25 again, but they do want to live life to the fullest. They want to remain healthy, and live long lives. They want happiness, and realize there is a correlation between the experiences of the mind and the body. Each morning, this couple goes for a walk and they work out three times a week. This supplements the sports activities that they enjoy, which include golf and tennis. What they do not do is sit on the couch. What they do not do is cry in their soup about aging. They may not be in line for Botox to make themselves look younger, but they are trying to lead healthy lifestyles that will help them feel younger.

So this family will enjoy Las Vegas and its sights and sounds while on vacation together, just as they enjoyed the family cruise the year before. But it will not just be about the vacation. It will be about spending time together as a family. The children like it when their parents tell stories about their families. They love hearing about the uncles and aunts that came before. They like it when their parents tell stories of their youth, like how they met and courted. They appreciate stories about their grandparents and great grandparents, especially the ones that involve how their family ancestors came to this country. They love to listen when their Baby Boomer parents recall and talk about their favorite movies or sporting events that shaped their lives.

What this couple tells you a little about is the life and times of Baby Boomers. Baby Boomers, who remember a slower time from their youth, have now learned to navigate the technology of the 21st Century. It is a couple that is proud about the fact that they were the first ones in their families to get a college education. It is a couple who can demonstrate what working hard to build a life can result in. It is a couple who thought carefully about how they wanted to live out the remainder of their life and then researched how to execute their plan successfully.

One final example of this Baby Boomer couple as it relates to the 21st century involves relationships. This is a couple that wants to maintain longtime friendships that they have cultivated. These types of friendships help Baby Boomers recall the past, but also help them focus on the future. In some ways the Baby Boomer generation is in transition, from what was, to what is, and to what can be. This is a transition in all areas of their lives, may it be family, friends, work, career, or a second career. Baby Boomers are trying to determine the here and now, while being steeped in their rich history as a generation.

Thursday, January 19, 2012

Top of the Hill and Bottom

This is a story about the life and times of Baby Boomers. The title, "Top of the Hill and Bottom," reflects the changing conditions that have taken place. Like many columns, this story is the composite of many stories. But through the composite comes the shape of what has happened to a generation.

Life in the suburbs was pretty good with friends, sports, and fresh surroundings. Of course, you were going to go to college. What was this, the dark ages? It was surely a great time to go to college; we were a thinking generation, a change generation, and we certainly did not want to be like our parents. Those parents had crazy notions like pay-as-you-go and sleep easy with no debt. We were idealistic and our music reflected it, as did our appearances, and our "rebel without a cause" attitude toward the establishment.

Oh, how quick one's mindset can change when faced with making a living. Where were all of those jobs during the Carter administration? Are those gas lines that I am in? How is that possible? This is America! But then, there was morning in America, and corporate life was the new badge of honor. Is it possible that the same person who marched in candlelight on the campus of his state school now identifies with President Reagan? Well, corporate life has a way of providing influence on one's life. "Greed is good" is not just a movie line, I am afraid, for Baby Boomers went from inspiration to consumption. They went from living off the land to owning the land. When exactly did "take no prisoners" become a good thing?

Here are examples of excerpts from a typical conversation that you would hear from Baby Boomers as we welcomed the first Baby Boomer president, Bill Clinton: "What Country Club, are you joining?" "How many vacations do you take?" "Where is your second home?" "Who is your broker?" "Do you have a Gold Card?" "How do you handle your debt service?" "What about tax shelters?" One key subject absent from the mix was savings. Just pay the minimum on that card. "Did you see the latest review of the 'can't miss' restaurants in *Boston Magazine*?" "Did you hear? Bob lost his job!" "Denise is heartbroken she won't be joining us on the Vineyard this season."

"Did you stay up to see the results?" "I think Gore won." "No, Bush won." "Does it matter?" For the house will always go up in value, and stocks will continue to rise. "Who needs those dividends? That is not enough of a return." "I know a hedge fund manager with houses in the Hamptons, Aspen, and a villa in Tuscany." "Can that news report be true? Are the major banks about ready to collapse? What happened to my portfolio?" "My position at the firm is on shaky ground, a lot like my home." "Those mortgage payments come more often than they used to, it can't be a month already." "What do I truly need?" "What is important to me?" "My dad died; where is my support system?" "Please God, don't let me have to move in with my daughter." "I just want to be happy." "Who are my true friends?" "My parents were not so out of touch after all."

Wednesday, February 15, 2012

A Time For Us

Amidst the great recession that Baby Boomers are likely to remember, like many who had the indelible mark of the Great Depression, there comes hope. For two years, traveling the country and fielding emails from my contemporaries, a steady stream of bad news accompanied the introductions and correspondence. It seemed that every Baby Boomer had a story to tell of a lost career, being pushed out of his company, or wondering how the world looked so dark all of a sudden. But the sun is starting to come up in "Baby Boomer Nation." To use a catchphrase, many Baby Boomers report a "light at the end of the tunnel."

Statistics support the anecdotal reference. In many parts of the country, the unemployment rate is dropping. There is a clear signal that new small businesses are being formed and, for the first time since 2007, people are feeling better about themselves. While this is general data, the broad picture applies to Baby Boomers. Baby Boomers are indeed going back to corporate life, starting new companies, and finally feeling upbeat.

It has been a struggle. While we are not out of the woods yet, and many who will read this column and are still suffering will cry foul, it is time to look at some lessons learned and then share some thoughts on the times in which we are living. Remember when people would tell you that you will know whom your friends are when the chips are down? Well, truer words were never spoken. It's sad, but Americans like winners. Everybody is your friend when you are picking up the check. It is like health care: want good medical treatment? Do not get sick. Want friends for life? Then never reveal you have a problem.

I remember the great basketball player Earvin "Magic" Johnson saying that, after he contracted AIDS, nobody wanted to play one-on-one basketball with him. Everybody had an excuse. "Friends" is an interesting term. Many people think that they have a multitude of friends. Others are wise enough to realize that only a few of their "friends" are real friends. Sometimes family members are no better; they run for the hills when the shine is off your résumé. So, the lesson learned by Baby Boomers over the last several years of economic drought is that "you know whom you can count on in the difficult times."

Baby Boomers also had to learn the hard way that life was not "a bowl of cherries." You face difficult times in life. Parents age and die. Marriages do not always work out. Companies go bust. Stocks can go down. Houses, as an investment, work out better when the bank is not sending foreclosure notices. Baby Boomers, once thought of as the spoiled generation, had to figure out what resilient meant. Guess what? They are bouncing back. Baby Boomers are stronger, have more fortitude than they are given credit for, and, most importantly, they do not give up. When history is written, and comebacks of the average Baby Boomer are as well-known as "The Comeback Kid," our most famous Baby Boomer, Bill Clinton, Baby Boomers will indeed be commemorated. It will be like Harry Truman who left office with a 28 percent approval rating, but history has been a much kinder barometer to his record.

Congratulations to Baby Boomers who dug in, kept fighting, and believed that things would be good once again. They are different, but good, because the days of "letting the good times roll" have gone the way of Chrysler – formerly great, suffered hard times for sure, now back to profitability, but not looking like they once did. In Chrysler's case, they now are attached to Fiat as part of the auto bailout. Baby Boomers, as a population, have gone through the process now and have to change their ways to remain solvent.

To many Baby Boomers, change is a good thing. Baby Boomers must get off of the treadmill from a spending point of view, and on it for health and wellness. Baby Boomers want to live free and clear now. Credit card debt is indeed the enemy. Baby Boomers have discovered this new phenomenon – it is called cash. Baby Boomers have discovered this new inner feeling – work for the satisfaction of the work rather than for the paycheck that buys "stuff." Baby Boomers have found satisfaction in their own inner voice. Suddenly, people who you thought have it all (well, in their opinion) just don't matter that much. Many Baby Boomers have discovered the interesting phrase, "Who cares what others think?" For when you had nowhere to turn, it was only your own ingenuity that counted.

So that brings us full circle – back to the top. This experience that Baby Boomers have gone through has shown that Baby Boomers have "one more good run" in them. It has been shown that life lessons coupled with new education can bring true happiness – the happiness of accomplishment measured by knowledge that you indeed are a person of quality that can produce a success story. But, Baby Boomers, one final thought: if this is indeed a time for us, you are going to have to change your mode of operation. You are going to have to discover teamwork. You are going to have to understand that modesty is a good quality. And, this may be the most important thought of all: you are going to have to accept help. The stranger whose help you receive today might turn out to be the friend and business partner of tomorrow.

Tuesday, February 21, 2012

A Day in the Life

Hello Baby Boomers! Did you ever wonder what a day in the life of one of your peers is like? Well, try this on for size. Baby Boomer Bob (not his real name) starts his day with a walk with his favorite girl. They have been dating and are serious, but taking it slow. You do not rush things at this stage of life. It is a mixture of companionship and future. What a romantic Bob is, though. He stops at a lilac bush and puts a little bouquet together that his favorite girl takes to work and puts on her desk. He has an interesting day ahead. His lunch partner is his 92-year-old friend, Murray. They share a wonderful friendship. They talk baseball, family, and food. It is really like an uncle and nephew getting together. To give you an idea of the nature of a man who is beating the clock and giving all Baby Boomers hope for health and wellness, Murray will do the driving on this day.

The first stop is Costco for gas. Murray did not acquire all that money without being a spend thrift – perhaps another lesson for Baby Boomers. Of course, they drove ten miles out of the way for the savings. But have you looked at the price of gas lately? A penny saved is indeed a penny earned. The drive, though, provides a further Baby Boomer lesson. Murray mentions that his daughter will turn 65 this year. She is very interesting, Murray contends. She was a student at UCLA when she met a man of equal age. She called home one night and said she would like to transfer to Cal Berkley to be closer to her new boyfriend. Murray and his wife Cecelia were not thrilled about the idea – especially upon meeting the long haired, bearded, VW-bus-driving hippie. His daughter, now a flower child, was in the heart of the protest scene. Baby Boomers remember those days well. Murray and his wife reacted like most parents of the day would; they refused to pay for her tuition if she transferred. Their daughter did what most daughters of the day would; she transferred anyway.

The rub between parents and daughter continued until graduation. Murray, a soft hearted guy, gave his daughter a lump sum of money upon completion of her education. It was to clear her debt and travel Europe, maybe with the hidden benefit of getting rid of the boyfriend. Yes, you guessed it; she took him to Europe with her, later married him, and had a wonderful son.

With the tank filled up and our Baby Boomer on an outing, he asked Murray to fill him in on the rest of the story. Well, Murray's son-in-law eventually joined the service to complete his medical experience. Sometime in the 80s, he became a conservative, and today, he is to the right of Newt Gingrich. His daughter, once subservient to a man, went on to get her Masters in social work, and today is a strong woman doing strong things in the community. Today, she is an independent thinker, with her politics to the left of Nancy Pelosi. The loving couple is now divorced, but their marriage did produce a great son, who is very respectful to his grandparents.

It is time for lunch now. Murray finds one of his little haunts. The sandwiches are good, the conversation even better. Murray had brought with him a wonderful scrap book of baseball clippings to show Baby Boomer Bob. Babe Ruth, Dizzy Dean, and Joe DiMaggio graced the yellowing pages. There sat the Baby Boomer and the member of the Greatest Generation, debating Cobb versus Rose, Hubbell versus Koufax, and Joe McCarthy versus Tony La Russa – each era of baseball familiar to each generation. Where was the Baseball Hall of Fame Executive Director to listen in on such a rich conversation? The sandwich shop closes at three. They helped the staff wipe down the tables, figuratively speaking. They closed the place.

On the way back, Murray pulls over and announces "one more stop." It's Lou's record shop, a legendary place. At Lou's, vinyl is still king. Somehow, in this shop, Perry Como is always in style. On this day, a turn table is a modern appliance. As for "Lou," well, he is indeed very real, for he is the "answer man." "Yes, we have Jonah Jones," Lou informs us, and thankfully, he is not confused thinking the question was about Norah Jones. What a place this is! They have all of Tony Bennett's albums, even the one with "I left my heart in San Francisco." While it is easy to get lost in the eras of music, your energy is kept alive by the Reese's peanut butter cups, the Snicker's bar, and Coke. You see, Lou sells all your favorites to enjoy as you peruse the store.

It is 4 pm now. Murray and Baby Boomer Bob shake hands, speak of the great day, and recall one of the lines that brought on laughter. The day may, in some ways, seem complete, but in reality it is just starting for our Baby Boomer, for now he must go to work. Real life, how about that? The present - yes, responsibility calls. But for a few hours, a Baby Boomer and a member of the Greatest Generation met, talked, ate lunch, and realized a good time was had by all.

When you began reading, is this what you expected? Probably not, but sometimes, a day in the life of a Baby Boomer can take you down an unexpected path.

Friday, February 10, 2012

Progress and Transformation

She was born "prior to 1964 but after 1946"; this is her coy way of saying she is a Baby Boomer, without revealing her age. She is not conscious of things like this, but it is her playful way of inserting her personality into the conversation. Truth be told, as I observed this woman turn more serious, it became clear that she was a product of college life in the 70s and reflective of women of her generation. She is an executive, who has been married and divorced. She has one child, a daughter, who is just now finishing college. The daughter just frustrates her, for she is not "driven." Can you imagine how she could think that getting married and being a mother is enough? So goes the introduction to our profile person named Carol. Carol is just one person, but her story could be the face of millions of Baby Boomer women.

When Carol came out of school, she went to work as a Marketing Representative. After a few short years, she went back for an MBA. Once back in corporate life, she climbed the ladder. With each new promotion came more responsibility, more stress, more travel, and less time with her family. By her own admission, when she got married she hardly knew herself, and certainly was not prepared for the partnership that marriage is supposed to bring. But the union did produce a lively offspring, even if there were few sparks on the 4th of July of life. As she put it, "My ex, and don't you hate that term, was basically someone that I met, and because all my friends were doing so, we just got married." Soon, frustration, anger, and lies began. Not lies of infidelity, but lies that "one should stick it out for the child," or even more simply, "because we've been together for a while."

But eventually, the couple found themselves going in two different directions. This was true in terms of career, mental state, interests, and financial resources (she made more than he did). Soon, they discovered divorce court. Time passed, and now she sits and wonders what she missed out on in life. Why is this so? Because she hates the battle cry of the sisters of her generation. They said, "We can have it all." Maybe the battle cry should have been, as a woman who we met in San Francisco commented, "You can have it all" at different stages, but not all at once. This commentary hits you like a ton of bricks. Anybody that remembers the 70s will recall the women's protest marches, Gloria Steinem and Cosmopolitan, and Billie Jean King beating Bobby Riggs, "for all women." Glass ceilings needed to be broken, Title IX needed to insure equal opportunity in sports. The modern woman was told in the 1970s: "Don't be June Cleaver. Be all that you can be. Fight for your rights in Corporate America." The Woman's movement succeeded, not because of the number of women in the work place today, although that in itself is a winning score. No, the reason that it succeeded is because Carol's daughter now has a choice: Do I work and pursue a career, or become a stay-at-home mom? She can make these decisions void of repression.

Carol notes she is a different person than she was thirty years ago. She claims to know herself, which one would not doubt. She would like to meet a nice man. Someone who admires what she has accomplished, someone who would respect her, and someone that she could have a conversation with. She is ready for that now, she concludes. She goes on to explain that she has had the career, and she has a wonderful daughter. She has nice friends, especially her best girlfriend. She states that her life would be complete if she could find someone to share the rest of her life with, someone who has similar goals. If that were to happen, Carol thinks her life would be complete, and she indeed would have "had it all," but at different stages of life. She feels that she has made progress with her life, met her goals, and made the transformation to be a complete person, ready for love. To many Baby Boomers, this story will sound very familiar.

Saturday, January 28, 2012

Marco's Dad

At a high school outside of San Diego, a 16 year old student by the name of Marco graces the campus. He is a skate border, a Social Media Maven, and a permit driver in search of a license. He is by all accounts a good kid, studies hard, and with some degree of manners, has asked a nice girl to the school formal. He is hoping to get an upper-classmate to double date with him, so his father will not have to drive him and his date.

It was not that he and his father are at odds; quite to the contrary, they have a wonderful relationship, and this provides the genesis for this story. Marco's father is 56, and his mother, also the same age, gave birth to him at 40. The parents are Baby Boomers. The loving couple, parents to Marco, lost a daughter earlier in their marriage. He became the reward after the initial sadness. So, while most Baby Boomers are starting to play the grandparent role, Marco's parents are still thinking about how to pay for his college tuition. It will work out though, because the good news in having a child later in life is that it has provided the time for Marco's parents to acquire a nest egg, not only for tuition, but also for the plans that they have beyond parenting.

Marco seems to think that Baby Boomer parents are cool. He likes to watch, what he refers to as "old television" with his Dad. Like, Gilligan's Island, where the debate continues on, "Mary Ann or Ginger?" Marco reports that they watch "Mr. Ed" and "the Brady Bunch." Somehow, Wilbur still provides laughs as the straight man to the talking horse. With "the Brady Bunch," he, like his father, understands, "Marcia, Marcia, Marcia."

Marco thinks that his Dad has fun taste in TV. It is what seems to bind them, it is something that they do together. That is a "good thing." Their favorite old program seems to be "Green Acres." Eddie Arnold and a Gabor sister are still getting it done as the socialite couple from New York, causing havoc on the farm. Marco said that they watch a great deal of "the Beverly Hillbillies." When I pointed out that the character of Jed's son was played by Max Baer Jr., the son of the former heavyweight champion Max Baer, Marco, of course, had to get on his phone and do a search to check out the facts.

What I find interesting about this family is that the parents embrace their age. They are not trying to run away from the past. In fact, the parents are exposing Marco to all the likes of their generation, from movies to TV to music.

"Did you know," Marco asked me, "that the Beatles were on the Ed Sullivan show?" Yes, Marco, I seem to remember that.

Saturday, October 22, 2011

Thinking of a Move to a New Place

One subject that Baby Boomers talk of on a regular basis is that move to a new place. Say, for example, you live in Chicago, Illinois, and you are thinking of your retirement years, or a second career, in which to stay active. You have weather on your mind; the winter can be difficult to endure, especially as you get older. What are some of your fellow Baby Boomers doing to plan ahead? They began by assessing their goals. How do they think they want the remainder of their life to play out? What are some of the considerations? Do you want to downsize? What kind of new community do you think that you would enjoy, and for what reason? Your fellow Baby Boomers then begin the research process, from periodicals to online data, trying to gather information for an informed decision. What seems to have worked is then making a list of the top five communities that seem to be best based on your criteria. The next part of the phase is perhaps most novel.

Go try the places out. Perhaps start with a vacation, and then advance to a tryout period that involves every day activity, simulating what it would be like to live there. This approach will give you the best chance to make an informed attempt at your future.

In a related topic of discussion, here are some of the reasons that Baby Boomers have chosen the place they moved to. They know other people who live in the community, so the new place is not a cold start. It is in a University town, taking advantage of the resources for the mind and body, as well as the entertainment value. You want to find a place that will keep you busy. You may want to find a place to start a business and enjoy the fruits of a job related to a second career. You may want to choose a place based on your desire to do volunteer work at a hospital or library. I met a group of women from Del Mar, California, who take a lot of pride in the local garden club. This was similar to volunteer work that was done by Baby Boomer women in Santa Barbara, California.

Finally, and paramount to Baby Boomers, it always comes back to the weather. May it be for golf and tennis, may it be for your daily walk, or may it be just for the ease of everyday life. Baby Boomers: good luck with the process. If you find yourself in the situation described, know that you are like many other Baby Boomers in the current times.

Thursday, October 6, 2011

Baby Boomers lose an Icon [Steve Jobs]

When you lose someone from your age category, it is always difficult. You look at the person's life through the prism of your own life. Steve Jobs, to all but a few of the readers, is just a familiar name with a history of accomplishment. Yet Baby Boomers will feel the impact, because in a way, we think that we know him. We have a shared experience with him. He pioneered the personal computer, and we used it. He wore jeans as a signature of his management style, and we had "Casual Friday." He was one of us that made good. He lived in our times. Steve, because he loved the Beatles, named the company that he helped found after their record label, Apple. The Steve Jobs that Baby Boomers know, or most identify with, is not the "iPad" Jobs, but the "Apple II" Jobs. You see, he is from our generation, having gone through the same shared experiences of the times. If you listed the ten Baby Boomers who achieved the most, Steve Jobs, of course, would be on that list. He is "The Henry Ford" of the Baby Boomer generation.

Even though he was sick with pancreatic cancer, he seemed to age gracefully, and Steve Jobs was still making a contribution to his dying day. We measured ourselves by him. We cheered his comeback to Apple, and analyzed his mercurial style of dealing with employees. Baby Boomers, maybe more than any other generation, have taken business leaders of the same age and stage, and created a relationship. The relationship might have been at arms-length, but somehow, they seemed like our next-door neighbor. He is like us. He went to school at the same time as us, and he knows what we know because we grew up together. Steve Jobs will be missed on the Baby Boomer landscape, for Baby Boomers have lost an icon.

Tuesday, August 2, 2011

What is most important to Baby Boomers

In an informal survey of over three hundred Baby Boomers from around the country, when asked at this stage of life what is most important to you, an overwhelming percentage said "family." In talking to Baby Boomers from a diverse economic spectrum, there was universal agreement that family was the aspect of life that stood out. Financial security, retirement, a second career, and finally, how and where they wanted to live in their "Golden Years" rounded out the key mentioned topics. These, while widely talked about and important, did indeed trail "family."

When you ask follow-up questions in interviews, or ask for an expanded answer, it becomes very interesting. For example, a lot has to do with where you fall in the age category of Baby Boomers. An older Baby Boomer might speak of their aging parents and the decisions about their care. Another set of Baby Boomers, just a bit younger, mention the college education of children and their children starting their lives in the work world, as well as contemplating marriage. The complicated Baby Boomer might be working on the multi- generational issues, such as health issues for parents and college tuition for children.

Recently, a Baby Boomer flew across country to visit his parents, who are living close to his sister. The parents live in an upscale assisted living facility within miles of their daughter. As the brother takes the plane ride and looks forward to interacting with the close knit family, he leaves behind his wife, who will spend time with his son and two young grandchildren while he is away. His other son studies in Europe. All these forces meet in the center of the Baby Boomer priority spectrum. Life for Baby Boomers has become reflective. Baby Boomers have spent time recalling their youth and thinking about the family gatherings that were so much a part of their up-bringing. They miss those days when the aunts and uncles came over, and time was spent with their cousins. They recall with fond memories the way that their parents interacted with the friends of their generation. One Baby Boomer reported that the house he grew up in always seemed alive.

As the parents of Baby Boomers have aged, the Baby Boomer tries even harder to hold on to the memories, as they do everything that they can to support their parents with care and dignity through the transition. Baby Boomers as a whole have come to the conclusion that their parents deserve their respect and caring, because for the most part, the parents sacrificed so much to give them the life that they have now. Baby Boomers also seem bent on passing on family traditions to their children. They look to reconnect with extended family. The cousin in Buffalo is important because of the shared bond of the Easter holidays of the past. You remain loyal to the cousins that you saw grow up, over the years of celebrating Christmas Eve together, and you care about them today as you did yesterday. In fact, now you want to grow to care about their children because, after all, these are not strangers, they are family.

Baby Boomers report having conversations with their spouse at the conclusion of a day, mentioning how they received Facebook messages from family. The messages received come from their children, their siblings, their cousins, and maybe even their aunts and uncles. It can be said this is family unity of the 21st Century. Of course, many Baby Boomers have lost many of the important people in their lives. This difficult dimension fosters a need to give of yourself to the people who are still in your life. Baby Boomers report a great sadness upon the loss of parents, and they are heart broken when they lose a sibling. The loss of a spouse is devastating. This reinforces the belief system, in Baby Boomers, to love the ones who are here.

So it is no wonder that the busy professional will fly across the country to make that precious visit. What Baby Boomers have most reported is that when you finally see, in person, that extended family member who you care about but have not seen for a long while, it is not uncomfortable. Rather, the opposite is true; it is like riding a bicycle or not missing a beat.

The good feeling upon the return from such a trip is like the feeling of fresh spring water after having been in the desert.

What is important to Baby Boomers of the 21st century? Some may argue that the reply to that question is an obvious one, or that the reality of the economic times makes you focus on the basics. Maybe both are true, but it can also be said that Baby Boomers have come to realize what is important. Maybe that is why "family" is front and center of the things most important to Baby Boomers.

Wednesday, May 11, 2011

The Aging Process for Baby Boomers

When you walk around the campus of Florida State University, in Tallahassee, you are impressed with the surroundings aided by beautiful weather, outstanding athletic facilities, and its leading department on the aging process. In the same building that houses the Childs Museum, named for the famous Florida politician, professors are hard at work on the human condition over time. Their research is topical for Baby Boomers, because the subject is part of the Baby Boomer human condition. Baby Boomers who have redefined themselves throughout their lifetimes are now setting their sights on giving all new meaning to the Golden Years. They are the ones going to yoga classes, walking in the morning, and going to the gym. In the 55-and-over communities, Baby Boomers are more concerned now with athletic facilities than any other part of the glossy brochure. The media is all over this subject. They have recognized that Baby Boomers want to continue to live an active lifestyle for as long as possible. Baby Boomers, always quick to invent terms to explain their actions, now say things like "60 is the new 50," much like they once said "don't trust anyone over 30" when they were 25. The grandparents of today would rather rock the worlds of their grandchildren than rock them to sleep in their rocking chairs. They dress with style, seek to travel freely, and will say to their children that they love their grandchildren, but they are not their built-in babysitters. Contrast that with generations gone by, in which a live-in grandmother just rested in the afternoon and went to bed early. These active Baby Boomers are not looking for the early bird special in the Florida retirement community; they are practicing for the 65-and-under state tennis tournament. As Florida State faculty would contend, people are living longer, healthcare is better, and people live more active lifestyles. But one also must conclude that mindset has a lot to do with it. A Baby Boomer now simply asks, "Why not?" He asks, "Who told me I can't start a business at 55?" "Who told me I couldn't rent an RV and travel the country?" "Who told me I couldn't join the Peace Corps?"

The mindset consistent with the aging process of Baby Boomers is, "My life is still ahead of me." It is not a quitter mentality. The people who study the aging process for a living will tell you that attitude and support are important parts of the equation. Simply put, an active Baby Boomer is likely to be a healthy Baby Boomer. Naturally the aging process has its limitations, so it is possible that people who study aging for a living might agree with the Baby Boomer who says, "I am not trying to be 25 again; I just want to be the best 55-year-old that I can be."

April 19, 2011

Three Baby Boomers from the West Coast who "Get It"

Al is a retired executive from The Boeing Company, but like most managers from Boeing, he wanted to continue contributing to society. Although he is a member of a country club, Al wanted his post corporate career to be productive and to leave the golf to weekends. Always thought of as leader within the company in the field of Ethics, he chose to start a company providing support to other corporations around the world. His consulting, which is so valuable to corporations that view ethics as a major component of their mode of operation, is aided by his expertise. He has even spent a considerable amount of time in China, where ethics is a major topic. Al is a good example of AARP's campaign to highlight post work life for Baby Boomers. Al lives outside Seattle with his wife Nancy, who is a cancer survivor. They have raised a family and their adult children are successful in their own right. They remain close to their children, even though the children live all over the country. Al can be seen at Seattle Mariner baseball games or at the charitable activities that he and Nancy support within the community.

If you find yourself in the international terminal at the San Francisco airport, you might run across our next profile subject. Mike is a policeman who looks every bit the cover boy for the SFPD. He is fit, probably due to the fact that he covers the terminal on a bicycle, and he is everything a policeman should be. He is well-mannered and well spoken. As he keeps the airport travelers safe, he also views himself as a representative of the city who wants to make sure that you come away with a positive impression while visiting. He is proud of his work, proud of his city, and proud of his family. Mike is a good example of Baby Boomers who get up every morning and go to work with the idea of "being the best that they can be." Retirement will come someday, but like a lot of Baby Boomers, he is in no hurry. He will be ready when the time comes.

And then there is Jane, who lives in Palm Springs. "Lives" there is actually a bit of a misnomer because she is hardly ever there. You see, Jane's ambition has always been to travel. This desire to live her life as she always wanted must agree with her because she looks healthy, and if you did not know better, you would never think of her as a Baby Boomer. She chalks that up to her daily morning walking routine and good solid nutritional eating habits.

Jane also takes part in a growing travel outlet for Baby Boomers known as "Elder Hostel." This Program allows like-minded and people of a similar age to continue educational pursuit, while also incorporating travel. A Baby Boomer can sign up for one of their programs, which are usually a week in duration at a destination that you are likely to want to visit. While there, your sightseeing is supplemented with lectures, discussion groups to stimulate your mind, and the ability to pursue continuous learning and improvement. Jane is a good example of a Baby Boomer who has decided that travel is important, but also bent on stimulating the mind. Both of these are key elements for Baby Boomers.

Finally, there are some things that these three individuals have in common. They all are nice and have positive attitudes. They are comfortable with who they are and the choices they have made. They all keep themselves fit, they all have planned well for retirement, and they all have a desire to be the best that they can be at their age. They see their golden years as very different from those of their parents'.

Monday, January 16, 2012

Skills for the 21st Century

The following is a composite of what Baby Boomers believe are the skills that they will need to compete in the 21st Century. But before we list them, we will have a short discussion as to how this came about. Baby Boomers will work longer than they expected. Most could not retire if they wanted to. Some will work to an older age, because the portfolio that looked so good in 2007 just does not measure up so well in 2012. Other Baby Boomers simply want to continue to make a contribution to society. The thesis statement has to answer this question: if Baby Boomers are going to be in the workforce, what skills will they need? Here are some possible answers.

Did you think the number one skill is technology? Well, it is right up there, but second to communication skills. Companies hungry for people who can work as a team would like to see the employee of choice be able to relate to others in the organization. Baby Boomers have life experience on their side. They have to use that asset by being able to get their point across, to listen to others, to relate to buying signals, and to present and persuade. These skills should be Baby Boomer staples. Baby

Boomers must work at this and not assume that because they are good at conversation, small talk, and banter, that they are communicators for the business world. Business today is pressure-packed; time is at a premium, so messages have to be received and delivered with crisp precision.

Yes, technology and all of its subgroups must be part of the tool kit of the Baby Boomer. Familiarity, ease of use, and terminology make up the foundation. Baby Boomers must fight a perception that they are from days gone by. They need to demonstrate capability without insecurity. Be active on social media. Know how to use Facebook without confusing business with the family vacation. Know LinkedIn for its power of business, Google+ for its range, and Twitter for its audience. Understand all the tools available, such as the power of the mobile phone and its apps. Be talented at the power of contact through emailing. In fact, work hard at your image on both; do the simple things. Do you know how to leave a succinct voice mail? Does your email get your point across? Finally, on the subject of technology, do not try to be something that you are not. Embrace the latest, but use what is comfortable. Above all, when asked about a technology in an interview, do not ever pretend to be more knowledgeable than you really are. The world is too cruel and too fast for a bluff.

A skill that is very underappreciated, but necessary, is to fit in without losing yourself to the corporate culture. Baby Boomers must welcome diversity, the ability to work in multi-age environments, and dress not only for success, but for your workplace as well. The days of the IBM, one suit fits all, are as relevant today as an episode of "Bonanza." Being able to work with a supervisor the age of your son will determine your effectiveness. The inability to share the workplace with different cultures without pre-judging, or with a lack of sensitivity, will not only be devastating, it will get you fired.

The assumption made for this column is that a Baby Boomer is applying for a job at a company, and that he hopes to be gainfully employed. These skills will also serve you well in non-profit settings or your own business, if you go that route. But the majority who responded to help bring about these conclusions did so, because of these three steps: apply for a job, get hired, and exist in the today's workplace. It is very interesting: Baby Boomers, if pushed to the wall, probably never thought that improving skills at this stage of life was going to be part of the action plan. Many lament at having to stay in the workforce. However, Baby Boomers who are succeeding in the 21st century are doing so because they are approaching the times, the situation, and the education in life as continuous improvement. They are looking at skill enhancement as growth. They are looking at life with a positive attitude. Baby Boomers, contrary to news reports, are indeed winning the battle and being productive in the workplace. Did you expect any other result?

Friday, July 15, 2011

Social Media versus Books

Do you ever turn to the Marketplace section of the Wall Street Journal? Well, on Thursday July 14, 2011, it was of interest to Baby Boomers. The section front page had two articles that were a bit of the old and the new. Toward the top was an article about Facebook with its ever increasing valuation, which has soared. Toward the bottom was an article about Borders, the Bookstore chain on the brink of liquidation. What to make of this as it affects Baby Boomers? Baby Boomers are perhaps the one generation that is fond of both mediums. For example, a Baby Boomer will go to a bookstore and sit for hours reading a favorite book. As a matter of fact, Baby Boomers report that at this stage of life it is one of their favorite things to do. But conversely, Baby Boomers are one of the fastest growing user bases for Social Media. On Facebook, Baby Boomers are reconnecting with family, staying in touch with friends, and perhaps with old college roommates, as well as using the tool for their second career. Baby Boomers have adapted to LinkedIn for business. Baby Boomer Katie Couric states that she uses Twitter as a key component for her career.

What do these two Wall Street Journal stories tell us about the world Baby Boomers live in now? Well, for one, young people are addicted to technology, and especially like to use it as their key communication and peer group tool, so much so, that schools are incorporating it into the curriculum. Teachers report that a student is more likely to concentrate and write a good paper if friends from class are going to review it in a shared Facebook-like manner as opposed to turning it into a teacher. There are states that are looking into eliminating books, and even considering stopping the practice of teaching penmanship. These are under consideration in California and Indiana respectively. It is doubtful that the average 13 year old is going to lose a lot of sleep over the closing of Borders bookstores. This is a shame because society is leading us to the conclusion that we can get our knowledge through eBooks and that brick and mortar book stores do not count. That thinking goes against the grain for Baby Boomers. Baby Boomers are buying the Kindle and Nook devices, and they love the products from Apple. But they love also going to Cape Cod for summer vacation and taking those hard copy books, with all the touch and feel that makes reading an enjoyment. Thus, the Baby Boomer comes to the conclusion that they must exist in both worlds. They must "tweet," chat, and read. Perhaps, it is the full complement of options and avenues that make the world so diverse and fun for Baby Boomers. A Baby Boomer uses the 140 characters available on Twitter, while also exploring the character of Ernest Hemingway. Those two worlds should not collide for Baby Boomers but, to coin a term from the past, there should be "peaceful coexistence" and a little bit of learning along the way, learning that includes the old and the new.

Tuesday, June 21, 2011

A Vacation Location for Baby Boomers

The warm gentle breeze coming off the Gulf of Mexico, the white sand, and the apartment with the water view – this awaits you on Siesta

Key in Sarasota, Florida. As you make the turn and cross the bridge you are in a land of paradise. Your day starts early with the walk along the beach, and after breakfast at one of the cute morning spots, you settle into a day of relaxation with tropical conditions. Your evening includes a vast choice of restaurants in this oasis of community. Sarasota also offers great golf and tennis. The shopping at the famed St. Armand's Circle is a cross between Rodeo Drive and a small shopping village.

As you drive into Sarasota, you encounter some other great areas. There is the long and well-manicured Long Boat Key. Many who go for a tennis vacation stay at The Colony Beach and Tennis Resort, which is always listed as one of the finest tennis resorts. The Resort at Longboat Key Club, with its golf course visible from the road as a part of your scenic drive, is your place for villa and apartment living. It has the golf course and the beach on either side of your accommodations. Some Baby Boomers report that they went to Sarasota on vacation, then decided to make it a second home location. Some have taken it further and have chosen Sarasota as their place to retire.

If you are a boating enthusiast this is also the community for you, with Bird Key being your destination. This is the place to buy a home on the canal and have your boat in the slip attached to your home. Some Baby Boomers have purchased an apartment in downtown Sarasota overlooking the water. This high rise effect living gives you the beautiful apartment with the panoramic view. But it all comes back to Siesta Key for that week or two away. It is the place to go and relax, lie on the beach, and leave the laptop behind. And if you go, you will see a sunset like no other, which you can enjoy from the beach or perhaps from the veranda of your apartment. One feature that Siesta Key also has is the rows of villas. These well-appointed two and three bedroom accommodations give you the feeling of a bungalow with the decor of interior design home.

Siesta Key was largely created in the late 60s and early 70s, and the villa like lifestyle of building prevents the place from ever appearing over crowded. Sarasota is home to some of the best grocery shopping with the key store being Publix. It is also home to some outstanding Italian eateries, places to enjoy fresh fish and some outstanding places to dine with a view. In the center of town sits the luxurious Ritz Carlton Hotel, with one of the greatest Sunday brunches anywhere. If you go to Siesta Key, Baby Boomers report two favorite places to stay. The first is "Island House Beach Resort," best for the apartments on the beach. The second favorite is "Horizons West" for the nicest in villas.

This is what Sarasota is all about for most Baby Boomers. They usually do not go just once, and sometimes they end up staying.

Thursday, June 2, 2011

Baby Boomers, Technology and Family

Baby Boomers have discovered that to stay in touch with family, they must use technology. A grandfather from Indiana says "nobody calls me anymore." Sometimes the phone on the wall in the kitchen looks more like an ornament. He refuses, no matter how much his daughter pleads, to get a cell phone. She argues, "but Dad, how about in the case of an emergency?" He walks down the street and goes to the post office, but he rarely buys stamps, because his letters do not get answered. He complains to longtime friends that grandchildren are not as respectful as when he was their age. Granted he is the oldest of the Baby Boomer spectrum, but his mode of operation is simply outdated.

The grandmother in Oregon created a Facebook page when her granddaughter was born. The grandmother in California communicates with her daughter in Colorado with such ease that they could be neighbors, but they never leave Facebook. They post so many pictures that friends in the state of Washington can tell you what is going on in their family. The California grandmother received a call on her cell phone during work from her daughter and almost did not know how to react outside of their virtual comfort zone. Recently, Baby Boomers report that families are doing more sharing amongst each other especially with extended family. A close knit group in Chicago may not have reached message board status but they do share family email messages, and comment to all copied when someone writes. A cousin in Illinois can comment when a fellow cousin writes about cherished memories, and then may even suggest a follow up idea, like when she thought they should create a family cookbook. This came about because extended family was talking, via email, about who some of the great cooks were of family members past.

What Baby Boomers report is a sense of positivity in their lives because of this type of interaction, which is easier now thanks to modern technology. The 3,000 miles between them do not seem so far, and people can communicate at their own time and pace. An uncle who has a nephew studying abroad can show interest, and the busy nephew can get back to him within the framework of the day. But you need to use the tools. You need to make the calls on Skype and have an account on LinkedIn. You need to give a thumbs-up on Facebook, and comment when posts hit your news feed. Recently, a Baby Boomer was known to say, "I am on Facebook because my granddaughter is on Facebook." That is a good thing. Baby Boomers who might have been attracted to Social Media because of use in their second career have found the hidden benefit of its use to connect with family and simply just stay in touch. Recently, the San Diego Union Tribune addressed this topic in a story about how older people were adopting technology into their lives. Baby Boomers who once dictated letters in the office to an administrator are now typing regular emails to family all over the country.

The California mother and grandmother will tell all of her Baby Boomer friends, "If you need any help, let me know," because she has turned into a regular Facebook Maven. When she is on her break during her workday at an eating establishment, she can be seen with the laptop fired up, sending messages to her sister in Idaho and to her niece at college in another part of the Golden state. She is posting pictures of a party at her house for her multiple siblings, numerous cousins, and friends who are like family. An older Baby Boomer laughs; when once he thought of himself as being on the cutting edge, he now contacts his young cousin to give him help in building his website for his emerging business. It is a new world order and Baby Boomers who have adopted technology to aid them in their family interaction have been rewarded. That feeling of being "out of touch" is gone. That resentment of feeling forgotten is lessened. Those old feelings that were at the foundation of their youth, about the family that they loved, have now returned.

Tuesday, December 6, 2011

Baby Boomers – Teamwork – Communications

Baby Boomers, in general, feel the corporate world of today is lacking in the key areas of teamwork and communication. Baby Boomers who are still working in corporate life feel a sense of frustration. They remember what it was like when they first started, and they lament the present conditions. Baby Boomers, for the most part, feel that they are team players. The definition of that term, while up for debate, has more to do with actions rather than words.

Baby Boomers suggest that their experiences and environment growing up helped prepare them to be able to function well with fellow employees. They point out that good communication skills were developed early on as a natural part of family life. For example, the family dinner table was a place for sharing, where one could talk about their day, receive feedback, and do it in an atmosphere of common ground. It seems that for later generations, family meals together are more often the exception rather than the rule, and thus this learning opportunity is less common. Growing up, Baby Boomers also did not have their life planned out for them. Instead of scheduled "play dates," they could spontaneously go down to the park, meet up with their friends, and co-exist. Additionally, many Baby Boomers played sports, always a good pre-requisite for working in a corporate team environment. Remember that it was Baby Boomers who ushered in Title IX. It was a time when playing in a pick-up game was common place, and before a basketball player was identified as a "prospect" in the 7th grade.

Let us also not forget, and this might be most germane, that what is being described as part of the Baby Boomers' background, took place before the days when sitting in front of computer screens, playing video games, and checking your cell phone ruled the day. Do employees coming into the work place lack teamwork and communication skills, in part due to the times in which they were raised? Poll most Baby Boomers, and they would say that it is a major factor. Do employees entering the work place now need to be coached on communication and teamwork skills? Baby Boomers would vote to the affirmative. That is why multi- generational employees are the next big "hot button" for Fortune 500 Companies. Are all Baby Boomers team players? Absolutely not; in fact, Baby Boomers at the top of corporations can be as cut throat as any. Are all Baby Boomers good communicators? Judging by the average CEO, who is a Baby Boomer and who cannot seem to share the vision, mission, goal, and objectives across the enterprise, the answer is "no." But the average Baby Boomer understands the concept, knows it when they see it, and their upbringing provides a basis for teamwork and communications within a company setting.

Professor Winston Brembeck, long retired as the pre-eminent scholar on the subject, felt that these skills could be learned. This legendary University of Wisconsin teacher thought with identification of these communication skills and seeing examples in practice, teamwork and communication could be accomplished. He thought that teamwork and communication was essential for a corporation to succeed. He questioned why companies could not recognize these essential elements. He would be sad to see that little progress is being made on the whole and that only a select few have gotten the message, aided by experts. Guess what? Companies that emphasize teamwork and communication see it reflected in their stock prices. Baby Boomers, always forward in their thinking when it comes to corporate life, would like to see teamwork taken out of the soft skill category and made a standard corporate practice.

Thursday, March 1, 2012

Are We Our Parents?

Barbara, a 63-year-old Baby Boomer, is having an interesting morning. She was up at 5 a.m. – not by choice, but because she is having a performance review with a new manager who was just hired. She decides to get up and go into the office early instead of continuing to turn and twist in bed. Perhaps she will make some notes and outline the meeting – she wants it to go well. As she enters the office, she encounters some co-workers and details her day ahead. She tells them that she will join them for coffee in a short while after she gets her computer to work. Technical support is not in yet. Barbara, by her own admission, is not computer savvy. She bought a laptop for herself for Christmas… and it is still in the box.

Barbara decides not to let the frustration get to her regarding the computer. She wants a clear mind for the upcoming 9 am session. She anticipates that the new manager will want a full assessment of her responsibilities, which she is prepared to give. But on this morning her back hurts from holding her grandchild most of yesterday. She was on babysitting duty. She remembers when she would drop off her kids at her mother's house. Now, she is the recipient of the hand-off. She made dinner for her grandchild and played games with the loving young girl. When the afternoon came to a close, she looked in the mirror and asked the question: "Am I becoming my mother?" This is a question being asked by Baby Boomers across the land. Are we adopting the characteristics of our mothers and fathers? Do we look, feel, and act like the parents that we once knew? The answer may lie in your attitude.

Some Baby Boomers resemble their parents by choice. A man might say, "I remember my Dad liked whipped cream on his coffee as a treat.

I find myself doing that, part for sentiment and part to enjoy his tastes." Baby Boomers may find themselves modeling the actions of parents as they take on a new role. For example, just as many Baby Boomers brought their parents' marriages into their own marriages, they now are bringing their grandparents' examples into their new roles. For all that Baby Boomers talk of being different than their parents, they still remain our greatest role models. A favorite expression of Baby Boomers is, "I remember my mother and father doing it this way." As Baby Boomers age, they have a greater appreciation for their parents and tend to adopt their behaviors.

The slogan goes: "We are not our parents. We want to be more fit, we want to defy age, and we want to carve out a new meaning for being seniors." This is typical of a generation that has a codename known as "redefine." We have a history of this, for we defined race relations, civil liberties, and roles of men and women. But, for all the change that Baby Boomers are known for, they have comfort in the familiar – their mothers and fathers.

Wednesday, June 1, 2011

Baby Boomers reunite with the Library

Baby Boomers have found an old friend. They have become reunited with the library. In 1970, a high school student from Skokie, Illinois, North of Chicago, spends his evening at the Skokie Library. He, like many of his classmates, goes there to study and maybe do a little socializing. When test season comes around, this is where he could be found. It was a traditional place that was quiet, and where a well-trained librarian would help with questions, or maybe help search through the card catalogue. Those times hold special memories for Baby Boomers. But for most Baby Boomers, that is all they were, a memory. For some Baby Boomers rediscovering their local library at this age and stage has been a bit of an eye opening experience, and a pleasant one. You walk into a whole new world, even if it is a bit retro. The resources are extraordinary, of course, with books to read, but also music and movies. There are computers to use, and newspapers and magazines to read. Many Baby Boomers report that they gain a whole new sense of community by attending some of the many events that occur at the local library.

At the library in Rancho Mirage, California, you can go to lectures, movies and even see a play about John Adams. When a local film expert recently put on a film series, one was treated to not only the films, but also to some popcorn to match. At the library in Del Mar, California, you are greeted by friendly librarians who seek to know your name and who are so helpful that Baby Boomers are shocked to find out such courtesy still exists in the world. Like-minded Baby Boomers also make friends either through the monthly book club meetings, the music performance series, or just by conversations outside the branch before the doors open. Baby Boomers have even been known to bring their young grandchildren to story time at the library.

In Bellevue, Washington, the library is so big and expansive, so modern and up to date, and the technology so pronounced, that it is a center piece for the East side of Seattle. So what do you pay for this place to make friends, and read the latest "Reader's Choice"? Yes, the library is free. No matter how hard overzealous politicians try to ruin the quality of life with budget cuts to take away the service, the library system survives.

Andrew Carnegie, often referred to as the "Patron Saint of Libraries," envisioned the sense of community that libraries would foster, and used his wealth to back up his view that the citizens should have such a place. He founded 2,509 libraries in the late 19th and early 20th centuries. When doing a Google search on Andrew Carnegie, you will see a wealth of information; it is almost as much as the great wealth that he created. While his life story and corporate success are infamous, his lasting legacy may be his philanthropy, which centered on the library system that we know of today.

Recently, Logan Jenkins, the great writer for the San Diego Union Tribune, used his power of the press to reverse drastic cuts to the library system in San Diego. These were initially budget cuts being considered by the mayor. His effort to bring to light what libraries mean to the community, and to people like Baby Boomers, who have rediscovered the resource, forced the city council to reverse its course. It was the quality of the life that we lead that was the thesis for Jenkins' conclusions. So do not be surprised when, as a Baby Boomer, you ask your old college roommate where he or she has been spending their time, and they reply "the library." Baby Boomers have indeed reunited with an old friend, the local library.

Tuesday, May 17, 2011

Baby Boomers Warm to Social Media

On this day in San Diego, California, it is cold and rainy. The forecasters say that it might even set a record for "the coldest day." Of course, everything is relative, for the daytime high will still be in the low sixties. For Baby Boomers who call this community home, even the rain might not be so bad. It will give them a chance to continue to explore and use Social Media. Starting with a discussion about Facebook, Baby Boomers will tell you that they initially resisted getting involved. They perceived it as something for young people. But something happened along the way, and that was reconnecting with family and friends.

Baby Boomers who now operate new businesses or are self-employed, were told that, in this day and age, they need to be up on Facebook. Thus, these Baby Boomers began to explore the tool, and found the hidden benefit: the connection to family members whom they call far too infrequently. With the click of a mouse, the old friend who you lost touch with, or the family member whose interests have grown, is now part of your everyday experience. Baby Boomers like this very much.

The Baby Boomer in Eugene, Oregon sends a note to family in Washington D.C., maybe with the simple message wishing them a good weekend. The family writes on "The Wall" (Facebook) of the family member who is having a birthday. You see, connection, family, and the interest in how old friends lives have turned out are all things that are important to Baby Boomers. When the pictures go up on Facebook from the recent family wedding, it delights the Baby Boomer. Want to know how the grandchildren of your best friend are doing? It is there for you to see on Facebook.

The Baby Boomer who has charged ahead in that second career has found a partner in LinkedIn. Baby Boomers have reported the care that they have put into the building of their profile page. The hope is that they will build their new work interest through the LinkedIn network. One Baby Boomer who uses both tools, Facebook and LinkedIn, calls them, "a tool for the masses and one for the classes." Meaning, Facebook provides the social reach or mass appeal, and LinkedIn, being the business tool that it is, has the very specific verification for the business community.

Baby Boomers have also become interested in Klout. Klout is a San Francisco-based startup that measures Social Media influence. Baby Boomers note that Klout provides a new world of promotion, where your acclaim is now measured in non-traditional ways. For example, the photographer Charles Dastodd of Chicago is almost an overnight success based on the fame garnered by Social Media. His phenomenon was built by Twitter, but carried over to Facebook. By building a network within the like-minded world of fellow photographers, he now has a substantial business and ranks fourth on the top ten Klout power index.

Interestingly enough, unlike Facebook and LinkedIn, Twitter was initially slower to catch on with Baby Boomers, but has since risen dramatically in popularity with our generation. One key reason that Baby Boomers have warmed to Social Media, is that they were not afraid to try something new. Another reason Baby Boomers have adopted Social Media is that they are not resistant to change.

A Public Relations executive in Boston, a Baby Boomer, has the right attitude. As the world continues to evolve, he embraces the change and grows with it; perhaps this is why he is leading Social Media conferences for business professionals. Putting all the factors together, Social Media then becomes the tool for Baby Boomers to embrace the past and play in the future.

Wednesday, April 27, 2011

Paul Allen and Bill Gates, a Complex Friendship

If you come across the 520 floating bridge from Seattle, you will be on what is known as the East side. The epicenter is Bellevue, but it also includes such places as Kirkland, Mercer Island, Medina, and Redmond. Mercer Island is home to Paul Allen, Medina to Bill Gates, and Redmond is the headquarters for the company that they started, that being Microsoft. Microsoft is to the 21st century what General Motors was to the 1950s. They are big, well capitalized, and they are the modern definition of the corporate world. They make strategy decisions, move markets, and although innovative, are not as leading edge as once upon a time in their history. They are the establishment now. Long gone are the start-up decisions, the Personal Computer Revolution, and the battles with Apple and Sun Microsystems.

When Paul Allen and Bill Gates started Microsoft, people could never have imagined the world that we live in today. They were every bit the Ford and Edison of their generation. In 1975, when they founded Microsoft, computing was about games on Atari. That was followed by early leadership from Apple, mostly in education, and Commodore, an early player for computers at home and work. Microsoft had a secret: they were about the software. On the other hand, companies like IBM and Compaq, and others who would follow, were about the hardware. Most Baby Boomers can recite the progression story from $14,000 word processing systems to desk top computing. The leaders in computing at the time, companies like Digital, missed the significance. Ken Olsen, founder of Digital, and one of the great contributors to the history of computers, never entered the market. It was the equivalent of the thinking that the horse and buggy was here to stay. The Microsoft story is widely known, but the founders and their history together is still debated.

Now both men, in their mid to late 50s, are reflective in their journey. For example, Paul Allen recently wrote a memoir "Idea Man," where he looks back on the years from founding Microsoft, to his departure (while staying on the board), to his post-Microsoft life. The press has already pounced on the debates, the arguments between the two men. Paul Allen brought a little of this on with his frank account of their history. These were two best friends joined at the hip from the early days at the prestigious Lakeside school, who went through the pressures of starting a business and reaching iconic fame. Who could possibly go through life without an argument? Let us be fair. Unless, as a Baby Boomer, you were left behind on the moon by Neil Armstrong, you know the names of Paul Allen and Bill Gates. But do you know them in the way our culture dictates? Besides business competition, can you recall behavior that has been embarrassing?

Sure, when they were young, they were aggressive in their business dealings, especially Bill Gates. But it is not easy finishing first. In 1983, Allen left as an employee, but stayed on the board until 2000. And yes, Bill Gates had the greater passion for Microsoft. Bill Gates had a drive like no other, whereas Allen has more varied interests. They both got what they wanted. Bill Gates will always be associated with Microsoft, like John D. Rockefeller with Standard Oil. Paul Allen is more like Howard Hughes, without the drama. He owns two sports teams, a communication company, real estate holdings, and more. It is what some call a diverse portfolio. One man, Gates, is consistently the wealthiest American, and at last count, Paul Allen was 17th, but has been higher. Make no mistake, these two men are good friends and they have more in common than most. Allen himself reports that they have seen at least 500 movies together. They are both great citizens of Seattle. Both share a passion for giving back, and are committed to philanthropic endeavors.

They are like many Baby Boomers, reflective, and with an eye on making sure their life has counted for something. Allen, for example, has given his energy and resources to the study of the human brain. Bill Gates, of course, is devoted to the Gates foundation of charitable giving. By the time he is done, he will surpass anything that has ever been done from a charitable foundation standpoint, far exceeding the gold standard Rockefeller Foundation. While admirable, the Rockefeller legacy of charity, like Vanderbilt, crossed a generation. Meanwhile, Bill Gates will have achieved business and philanthropic heights in one lifetime. Paul Allen, who has funded manned space travel, is a true explorer. Maybe that is how these two men changed the world. They had a shared goal, a like-minded thought pattern, a passion for friendship, but the two men had enough of a difference in personality to get the best out of each other. By the way, that is how most good relationships work.

Paul Allen said that he wrote the book because he has been diagnosed with Hodgkin's lymphoma, and that occurred in 2009. Perhaps he just wanted to tell his story, or maybe he just wanted to reflect again on friendship, accomplishment, and a life lived. Paul Allen and Bill Gates have a complex relationship based on history. But as Baby Boomers would certainly agree, many would have liked to have taken the ride with a friend, even if the result was far less of a result than Microsoft.

Summary – Chapter 1

Baby Boomers in the 21st Century

When I was growing up in Chicago, I lived and died with the results of the Chicago White Sox. I loved baseball, and I loved participating in Little League. I just enjoyed my youth and times with the extended family, especially the hallmark: the Christmas Eve tradition. I was fortunate to have my grandparents as a presence in my life. I was extremely lucky to have supportive parents, before the term "supportive" became fashionable. They gave my brothers and me unconditional love, in their generation's mode of operation. Like others of their generation, my parents were modest in their actions, modest in their own wants and needs, and generous in their sacrifices for their sons.

When I was in college at the University of Wisconsin, it was a time of awakening. It was partly due to the circumstances in the country and partly due to my own growth as a person. It was a time of change. The turbulence of the 1960s led into the massive shift in the 1970s, where institutions truly became a question mark. As college life turned into corporate life, and corporate life turned to touches of gray, the calendar now was the 21st Century. Suddenly, the world was upside down with children taking care of parents, trading the Social Security office of those parents for your own retirement planning. Now Baby Boomers think to themselves, what is next?

For my part, the next chapter in life is similar to that of my peers. This commentary is about talking to Baby Boomers from the perspective of a Baby Boomer. My world and that of other Baby Boomers centers around five areas. First, there is the continued growth of the relationship with that special someone in my life. Second, the continued respect for family, which has always been such a part of my life. Third, it is important to feed the social relationships with friends, especially my best friend, who wrote the foreword to this book. Fourth, like other Baby Boomers, I have chosen and have developed my second career, which is as a spokesperson for the Baby Boomer generation. And fifth, the realization that planning for the future is paramount. That includes the best place to live out my life, the travel destinations of the future to aid in our happiness, and to take care of myself. That means that health and wellness are not evil words.

Baby Boomers across this country continue to look for happiness. They are an optimistic generation. They buy into the theory that better days are ahead. They also welcome the discussion that they can only worry about what they can control, so they have adopted a lifestyle of continuous improvement. They are trying to live each day to the fullest. The 21st century is not the swan song for Baby Boomers, but a time when they will keep making an impact on society, just as they have done all along during the rich history of the Baby Boomer generation.

Chapter 2

Caring For Elderly Parents

I often relate to, and use, this phrase in communication: "When the children become the parents, and the parents become the children." I feel it is a gripping statement with a sobering meaning. It is a concept that Baby Boomers across the landscape can easily identify with. A parent, once so strong, the rock of the family and your go-to person for advice, now struggles. I once saw my own father, a strong and independent man, torn with sadness as he struggled to put his shoes on. I once saw my mother cry, not from the softness of her heart, but from the dependence on my older brother in her time of need. Our family story is the story of Baby Boomers and their parents.

They are called the "Greatest Generation," a phrase made popular by the book by Tom Brokaw, journalist and former NBC television anchor. Tom Brokaw has had a stellar career, from covering conventions as a young reporter, to taking his place on *The Today Show,* to eventually being the face of NBC, as the leader of the nightly news. His greater contribution to society, however, may have been his study of this time-honored generation. This group of people bridged the gap between their own parents, who had come from what was referred to as the "old country," and the Baby Boomers: they were the advocates of FDR, the patriots in World War II, and the matriarchs of the growth of America. But most of all, for our purposes – the Baby Boomers – they were our parents.

My father was born in Simbario, a small town located in the Calabria region of Southern Italy. He used to like to say the town was so small and so hidden, that with all the wars that Italy fought, nobody from the town was ever drafted, for the Italian government did not know it existed. His father crossed the Atlantic Ocean to find a better life for his family. As with many Baby Boomers' parents, it was the promise of a better life in America that brought him through Ellis Island. Once in America, these parents struggled to find work and provide for their families. They were thought of at the time as immigrants. They were the Irish, who settled in Boston, the Russian Jews, who found a colony of life in New York, and Italians, like my family, who first went to Michigan, and then gravitated to Chicago.

My grandfather worked in the mines in the Upper Peninsula in Northern Michigan. That is what Italian men of his day did when they came to this country. It was hard work, even grueling, but he did it to provide. One day, my Dad, who came over as a child in 1921 and was a great athlete and student by high school age, and who was now proud of the way that he spoke the English language, had to go see his Dad in the mines. It was a day that would change our family forever.

My Dad, who loved his father, used to make his lunch. One day, my grandfather forgot his lunch, and my father, who did not want to see him go without sustenance, went to the mines to bring him his lunch. He took the cage far below ground and saw the conditions in which his father had to work. The pain that his father had to endure became the inspiration for improvement. His sadness at seeing his father work so hard for very little pay, and in such dirty conditions, drove him. On that day, he gave up any hope for college and boarded a train to Chicago, where he worked for four years until he could bring his parents and siblings to a beautiful apartment on the South side. In a letter to his family, he said, "Just come with the clothes on your back."

It was there, in Chicago, that the family gained its traction, its full measure of life in America. My father was a popular man amongst his peers and served as President of an esteemed athletic club in Chicago for many years. He and his older brother ran a pillow company for 52 years, during which time it became the largest and most prestigious firm in that industry. In 1939, my father married my mother. They were happy, worked as a team, and would find 60 years of marriage a blessing. They were to have four children. Their eldest, Patricia, died as baby. They went on to raise three sons: Robert (known as Bobby), Raymond (who is called Ray), and myself, the youngest, Richard (currently known by most as Rick, though, as a child, I frequently heard the more popular family moniker of Ricky). This was a family with a great history and cherished memories that walked the sands of time together.

Frank and Mary Bava, my parents, part of the Greatest Generation, were representative of the times. They sought to educate their children, they were devoted to extended family, and they were loyal to their friends. They wanted to own a home, they bought a Chevrolet Impala, and they made sure that we had a color television for the Rose Bowl. They enjoyed the family dinner, they enjoyed the company of friends, and they especially liked to entertain those friends. They looked forward to holidays with family. They were supportive parents before "supportive parents" became part of the popular vernacular. They were like many people of their times, who understood President Roosevelt's declaration for Social Security, and who would one day see the fruits of that benefit. They, like others of their generation, wanted to reach their full potential, as was the promise of the post-World War II times. It was the generation of big bands, Joe DiMaggio playing centerfield for the Yankees, and the move to suburbia. It was a generation that got up every day, went to work, never seemed to complain, and were the strength that Baby Boomers would so identify with as they looked at their parents.

These parents of mine, and yours, were the parents of Baby Boomers; they always seemed to "be there for you," as the saying goes. You could call them, seek their advice, and value their wisdom. They would always be strong, always be in your life, and you could always depend on them. But then one day – and most Baby Boomers will recognize that day – something changes. Your parents begin to slow down, as their memories fade and their energy decreases. One day, the laughter shared with parents while shopping in the grocery store changes to long discussions about prescriptions. One day, the discussion changes from the summer vacation to a conversation about rest. One day, you begin to worry about what happens when you call your parents. One day, they need your help, and you are scared, because now you have become a caregiver. Your only thought is, "I just want it to be like it once was." You begin to realize what your parents have accomplished in life, the respect that you have for them, and how you will hold on for dear life to preserve their lives. You are now a driver on black ice, hoping that the end is not near. You want your parents to last forever.

So now your job as Baby Boomers begins, when your time with that beloved parent is about caring for them. Your thoughts are about making them comfortable, helping them, and making their lives sustainable. You become a practitioner of Medicare, and of health benefits and services, for you need to take care of your parents. Baby Boomers across America are in this category. This is what they are thinking: "My parents were so good to me; they gave me the life I have; now I have to step up and assume responsibility." This burden can be overwhelming, the issues complicated. But, like Baby Boomers who once wondered about their draft lottery numbers, who once saw fellow students streak on the college campus, and who remember the day that they started using email, now comes the time of the great Baby Boomer challenge: caring for elderly parents.

What is it like to have parents begin to fail, to sit with them in hospitals, or to have them forget your child's name? What is it like when you have the debate with your siblings about whether parents should stay in their homes or seek assisted living facilities? What is it like when siblings, so close all their lives, now fight over whose responsibility it is to take care of Mom and Dad? The question becomes: Are you doing enough? What is it like when your parents are not nearby, and the burden of caring falls on a sibling? What is it like when the balance of work, marriage, and caring for your parents becomes so great that you wonder how can you escape? But, in the end, the conclusion that Baby Boomers meet every day is, "It is now part of my life, for I am now the parent."

Saturday, December 10, 2011

They call it Assisted Living

I made a new friend recently – who says Baby Boomers cannot make friends at this age and stage? However, Baby Boomers do complain about it enough that I wrote a column about it a while back. But I digress – this new friend was telling me that he is putting together a consortium to build assisted living facilities. He hopes that their initial location will get off the ground next year, and that it will be the model for locations over the life of the business plan. This man, a financial expert by background, wanted to show me the concept, because, as he said, I am the Baby Boomer guy, and every day, 10,000 Baby Boomers turn 65. As he went over the plan with what they called some new ideas, I began to daydream. Not about my possible future in one of these places, but of the experience we went through as a family caring for my elderly parents before they passed.

It started with my mother. After the Harvard-educated doctor botched her surgery, she was confined to her bed. My brother Bob, a retired banker, moved in and became the caregiver for both my mother and my father. My mother passed, and my saint-like brother cared for my father until he died at 92. This process went on from 1998 to 2004. There are three brothers in our family: I am the youngest, and my brother Bob is the oldest. There is no question that my middle brother, Ray, would agree with me when I say that our older brother, Bob, supplied the brunt of my parents' care.

One Saturday, as my father began to fade and taking care of him was becoming difficult, my brother Ray and I visited several facilities, just to see if any could provide the loving care for Dad, and spare our older brother the burden. Although Bob never complained, you could see the strain and the years of devotion starting to take their toll.

In 2007, Bob died of a massive heart attack when he was just starting to enjoy his retirement years. He did not smoke, drink, gamble, or have any vice of note, but he did love to eat. The night before his funeral, my brother Ray and I talked of his devotion to my Mom and Dad. But we also talked of the visits to elderly care outposts. What a crime in this country, that these places supposedly operating as places of care, treat the elderly like people parked on their way to death. Yes, there are some that offer outstanding care, but you need a bushel basket of money to get the kind of care that would classify as respectful. The picture that we get from corporations of assisted living looks more like an over-55 community than elderly care. Yes, if one is healthy enough to make it to the dining hall, or to the bridge game, then there are plenty of answers. It is when sickness becomes part of the story that things get tricky.

Once upon a time in Northlake, Illinois, there was a place called Villa Scallabrini. It was home for aging people of Italian background. For years, they cared for the residents as if they were their own grandparents. Italian women would donate their time, and my Aunt Helen was one of those volunteers. Each person had his own room, and there was the chapel, the food, the culture, the surrounding gardens, and the individual attention. Italians, always conscious of respect for their parents, were said to be able to place their parents in the Villa, guilt-free. I remember visiting when a wonderful elderly cousin was placed there, and the way she was treated was remarkable.

So, when my brother Ray and I thought of our situation, we thought of checking out the Villa. The result of that morning will stay with us forever. The Villa of 2004, along with its current stench, had a new corporate owner. There was a notable reluctance of the manager to give us a tour, as he clearly wanted to keep us in his office, in the lobby, or in what are known in the trade as the common areas. Oh yes, the chapel was still there with its shiny pews, but everything else would make you cry. How do I know this? Because after we received the booklet and the contract, and saw the video pitch, we did our own homework. Once the manager thought that we were out the door, my brother and I went back in and saw the place as it really was. We saw the rooms with the multiple beds, and the darkness, and the lack of staff. We saw the people just waiting to die. But I will bet the return on investment was good. There was this one area, like a hallway, separated with curtains, with army cots for beds – disgusting. Yes, this was the worst case; others that we saw were better, but not much better. Yes, the overworked staff probably felt like they were doing a good job, but they were stressed. Recently, I read in the paper about a case where a son questioned a staff member as to why he was calling his mom "granny," instead of by her name. The response was, "Your mother is so out of it that she would not know what I am calling her."

As for The Villa, who knows, maybe they have upgraded their care since 2004. I tend to doubt it. I do know this: my Aunt Helen's daughter, a Baby Boomer, never talks of donating her time there now, even though for years she would go there to pick up her mother, whose efforts she supported. Although the name remains the same, this is not the Villa Scallabrini that she would remember from her youth.

I can already anticipate the feedback, because many people from the assisted living industry are followers of my work with the Baby Boomer generation. They will say that their facility is nothing like what I described. They will say that their staff-to-patient ratio is among the best. They will say that they deliver an outstanding service and make a contribution to society. They are right, but at what cost? The average person could never afford the care that they will describe. Perhaps, your parents did well in their lives, and hopefully the kids have care more prominently on their minds than what they are going to be left in the will. In that case, your family might be fine. Our Baby Boomer friend, Bill Gates, who loves his father dearly, will be fine if it comes to that for his Dad. Currently, though, we should be ashamed in this country for the way that we care for the aged.

So finally, coming back to the original premise about my new friend going into the assisted living business, let us hope he gets it right.

Wednesday, April 13, 2011

When Your Time Comes

One of the difficult things taking place in the lives of Baby Boomers is figuring out how to care for their aging parents. Where is the manual for this sensitive set of circumstances? Father and mother, or a parent who is widowed, often want to maintain their independence for as long as possible. They are also accustomed to being leaders in the family and giving advice. When the roles reverse, it can cause tension even in the best of families. What also complicates matters is when there are siblings with different ideas on what actions should be taken. Baby Boomers reported that, if these situations are not handled correctly, brothers and sisters can become distant when one feels that they are doing more than others. The sister who lives close by and drives dad to the doctor and cooks meals for mom, can come to resent the far away brother who seems detached. Initially, things seem fine while the parent continues to live on their own. But when the next stage takes place, complications set in. For the chosen few with deep bank accounts, many options exist; however, for the vast majority decisions need to be made. Will a child take the parent into their home? Does the parent go to a facility, if a good one can be found? Most Baby Boomers want to do the right thing. The overwhelming feeling is "my parents were there for me, now it is my turn." When my grandfather died and my grandmother could no longer live in her third floor apartment, my parents, aunt, and uncle just talked it over in a civil manner and divided the responsibility. My grandmother never saw the inside of anything other than her children's homes. She remained free to experience her life to the end with nothing but the enjoyment of grandchildren, family friends who came to visit, and children who allowed her to continue to be the "CHIEF." Wouldn't it be nice if this peace and harmony could someday exist for the Baby Boomer generation when it is not their time to do the caring, but to be cared for? Baby Boomers, you will want your children to see how you care for their grandparents, because they most likely will mirror your actions.

Summary of Chapter 2

Caring For Elderly Parents

As the cold night falls on Chicago, two Baby Boomers enter Northwestern Hospital. The challenge that they face is great, for their father suffers with skin cancer, compounded by early stages of dementia. Their mother, meanwhile, attends rehabilitation as she recovers from a serious pelvic injury, compounded by the discovery of a large mass in the rectal area. Two parents whom they love, two parents who defined a success story, two parents who have made philanthropy a cause, are now weak, confused, fearful, and looking at the clock on the wall. The Baby Boomers, a brother and sister, march to the call, talk to the doctors, and communicate with extended family. They are to be admired and appreciated, for their role is a difficult one, and their dedication to their parents is profound. To these two Baby Boomers, their father is not a prominent attorney; he is Dad. Their mother is not a famous singer, but Mom. Their father is not arguing before the Supreme Court; he is struggling in the court of facilities, and they love him in either role. Their mother is not a board member at a music school; she is singing for her supper at 6 p.m. in the kitchens of patient care, and they love her. They are to be admired, this brother and sister, for they represent a growing breed of Baby Boomers who went from attending luncheons honoring their parents, to having the honor of supporting these same two people who they care about so much.

They began one day by taking over the wheel when their loving parent did not want to drive. They continued, as the host of the family Thanksgiving, once held at their parents' home. Then one day, they began making doctor visits, as an aid for their parents' ailments. One day, they helped their father close his office, a painful reminder that high-profile law cases have been replaced by idle time. One day, their mother, a famous opera singer, walked in the door with a CD with recordings of her singing for the grandchildren. The reality was hard to accept – that this would someday have to replace her live performances that her children had grown up with and cherished.

What is interesting is that these two wonderful Baby Boomers do not seek glory. They are not looking for a pat on the back. They are just doing what they believe is right. They absorb the heartache and the long hours of duties, because they once saw their parents care for their own parents, and attend to their own siblings.

Is it hard on Baby Boomers to now watch their parents struggle, to not see them as they once were, to see them age? The answer is yes. When Baby Boomers gather now, amongst friends, they might talk about James Taylor, they might talk about the best place for dinner, but more than likely they are comparing notes on something that is front and center in their lives: caring for elderly parents. As an observer of my generation, I do not see spoiled individuals, self-absorbed in their ways. I see kind, considerate peers trying to return all the good that they once so appreciated receiving, to those strong rocks of people called parents.

Chapter 3

Losing Loved Ones

Of all the chapters in this book, this one is the hardest to write. I am a Baby Boomer who has lost both my parents. As you know from the previous reading, I have also lost my older brother. The loss was painful. The focus of this chapter centers around the loss of parents. We have seen that many Baby Boomers are spending a great amount of care, time, and effort supporting their elderly parents. For those Baby Boomers, the experience is difficult. However, the Baby Boomers who still have their parents can count themselves to be very lucky. This area of discussion, watching your parents age, suffer from illness, and then pass away, is a very hard thing for most Baby Boomers. They have trouble coping with the process. Many Baby Boomers have shared the grief that comes over them, as the finality of parents becomes a part of your life. In this chapter, I will converse with the readers about my own dealings with the loss of my parents, as a microcosm of the composite of stories that I have heard from Baby Boomers.

My parents met in 1937, and they "courted proper," as the saying goes. They had a big wedding. My mother and dad had numerous bridesmaids, groomsmen, and flower girls. Their wedding was an event. They were two like-minded people who saw marriage as important. They came to the marriage respectful of their parents, and loyal to their respective extended families.

Like people of their generation, they wanted to work hard, raise a family, and seek a better life than that of their parents. They achieved that goal. The statistics show that they owned their home, lived debt free, and lived within their means. Through further examination, it can be pointed out that they were like athletes who got the most out of their talent, and thus the most out of life. They were, by all accounts, happy. They worked as a team, had great communication as a couple, and made decisions jointly. Friends who knew them referred to them as "Frank and Mary," as if they belonged together. They, like most, were not without hardship. Early in their marriage, they lost their first child, Patricia. They were to raise three sons, of which I am the youngest. They relied on friends, who for the most part helped in many ways, because in their time, people did pull together and were better for it. It gave their life a sense of community. But what it also showed is that, like many of their time, they did more with less.

They lived their life with principle. Their life had meaning because they had ethics. They never showed their problems, were good natured, and brought a smile to everyone they encountered. They were simply good people. My parents believed in the basics: respect to their parents, a loyal regard for their siblings, and showing leadership to their nieces and nephews. They knew how to be a friend, and in their own way, made a contribution to society. It was these kind of values that they imparted to my brothers and I. When I went to college, I remember talking to my classmates about their families, and being proud of the family that I came from. It is so interesting; many Baby Boomers spent a great deal of capital trying to get away from their parents. Once away, they will tell others, people they meet, about their parents, who they were seemingly trying to escape.

Maybe that is why, as time has gone on, Baby Boomers have come to appreciate their mothers and fathers. Many Baby Boomers at a later stage of life found meaning in the relationship with their parents. As they got into the work place, they began to think about the sacrifices that were made for their education. It was their parents' sacrifices that gave them the foundation for the life that they were leading now. It is funny, all of a sudden, Baby Boomers, looked at their parents with a sense of gratitude. As a generation, Baby Boomers have tried hard, as they reached middle age, to give back to parents, to take them on vacations, and make them a part of their family. Most Baby Boomers had a renewed feeling of warmth for their parents. It is with that back drop that Baby Boomers are finding it so hard to lose these important people in their lives. The parents, who were their rock, are now represented by a grave stone, and this for many Baby Boomers is difficult to deal with.

My mother first started having problems with arthritis, and the pain became so problematic that it was recommended that she have knee replacement surgery. The surgery did not go well, and she never walked again. Shortly after the operation, she had a stroke, causing her to become bedridden. This turned pain into suffering and death.

I recall standing in church at Queen of All Saints, in the Northernmost part of the Chicago city limits. This church was the site of so many happy times, like midnight mass with family on Christmas Eve. It was the church where my parents renewed their marriage vows when they celebrated their 50th Wedding Anniversary. It was the church that was attached to the grammar school that put me on my way in life. It is a beautiful basilica. But on the day of my mother's funeral, it was the representation of sadness. As my Aunt Evie sang the "Ave Maria," and nobody does it better, the tears began to run from my eyes, as if they were to fill the empty well in my heart.

You try to take heart in the fact that you still have your father. But you know that things will never be the same. My father, a strong man of heart and body, seemed to die along with my mother. He stayed with us, but only as a physical presence. Within a few short years, he would lie next to my mother in Queen of Heaven Cemetery. I miss them both, and so wish they were still here for the guidance they used to provide, and the joy they brought to my life.

In October of 2012, I became engaged. I met a wonderful woman, the love of my life, the "one and only." My fiancée and I made the journey from San Diego, our home, back to the Midwest. We were to celebrate our wonderful news, with family. We wanted to spend time with her parents, back in Columbus, who we are fortunate to have in our lives. We were also going to Chicago, where my Uncle Joe and Aunt Fran were giving us an engagement party. Amidst that wonderful joy, was the feeling that my parents were not here to share in this happiness. They would have loved my fiancée Lisa, for she represents all the qualities that my parents would have hoped that I would find in a woman. Upon driving to the engagement party, a highlight in Lisa's and my life, my brother Ray and sister-in-law Sandy suggested that we stop at the cemetery. There we stood the four of us, Lisa and I, Ray and Sandy. We looked upon the grave that represented my brother Ray's and my parents. We stood as a family, Lisa and I, along with Ray and Sandy, and in that moment we shared the good news with my parents. For you see, the grief of losing your parents is there, but their memory is paramount.

Friday, June 17, 2011

Father's Day Weekend 2011

It is Father's Day weekend, 2011, and Baby Boomers are in a reflective mood. They are thinking about their fathers, the way that they grew up, and the values that they learned. This is interesting because many are now fathers and grandfathers themselves, and they are the recipients of the respect that they once delivered to their own fathers. But, like the Oregon father shared last year, even though his son provided a nice dinner and special day for him, his thoughts were with his own Dad on the East Coast. The Oregon family gathered, gifts were exchanged, and laughter was present. However, while appreciative of his son's respect, he felt almost reluctant to be the one receiving the honor and admiration on Father's Day. This is because Baby Boomers were sons and daughters first. Baby Boomers somehow feel more comfortable being the sons and daughters. It is like they feel more comfortable giving the card than receiving the card.

But there is another dynamic going on, and that is common for many Baby Boomers: their fathers were good and decent men. They were the type of men that made this country great. They got up in the morning, sometimes very early, went to work each day, and provided for their families. They worked hard to educate their children. They sacrificed to give their children better lives than the ones they had. These were the fathers that sent their children to college. These were the fathers who supported their children before there was a word for it, when going to a little league game was done out of caring rather than peer pressure. Most Baby Boomers simply loved their Dads. They liked spending time with them, and they relied on them for the critical steps that Baby Boomers would make during their lives.

While some Baby Boomers are lucky to still have their Dads, many do not. There is the woman in Boston who was very close with her father, and still feels the pain of his passing. When she confided her feelings to an old classmate, her friend could identify, having lost his Dad. Their mutual loss was a subject of interaction after not communicating for several years. For those fortunate ones who can have the multi-generational celebration this weekend, they should count themselves lucky. A Baby Boomer who can sit in their living room with their aged father on the left and their children on the right can count this weekend as a Hallmark moment. For golf fans, the U.S. Open always concludes on Father's Day. How great would it be to have a family barbecue, follow the golf, and celebrate as a family? But, for many Baby Boomers, the day will consist of a quiet moment, remembering the men that shaped their lives: their fathers._

Tuesday, December 13, 2011

The Christmas Eve Tradition

Her name was Rose Eraci. She and her husband Joe had three children. Mary was the oldest, Evie was a few years younger, and the youngest, also a Joe, was raised as "Joey," but spent his adult life as "Dr. Eraci." Evie, or the formal name by which she was called by her mother, Evelyn, became a famous singer. Later in life, she was a woman who gave back to charity. Mary, a school of music graduate, could play on a piano anything that you could whistle. She had every talent a woman could acquire to go along with a kindness that could never be duplicated. These three described above watched, as children, their mother and father, Rose and Joe, support and take care of numerous family members, which brought closeness to the entire family.

Rose with her sisters and brother, and Joe with cousins, were closer than any family could be. It was with that back drop that Rose Eraci would create a Christmas Eve tradition that would endure long after her life was over. Starting during the depression when families needed to come together just to survive, Rose Eraci thought that bringing family together on Christmas Eve was very special. So began the tradition of the festive night that was first centered around her sisters and brother. As years passed, her own children would marry and have children. The tradition continued, as the crowd grew bigger, and by now family members were taking turns hosting the celebration.

They observed the Catholic principles, thus only fish was served. But because they were Italian with some great cooks in the family, the food was mouthwatering. In 1939, Mary married the most popular man in the neighborhood; his name was Frank Bava. He was President of the famed Chi Armour club. He had three things that Rose would like for her daughter. He had a steady job, he was good to his parents, and he was, as she would say, "a good man." Frank and Mary were forever linked in July of '39. They would host Christmas the first year of marriage, something they would repeat many times. Those first years it was about Aunts and Uncles. But over the years families began to grow, marry, and form traditions of their own. But by then Rose Eraci's other two children would get married, each taking their turn. By the late sixties, the tradition was in full force. By now, all of Rose Eraci's children had children of their own. In fact, Frank and Mary had two older boys, out of a total of three, who were walking down the church steps, and then taking their turn in the rotation.

So what began with Rose Eraci wanting to be with her brother and sisters would now become the foundation for her family. It would become a "can't miss" event, full of laughter and truly good cheer. Rose Eraci had three children that were genuine, and their offspring embraced tradition. Anyone in this extended family in 2011 could tell great stories of wonderful memories. They would tell stories of food, singing, and "remember when…" "Remember when we had the grab bag?" "Remember when we went caroling?" "Remember when we went to midnight mass?" "Remember when Grandpa Eraci would give out the envelopes to the grandchildren?" "Remember when Bobby, the eldest grandchild, began kidding Grandma Eraci that she was the Rose Kennedy of our family?" "Remember the first year the celebration outgrew the hosting in a home?" A public place had no impact on the smiles, or the want to be there, or the "can't wait to see you" feeling. Now, new relationships were being formed because the youngest of the children were now grown, married, and with young children of their own. Aunt Evie was now leading them all in song, as she had done in the past for their mothers and fathers.

All families should be like this, where you have tradition on your side, where extended family likes each other and believes that being together is a good thing. Grandpa and Grandma Eraci would pass away, but the tradition lives on. Mary and Frank Bava have since passed, but the tradition lives on. Bobby and his wife Lenora, who once hosted a memorable Christmas in their new home in Naperville, IL, are gone, but the tradition lives on.

Raymond, Frank and Mary's middle son, hosted his share, took his turn, and just two years ago, his youngest son, picked up the baton, and took his turn to host the Christmas Eve tradition. Dr. Eraci's oldest daughter, Mary Pat, remembered her mother and father hosting in the family home of Elmhurst, IL. She had the entire family to her home in nearby Oak Park, IL just a few years back, as her sister organized pictures of Christmas past. It was a walk down memory lane.

Rose Eraci will never show up in a history book, but she created history simply because she believed that the family should be together.

Thursday, September 22, 2011
Breakfast with Mom and Dad

Baby Boomers report and write in about the impact the loss of a parent or parents has on them. Some Baby Boomers share their heart wrenching stories of trying to cope with the death of their parents, and their struggle during the bereavement process. This story is dedicated to you.

The story that you are about to read is fiction, different than other things read in this space, and is not based on direct input from Baby Boomers, or an actual case study. What can be garnered, though, are the impressions that Baby Boomers have provided, which create this composite story. The meaning of what is contained in this writing reflects the shared relationship between Baby Boomers and their parents.

In 2004, a Baby Boomer's father passed away, almost five years to the date of losing his mother. On a summer day, in 2011, the son visits the cemetery and stands by the grave, for what seemed like hours, the loss still weighing on his mind. Oh, how he misses his parents. Talking out loud, he says to the grave stone, "I have nobody to call." "I miss your advice and your encouragement." He realizes the hurt, as he remembers what his parents did for him, their sacrifices for his education. They were always supportive; they made you believe that you could accomplish and never let you get down. You were the apple of their eye, not spoiled, but made to believe that you were indeed part of a family. As the darkness sets in, a worker comes by to let you know the gates will be closing. So, with a tear in your eye, you bid farewell, leaving with only your memories, and the sight of the flowers that were planted. You drive back to the hotel, for your flight home is not until the morning. It seems that room service is enough for tonight, for you are tired and drained from your day, so you fall fast asleep.

You think that it is morning when you wake, but your surroundings look different. You are in a kitchen, the smell of bacon is in the air, the table is set with china cups and a formal white table cloth. You are seated, and when you look up, your Mom is pouring coffee. Sitting at the table is your Dad, he is smiling, with the pleasant look that is so familiar. As Mom joins you at the table, you butter the slice of homemade bread. There are homemade cookies for after breakfast. There is laughter. Dad, Mom, "I have missed you so." "Well honey, Dad and I wanted to just have one more breakfast with you. We wanted to hear everything that is going on in your life. Tell us about the job, and the kids, and how things are going with your wife. We just wanted to make sure you were happy. You're never too old, to get some guidance after all." "Yes, yes," the son cries out. "It is what I have been missing. I have so much to tell you both"

But the scene fades, soon the Baby Boomer is at the table alone, and with a blink of an eye, the room is now filled with the standard single of the airport hotel room on the 9th floor. It is now morning, and the shower feels good, pouring down on an unsettled mind. As the man of 55 finishes dressing, and proceeds down the elevator, he has one thought, and one thought only: "if it were only possible. If only one more time, I could have breakfast with my Mom and Dad."

Thursday, June 23, 2011

Two Baby Boomers discuss Loss

On an early Friday afternoon in Del Mar, California, two Baby Boomers became engaged in conversation. It was not a long talk, but one of meaning. The interaction spoke to what a great many Baby Boomers feel, as reflected in the dialogue between the two. It was about twenty minutes to 2 as they were both getting ready for a book forum at the library, when a discussion of loss occurred. It was the Friday before Father's Day and both were reflecting on the fact that they miss their fathers and, quite frankly, both of their parents.

The conversation was respectful and heartfelt. Both could identify with each other's loss. Both, it was obvious, came from loving families and it was clear their parents had an impact on their life. This speaks to the general issue of Baby Boomers who age, and because of the natural course of life, find that the people they hold dear will leave them. The impact can be anywhere from devastating, to at the very least, leaving a hole in the heart. It signals that, when you lose your parents, life will never be the same. Something is gone forever and never will it reappear. It signals the feeling that you, yourself, are not the same, and that age is not something that you just talk about, but something very real in your own life. It is a passing from youth to something else.

Most Baby Boomers will experience this feeling. Some will also experience the steps previous to this, like parents getting sick and needing care. They will watch their parents' health fail before their eyes. But nothing has the impact of death. There is such finality to it, but the pain lingers on, even as life moves forward. Baby Boomers cope, they learn to live with the loss, and they look to channel their love elsewhere. Some discover a closer bond with their own children. Some look to the next generation to impart the wisdom of their parents. Some find solace through a beloved uncle or aunt. But most, they simply remember; it may be in memory, through pictures, or in those visits to the cemetery.

But Baby Boomers do remember, and increasingly, they realize the sacrifices that their parents made for them, and the appreciation they have for their mother and father. So, as the two Baby Boomers concluded their talk, which was sometimes interrupted by the goings-on around them, they came away with a feeling of understanding each other and their shared experience. Further, they were examples of the larger scope of Baby Boomers who simply miss their mother and father.

Thursday, May 26, 2011

Baby Boomers and the Extended Family

Baby Boomers report an increased effort to reconnect with their extended family. If you talk to Baby Boomers, there is a heightened awareness that the need to find the relationships of the past is more than just a nice thing to do. The issue becomes one of needing a foundation to their lives at this stage. Why is this, why do Baby Boomers feel the need to renew bonds that may have seemingly slipped away? One answer is a longing for the past, when families were for the most part, all in the same general area, and holidays and special events were spent together with aunts, uncles, cousins, and other family members.

Another reason is that as Baby Boomers look back on their lives and do an evaluation of what took place, they recall, perhaps, an aunt or uncle that played a key role in their development. But, more than likely, the pendulum of life has swung back into the direction of family. For example, as Baby Boomers left college and began to find their way in the world, many had a steak of independence. They sought a different lifestyle than what they were accustomed to. They wanted to be on their own, see other parts of the country, and try new things. "Getting away" was the mantra. As a result, many Baby Boomers began to lose touch with their relatives. They were busy with corporate life, and not interested in extended family life. Baby Boomers began to stop going home for Christmas, while starting their own new traditions. Everyone seemed to have his or her own life, career, and house, and the years just passed.

Then one day, the world begins to change, your parents become ill, and you have to return home. Subsequently, they pass away. Baby Boomers are left with a void; all of a sudden, maybe a sibling unexpectedly dies, and now one looks for support. Baby Boomers report that their reliance on friends, which had been the mainstay from ages 25-55, just was not enough to fill the void.

So, Baby Boomers began to rediscover the people that they still had in their life, maybe an aunt, an uncle, or a cousin, who could provide the emotional support, or allow you to see the present through the eyes of the past. The reconnection process, however, is not always easy. The woman in Del Mar, California sometimes finds little support from outreach to her mother's sister, or once favorite cousin. She feels hurt when her emails are not returned, or she feels awkward, because so much time has passed. A worse scenario is that people have changed and they are not as loveable as they once were.

But the woman outside Scripps Hospital, near Torrey Pines Golf Course, might have a better perspective. She reported, "I am moving back to New York. I have family there. I am going to go back, I will hate the weather, but I am going to invite my sister, her children, my aunt, and her children for everything from coffee to summer picnics, until we recapture what we lost." She went on to say, "I know my life will be enriched just being around the family." So it goes for Baby Boomers, just another step towards life at this age and stage. Baby Boomers thinking about their lives, now choose to find solace in the cousin that once watched them play little league baseball.

April 14, 2011

Baby Boomers and losing Parents

It was good for so long, and then things began to happen. Baby Boomers react to the fact that at a certain period of time in life, you start to lose the people you care most about. It usually begins with a parent.

The first time that you go through the process of a parent becoming ill, taking care of them, and then losing them, it has an impact. The Baby Boomer reports that justification takes place. You are incredibly sad about the loss of your mother, but at least you still have your father. But as he begins to fail, and then dies, you just know things will never be the same. You begin to face your own reality, and some say your own mortality. It is natural in this situation that you look to others for love and support. It may be your spouse, your children, your siblings, or extended family members who are important to you. Most say that what helps is to make sure that the dearly departed are given the proper respect in the final act, i.e. the wake, the funeral, the ritual of saying goodbye.

This is important on many fronts: it is unfortunate, but the funeral is the final way that one is remembered and creates a lasting impression, so proper respect needs to be paid. It also is a time of mourning, a process that one needs to experience. It also provides others a chance to show you they care by coming. Baby Boomers say that you know who your friends are when you lose a parent and others are there for you. The support means a great deal, and Baby Boomers note the appreciation. Baby Boomers comment that those few days from the impact of the death, to the planning of the funeral, to the final goodbye are amongst the greatest challenges that one will face in life. This is something that always stays with you.

Summary – Chapter 3

Losing Loved Ones

We said at the beginning of this chapter that this would be the most difficult piece to write. As you can see, through the messages constituted in this space, a great many Baby Boomers have experienced the grieving process. What must have been a sad chapter to read can also be looked upon as the wonderful aspects of memories.

As Baby Boomers have pointed out, the physical nature of losing parents, while difficult, is not the end of the story. The many experiences shared between Baby Boomers and their parents will live on in infamy. As one Baby Boomer shared in a grief counseling session in Palm Springs, California, parents are always with you even if they cannot answer the telephone on a Saturday night. May it be in life or loss, Baby Boomers have come to the ultimate conclusion: parents matter. Their hope is that the learned experience shared by their parents to them will ultimately be imparted to their children, and there is the continuum of the family chain.

Many Baby Boomers have had significant loss. Some have lost a spouse, which in itself, has been traumatic to Baby Boomers. Some have lost a dear friend, and that is hard to reconcile, when a peer passes away and your own mortality is brought into focus. But what seems to be the predominant issue facing Baby Boomers as of this point is the loss of parents.

Baby Boomers were of a younger age when their grandparents died. While that was sad, there was comfort in the fact that your life was still ahead of you. After all, your parents were there, and your extended family was together. Of course, those circumstances were far different. This is due in part to timing, and when your parents pass, things change, and there is realization that there is a different time on the clock on the wall.

I began to feel the impact even before my Dad died. With my mother now gone and my father fading, I sought to recapture days gone by. I sought to find lightning in a bottle. I wanted the fountain of youth. No, not the story book version; I was not searching for my youth, but the feeling of my youth, when a discussion with my Dad was meaningful again. My brother Bob, who has since passed away, was for all practical purposes the caregiver for my parents in their waning days. My brother Ray and I owe a debt of gratitude to our brother Bob, a bill that can never be paid – for he took care of our parents. They never saw the inside of a facility. We, as a family, are very proud of that.

My brother Bob had grown tired, not in a complaint sort of way, but he had simply needed a break. I came up with this idea of a father-son trip. I said, "Dad, where do you want to go?" My father surprisingly warmed to the idea, and said that Sarasota, Florida would be a great place, for it was the site of so many happy times that we had as a family.

We did this twice. The first time, my father was independent, and he could walk when we got up in the morning. For two weeks we reminisced. It was joyful, a true walk down memory lane. For two weeks we just spent time together, watching Baseball and seeing some of the sites that we had gone to with my mother. We had such a good time that we tried it the next year.

The second time was not so easy. My father had become frail, and the logistics in the airport, getting him from Chicago to Florida, were now monumental. It is amazing how the person pushing your Dad in a wheel chair across an airport, can become your best friend. On this last trip to Sarasota, I had the feeling that my father knew that things were coming to an end. I sensed that he wanted to share things with me, and it was my job to listen. I am glad that I did, because the end was near, and closure to his life would soon come, and there would never be another trip again. I tell Baby Boomers all the time, the ones who have their parents, do not think that the life of your parents will go on forever. Make the most of the time that you have with them, for the alternative is not pretty.

When you visit Palm Springs, California, there is much to appreciate. You can find golf courses. You can take advantage of the glorious weather, and you can find grief council. I first observed a Baby Boomer woman who was struck by grief. She shared with me the program at Eisenhower hospital that she took advantage of as a source of help. I also observed a Baby Boomer who would go to the Rancho Mirage library, a wonderful facility, and a staple of the Coachella Valley that encompasses the Palm Springs surrounding area. He would go to this wonderful world of periodicals, and take out a book every day on grief. It would provide solace. Some Baby Boomers who live in the Palm Springs area have gone to senior or community centers to take advantage of the grief services that are offered. Some prefer even to take advantage of individual therapy.

But most Baby Boomers who have sought out help benefit from the group sessions. They feel a sense of unity from others, to know they are not alone in the feeling of grief. One Baby Boomer said, while talking to him after I had attended such a group session, that he was reluctant to come. He did not want to sit around and hear others go on and on about what he considered a private situation. He was encouraged to come by a grief counselor that he had met. The expert said, "Try it. There will be people of your age, similar background, and who are going through the same set of circumstances." The Baby Boomer, while initially reluctant, now praised the experience of being guided by the shared value of community.

It is very interesting to me as a chronicler of our generation, the Baby Boomers, that members of this generation have always gained from the shared examples of their peers. The same generation that found shared value in music, who found shared reciprocity in politics, and who grew up together in an ever-changing world, now finds harmony with their peers when facing grief. When facing grief alone, your sadness can become paralyzing. Your feet feel like they are in quick sand when you get up in the morning. Walking to the shower, it feels like your feet are in a bucket of ice. There is something comforting about talking with others who are going through the same thing.

Baby Boomers who have lost loved ones have felt this deep sense of loss. Some have had to live with the sense of loss and some cope more easily than others do. Some can go on with their life, even though they feel the change inside. Some find it very hard to deal with, almost driving them to the point of becoming irrational. For some, the struggle to cope with the grief becomes some overwhelming that it can even lead them to quit their jobs, give away their money, and drop out of society. Their extended family members wonder what happened to them, and ask where they are. Friends worry because the conversations seemed strained, until there were no more conversations at all. A brother worries about your irregular actions, wondering what has come over you. He can't understand the impact that the grief has had on you, or why it would manifest itself in such extreme behaviors. This happens because nobody can measure the score card of another person's grief.

This escape may not be a good solution. But for some this becomes an answer. Many Baby Boomers realize they have to get back on the train of life by themselves. But help is a good thing, may it be grief council, the clergy, or the best anecdote of all, "someone special" that gives you your life back. One thing is certain, Baby Boomers, if you are going through this feeling in life, where you suffer from the loss of loved ones, you are not alone, because your fellow Baby Boomers can relate.

Chapter 4

Social Relationships

Baby Boomers across America lament the loss of the feeling of connection. They recall their college days, when groups of friends headed out for an activity together. They long for the days of early adulthood when friends seemed to come so easy. A Baby Boomer in Santa Barbara once revealed, that while his married life, children, and extended family are as good as they can be, he is seemingly without the friend to watch a ballgame with. Baby Boomers, because of busy schedules, the pace of life, and time having passed, report that the ingredient missing from their lives is friendship. The lives of many Baby Boomers have followed a similar course. Growing up, there were the friends in the neighborhood, then there were the classmates who seemed to help you through the puberty stage of high school, and later there were the friends who helped you through the transition to college. Baby Boomers recall the vast friendships in their early jobs, the ones that they would go out with after work. They recall that, even as their work life became more hectic and responsibilities increased, there was still always time for that coffee with a friend, associate, or even a person who was a little better than an acquaintance.

Now, however, at this stage of life, the lack of time, events of life, and responsibilities have made such encounters almost obsolete. This is a problem for many Baby Boomers. Some suffer from loneliness. Some just feel that it is harder to make a connection with someone new. Of course, the big culprit is time. Baby Boomers have so much going on, that the action item list is working in overdrive. You have the relationship with your spouse, the parents who need care, and the leadership that needs to be paid to children. There is the worry about finances, retirement, and the work place. Where is the opportunity for the added effort to meet, talk with on the phone, or cultivate past friendships and new relationships?

Another interesting aspect to this is the losing track of friends who were once so near and dear. What happened to them? Where are they now? How did you lose track of people who were so important in your life?

Many Baby Boomers who are now in new relationships due to divorce or death of a spouse, and those who are still searching for the "one and only," report the following typical conversations. They are out with someone, and they are trying to get to know each other. As Baby Boomers, they believe that they have a great deal to share with one another. Typically, one speaks of family, interests, and work. But very often, one begins to share memories, instances in life that are unforgettable. Very often, those situations involve a good friend from the past, someone that was meant to be a friend for life. Then it happens, the listener to the stories asks, "are you still friends, with that person?" Sheepishly, you say, "we sort of lost track of each other." That "sort of" stays with you – it bothers you.

This is not, of course, the case with all Baby Boomers. Some have had life-long friends; they are the ones who keep up with people and do more than just send a Christmas Card. These types of Baby Boomers do report a richness to their lives. A wise man, my father, once said that you need many kinds of relationships to round out your life. You need to be respectful of your parents, be devoted to your partner in life, and be loyal to friends. This is of key importance, for being there for a friend is a gift that should not expect a reward. There also should not be a score card, like who pays the check or how many times you were invited to a friend's home. There should not be a litmus test on who writes the e-mail, calls on the phone, or sends the text message. The important thing is the communication, the sharing, and the support. Baby Boomers have experienced so many things in their lives, most of all change. It is so hard to keep things consistent, constant, and regular. A friend keeps things in perspective. Sometimes, the conversation with that friend, who is just there to listen, can be a stabling force in one's life.

As Baby Boomers have reached a certain age, they are looking back and reflecting on their life. This is what the "old timers" used to call "taking stock in life." What has it meant? What satisfaction has been gained? What was it all about? Baby Boomers used to appreciate the comic tone of such statements as "when you die, nobody is going to put on your grave stone that you were a workaholic." The best that you can hope for is that someone will say that you were a good man. That is what the priest said at my brother Bob's Funeral. The night before, at his wake, friends came and paid respects, and they spoke of him as friend. There were people from his breakfast club of present day. There were friends who knew him from high school. One dear friend of my parents, having just lost her husband, also came to the wake. When we said how much we appreciated her coming, given that she had her own grief to deal with, she spoke of my brother calling the hospital to inquire about her husband, because they were important friends to my parents.

A best friend, and many Baby Boomers have them, can be a pillar of light in sometimes dark hallways. They help you navigate the troubled times, the sometimes depressing moments. They are fittingly the source of your pride; the ability to sustain an important social relationship is part of the fabric of life. They are the thread by which all stages of life are woven. They remember you as an insecure freshman in college, finding your way. You remember the day that you received the call, when their first child was born. They remember the day that you cried your eyes out when your mother died, and you remember the day that they celebrated their 35th Wedding Anniversary. It is part of the life experience, isn't it? These social relationships give your life meaning. Sometimes, the sharing with a peer can be so rewarding. Sometimes it helps you to understand, sometimes it helps you to relate, and most of all, it brings you a great deal of enjoyment and fun, which is what life can sometimes just be about.

Baby Boomers across America are reaching out; they are trying to reconnect with old friends. They are trying to see what happened to former classmates. They are calling friends who they have not spoken to for a while. They are joining coffee groups, and meeting in the early mornings for camaraderie. They are going to the gym, tennis club, or golf course, and meeting a friend for an outing. Men are having lunch with friends, and talking about the start of Baseball season. Woman are meeting friends for coffee, having a shopping or spa day, or just understanding the company of a friend. In this chapter, you will see reference to a couple in Santa Barbara. The husband, who was spoken about earlier, is missing his glory days of popularity. His wife, who wants him to seek those friendships again, is being supportive of his effort. She is a hard-working person, who spends long hours in a lab. She has managed to keep up with her best friend, and they do make time for a coffee at least once a week. This was not always the case, but she valued her friend. The social relationship was important, so she made the effort. Like many Baby Boomers, she would tell you that it has enhanced her life. She wants her husband to experience the value of friendship as well.

Tuesday, March 13, 2012

The Psychologist

She stands in the entrance of the restaurant located in the Hilton in downtown Palm Springs. She is there for a major conference; she, in fact, is a presenter. She has a big time reputation, a king pin in the University

Circle where the world is insular, sheltered and where a reputation is made by your ability to publish. Well, our Baby Boomer woman is a publishing machine. She is a magnet for the big time conference. On this day, though, she wants a sandwich, a to-go order to bring into the presentation room. You see, she is too busy to stop and eat at the nice comfortable chairs that adorn this cute little eatery. No, she is one of those on-the-go types, where every encounter is a sales pitch and personal relationships are confined to the service people who fill her order.

She explains almost immediately to the man she meets that she is rushed, very busy, and, of course, she brought along some students from her department to share in her glory, although she calls it a "good experience for them." The whole process of looking at the menu, ordering the take-out order, and receiving her turkey sandwich is much too long and tedious for her liking. The kind man, who has now become her companion in this journey for sustenance, becomes part-time foil, part-time distraction, and full time conversation in waiting. To her dismay, the waitress who took her order at approximately 11:30am tells her the bad news: it will be just a little while longer. Our professor reacts as if the world is coming to an end. She will grin and bear it, with more emphasis in the "bear" than the "grin." "What could possibly take so long," she blurts out. "There is nobody in the place and it is before the lunch crowd." So now the scene is set, the professor and her fellow Baby Boomer man, an empty eatery, and a waitress under the gun to please the mighty woman of lecture. The Baby Boomer man says, "You must be hungry coming for an early lunch." No, she contends. This is her only time on the schedule to get something and, in fact, she will eat while her students lead a discussion after her talk.

The Baby Boomer is curious. He wants to know if all days are like this. Her answer results in an affirmative. He wants to know how this came to be. Surprisingly, the woman lets her guard down; she explains that she has been on the treadmill for a long time. First, it was the Ph.D. thesis, and then, it was her appointment to her renowned University. Then, it was the building of the reputation. Then, it was the pressure to publish. And, as he meets her amidst a warm day in the Coachella Valley, she is to be the keynote speaker of an important conference, for she is a headliner.

The waiting continues, the talk goes on, the two Baby Boomer professionals move forward in thought – him in a way that defines being a gentleman, her in the curt tone of one who knows that she is famous in her field. The man, without any prompting, lead in, or introduction, asks if she is married. She is nice to look at, but his intentions are pure for he has another reason for asking. Interesting enough, she lets her guard down once again, and her professional facade drops faster than Danika Patrick can drive a race car. She blurts out that she has never been able to find a man. She would like too. She just cannot meet a nice guy.

Within seconds, her guard is back up. She turns quiet and distant. She leaves the man a mystery, a riddle to solve, a short discussion that gives this Baby Boomer Chronicler thoughts that will make him toss and turn. For now, the sandwich has indeed arrived and, like that, she is gone. What remains is for the man only to ponder as he bangs away on the keys of his lap top. He left the Hilton after his encounter with the professor and walked a short distance to the Marriot-Renaissance. He settled into the wonderful new laptop station they have and wrote, fully knowing there was more to the story.

Saturday, March 3, 2012

The Definition of Consistent

Two Baby Boomers are talking. One says, "I will be there for you, buddy. You can count on me." Until you call, that is. A Baby Boomer is dating a woman. She tells you things; you come to expect a certain mode of operation, until she does something that is not in keeping with what you both have agreed upon. Why is it that Baby Boomers have such a difficult time with concepts such as loyalty, being true to your word, and saying what you mean? Why do Baby Boomers fail to deliver today the same attitudes, opinions, and sense of action that they demonstrated the previous day? Why do Baby Boomers have a problem being consistent? To learn more about this, one needs to look at the previous generation. The parents of Baby Boomers more than likely had to work much harder to achieve their quality of life. They worked harder at friendships – partly out of necessity, and partly because that was where their fun was derived.

If you needed something fixed around the house, you called a friend, maybe someone who was handy. In those days, and in that generation, people pitched in to help one another. They worked so hard for the house and enjoyed having friends visit, just spending time together. Thus a trust was built up, lasting friendships formed, and a consistent thread flowed through the relationship. Baby Boomers came into their formative years in a time of distrust. A President who lied, a war that would not go away, and institutions such as government, police, the church, and marriage were all questioned. Baby Boomers were also a part of ethics breach in corporations and the breach of the vow resulting in high divorce rates. Baby Boomers report that finding a partner in life free of cheating is the greatest gift. Baby Boomers report that having a friend who is at the other end of the phone in a time of need is a true blessing in life. Baby Boomers report that the simple things now matter – the smile day after day of the manager at Starbucks, the person who always has a smile on his face as he greets you warmly, the person who is as kind to you when they do not need something from you.

Do you shop in a grocery store where the personnel are consistently nice, courteous, and helpful? And, are they like that day after day? Doesn't it just give you a good feeling to be able to count on their action time after time? Or, how about the restaurant that you take your wife to for special occasions, and each time you go, you walk away saying it is consistently good? When it happens, you come away thinking that it was money well spent. Ever phoned your brother at an odd hour of the night, not realizing the time, only to get the same warm greeting? Feels good, doesn't it? Ever dated a girl who, no matter how much she has going on at work, still manages to send you an e-mail to show she cares? That is the affair of the heart, and then some. Ever asked for a favor and had a friend do it just because you are their friend, not worrying about when it would be their turn to receive? What a secure feeling to know that you can count on someone.

Baby Boomers have grown up in a world where service has deteriorated, where someone actually doing what they say they are going to do is the exception, not the rule. Baby Boomers have told this writer over and over that it is very important to them at this stage of life for people to respond in a consistent manner: you are going to be the same tomorrow as today. Baby Boomers need to have the comfort of the behavior, a consistent behavior, for life is too short for the antithesis.

Friday, October 7, 2011

When Nobody Cares

There is a segment of the Baby Boomer population that feels down, blue, and unappreciated. In fact, you could go a bit further to include such things as lacking in confidence, beaten down, and longing for the better days of the past. Some Baby Boomers also report a feeling of insecurity due to circumstances associated with job and economic conditions. Furthermore, and most importantly, many Baby Boomers feel that nobody cares about them, that there is no one to turn to, or truly talk to. It is hard to gauge the true percentage of Baby Boomers who fall into the category described above, for it is hard for any Baby Boomer to admit to true feelings on such a sensitive subject. By all accounts, however, the numbers are significant enough for us to deal with this topic.

Throughout history, as people change as they get older, and the world around them also becomes different, it is natural for them to go through a feeling of loneliness. Also, there have been some grave times that test a person. But what makes what Baby Boomers' circumstances different is the rollercoaster ride. For so long, Baby Boomers had it so good, and then it seemed as if the light was turned off. Baby Boomers in America came into the world during a time of prosperity. Post-World War II was a time of great growth, job creation, and sustainable living conditions. Baby Boomers were the first generation expected to go to college. Many assumed a White Collar job, and invention played into the hands of the good times. Personal computers, software, computer services, databases, and storage technology were the Baby Boomer's playground. Life became limitless. It became about the pleasure quotient, five-star hotels, First Class travel, and Boston Magazine's survey of the top restaurants, which all of a sudden were "must try" places.

Baby Boomers bought homes, then upgraded to bigger homes. Private schools and private banking were also on the agenda. The broker was on speed dial because the NASDAQ just would not stop going up, and you needed to trade and win. And, to make matters even better, there were good times all around. For example, there were holidays with the extended family, could anything be better? The laughter could be heard for miles. There were the new traditions, like New Year's Eve with your best friend, no matter what the travel distance. Furthermore, everyone was alive: your brother for the golf trips, and your wife to apply meaning, substance, and to make your life worthwhile. You could now repay your parents for all the sacrifices that they made. The train was moving down the track, it was a high speed rail, and your destination was happiness.

What happened? I woke up one day, I am in my 50s or early 60s, and I am alone. I have had three jobs in the last two years, and yet, I need another one because I cannot afford to retire. The thirty-something who interviewed me yesterday thinks "old" when I say "experience." That I could probably deal with, the composite Baby Boomer admits, if only my support system was still intact. But my parents are dead and buried. The elder care took it out of me. In some ways, their passing was a relief. How criminal is that to admit? My wife, how I miss her, she was taken so young. My siblings seem so involved with their own families that my call to them seems an intrusion. Why did I lose contact with all those cousins, who were part of my youth? I do not even know the names of their children, or, quite frankly, what they do, where they live, or anything about them. And finally, I used to have so many friends. Was I just fooling myself? Were they friends, or simply acquaintances? What does it matter? I would not know whom to call now anyway. Quite frankly, I tend to wonder, does anybody care?

Sadly, what you have read speaks to a lot of Baby Boomers. Lucky are those who have lives, which can be said to be the opposite of the above. There are some Baby Boomers who fall into that fortunate category. But let us have compassion, as fellow Baby Boomers, for the ones with a lesser plight. Maybe the answer is to pick up the phone and call your best friend. Maybe the answer is to email a cousin, or wish your Uncle a Happy Birthday. Chances are they will appreciate hearing from you.

Friday, September 9, 2011

The Value of a Friend

As Baby Boomers get older, friends become more valuable. This is not one Baby Boomer's opinion, but that of the vast majority. This subject matter is about a real friend, the kind that stands by you and supports you. This is the type of friend who knows your faults, your problems, your issues, and still manages to stand by you. This is the person who is your friend even when you are something less than the "happy go lucky," pick up the check sort. The search for the true friend is elusive. There are some who say that in your lifetime, if you can count on one hand five people who you can identify as true friends, you are a very lucky person. Chances are, as you read this, as a Baby Boomer at this stage of life, you may be hard pressed to reach the magic number. Unfortunately, in life people seem to come and go. This is in part because people change; sometimes they have busy lives, and sometimes they just fool you. Baby Boomers, as it has been reported, say that they have trouble making friends at this stage of life. Two different things happen: first, your longtime friends sometimes disappoint you, and second, the new friends that you have made and known now for several months, seem to fail in their conviction.

The old friend, who you have poured your guts out to for 30 years, fails you when you need them most. The one time when you made the call, and needed help, they were not there for you. Oh, how that hurts! You have met someone who is at the same age and stage, and over the last several months, you have begun to say to yourself, here is someone I can trust, and so you do. Your likes, politics, and intellectual acumen seem to be so compatible that the next coffee session is anticipated. Maybe you each do minor favors for each other, until you come to realize, the person has a self-interest about their personality. You always talk about subjects of interest to them, and they seem to place little value in supporting the activity of your work; perhaps "under-valued" would be the term associated with their view of your goals.

You think that you can write for the New York Times; they think you are local newspaper material. Are they being honest and helpful with their assessment, or do they lack the credential of friendship, violating rule number one, which is support and encouragement? You see, Baby Boomers are not in the mood for reality check at the moment. They are looking for a friend who will help them overcome the trials and tribulations of current life. The young person calls it, "he or she is there for me." Street people call it, "They got my back." Educated Baby Boomers just simply call it a "friend." Baby Boomers need that friend more than ever. There are some things that a woman needs to talk over with a girlfriend, not her husband. Sometimes, a man just needs the advice and council of a buddy. There is a perspective that you get from a valued friend that can just make all the difference. There are many relationships that make a person whole. It starts with parents. Lucky is the man who has loving parents. It continues with siblings, and it is so valuable when a brother is behind you one hundred percent. Who needs sibling rivalry? Then, if you are fortunate, you might find happiness with a spouse. Who can deny how important it is to go through life with a partner that makes life all that more complete.

Researchers will also tell you that a happy marriage has an impact on your health. But, to make life complete, one should not underestimate the value of a friend. There is no greater feeling than when a friend comes through for you in the clutch. It is like an adrenaline rush when the friend follows up, and lets you know that a friend is like a sacred bond, worth true currency in life. When the chips are down, who can you call? Baby Boomers ask that question.

Friday, July 8, 2011

Baby Boomers and Human Interest

Human Interest can mean a lot of different things. It can be a curious nature, or a story in a magazine known as a "human interest story." Sometimes it can refer to the desire to study our fellow man. For the purpose of this story, it is defined as the human interest in fellow Baby Boomers. The preponderance of the evidence shows that Baby Boomers are interested in other Baby Boomers. They are interested in what they are doing and how they are living their lives. For Baby Boomers at this stage of life, it is not about keeping up with the Jones'. It certainly does not mean "how to" books that dictate how Baby Boomers should do things. If we know anything at all from Baby Boomers and their history, it is that they do not like to be dictated to. However, they are fond of case studies. If they are looking to retire, they might like to know about locations that are good as seen through the prism of other Baby Boomers' experiences.

If travel is their objective, and for most Baby Boomers it is part of the equation, they very much enjoy web sites that cater to their needs. If financial planning and estate planning are the Baby Boomers' priority, they may seek council from a firm who has helped fellow Baby Boomers. Baby Boomers respond to like-minded people and like-minded interest. It is what now binds us together as a generation. You, as a Baby Boomer, are living your life, and sometimes the game of life is not always a cake walk. So, to be able to relate to your peers, talk with them over coffee, to read a periodical that leads to identification, is a good thing.

Baby Boomers started their college years and the years after as a generation that wanted to go their own way. Today, they are a little more reciprocal. While Baby Boomers have not lost their independent streak, they have come to rely on the community known as Baby Boomers. It seems like everywhere you turn, a Baby Boomer is looking up an old classmate, or going on a tour within their age group, or just seeking out the new friend that can relate to their background and history. Now, more than any other time in the lives of Baby Boomers, the contact with that similar aged person is of utmost importance. Technology has helped with information, but human contact is paramount. Baby Boomers want to share information, and communicate on aspects that are important to them at this time in their life. They are hungry for knowledge about what other Baby Boomers are doing, and they want to relate on a multitude of levels.

Baby Boomers seek clubs, activities, and common interests with people of their generation. But what has been observed more than any other set of traits when Baby Boomers talk to each other, is that they love to recall the past, speak of events of their lifetime, and simply say "remember that?" And what a feeling when the other person responds, "I sure do." It is a bond of good will, created by human interest.

Wednesday, June 8, 2011

Baby Boomers Remember their College Years

Sharon spent the late sixties at Syracuse University. She looks back fondly at her college experience. To her, they were happy years with friends. It was a time to go from a girl to a woman, and her mind was challenged. To her, it was a great time in her life, and she likes to recall the memories even to this day. This is the sentiment of the vast majority of Baby Boomers. Many say that, although it was tumultuous time to be in school, it was also exciting. When Sharon was at Syracuse, campus unrest was paramount, but it did not change the kind of activities that are still prevalent in upstate New York. There might have been streaking outside the dorms, but there was also streaking on the football field, for football tradition runs deep. This is, after all, the school of Jim Brown, Ernie Davis, and Floyd Little.

In Madison, the capital of Wisconsin, and home to the main branch of the University of Wisconsin (founded in 1848), two friends would meet in the Lakeshore dorms and go on to become lifelong buddies. The friendship started in 1972, when two dorm mates with rooms across the hall from each other, quickly formed a bond that would, over the years, be brotherly in its association. Now, 39 years later, the two friends have seen a lifetime together. Over the years, as the changing faces of professional and private growth took place, they were there for each other, with each being a sounding board for whatever issue was confronting their friend. These two have been such good friends over the years that they rarely call each other by their first name, but would rather rely on the moniker "buddy."

The Badgers, as they are known at Wisconsin, are proud of their alumni, and proud of the college life that goes on at their campus. There are few colleges with a more loyal following than Wisconsin. It has a lot to do with the cherished memories that graduates have of their time in Madison. Recently, a Wisconsin student who was in the same class as the two friends already mentioned, reconnected with a classmate through social media. Their friendship did not miss a beat, even though so many years had passed. The reason for this may lie in the fact that the shared experiences of college are hard to replace when it comes to the joy factor. When the two buddies get together, for example at Thanksgiving dinner, the discussion of some escapade of the 1970s is not far off. Like other Baby Boomers, they wonder what happened to all those other college friends. A common refrain is, "what are they doing now?" or "how have they lived their lives since college?" It was suggested that a good idea for a reality television program would be to take a dorm floor from the Baby Boom era, and catch up with the former students. It would be sort of "now and then," very interesting. The credit for such an idea comes from one of those two great Wisconsin buddies, now a professor and charting the course for a whole new generation of students.

Baby Boomers who report attending alumni weekends have found it to be very enjoyable. Many Universities have active alumni associations and have been able to take advantage of trips to away sporting events, and a variety of vacation packages with like-minded and fellow Baby Boomers from their era on campus. One Baby Boomer, who frequently goes on such trips, reports that she and her husband have seen the world through their alumni trips and have even reformed bonds with former classmates. As for our two friends from Wisconsin, one puts it best. "I have been best man at the wedding, godfather for the first child, and my good friend's parents are like second parents." So, when you encounter a Baby Boomer and they say that their college years may have been the best years of their lives, as a fellow Baby Boomer, you can probably identify.

April 15, 2011

Baby Boomers need friends

Remember those great days in college when there was an abundance of friends? What happened? Something called "life" is the answer. Think about it: after school, one needs to build a career, form relationships that often involve marriage, and in many cases, have children. All of a sudden there are business trips, and relocation for a better opportunity. There are school activities involving your children, like a school play or a game to attend. There are homes to buy and college education to be planned for. Your parents need you, and your wife wants to go on a second honeymoon.

You get the picture. Sure, you have plenty of acquaintances: people from work, golf buddies, people that you see around town. But the friends so needed at this stage of the Baby Boomers life, many report, are missing from their lives, and it bothers most of the generation. Think about it, how many people can you truly confide in? Or, when the chips are down, whom would you call, and would they respond? The older one gets, for some reason, the harder it is to make those lasting relationships. But they are necessary. For a person to have a full life, many kinds of caring relationships need to exist. That is why the person who brags that the most important person in their life is their spouse, at the sacrifice of their parents, their extended family, and friends, suddenly reaches a point when they find themselves alone. Just like anything else, maintaining a good friend is work, but Baby Boomers who have them will tell you that their life is richer.

April 13, 2011

Dedicated to Robert Bava

Robert F. Bava was my late brother. In the family, he was known as Bobby. He received that moniker from my grandmother. She liked to add the "Y's." My Uncle Joe, a respected doctor, was "Joey" until the day she died. I am sure that gave the nurses at the hospital a smile when she would visit him there, not to mention his children. I, of course, became "Ricky," although I used to like to say it was because of Ricky Nelson (all Baby Boomers recall the Ozzie and Harriet show and their sons David and Ricky). My brother Bob actually liked being called Bobby, but then again, he was so good natured that he responded well to all things "family." When I was a young boy, our family was probably at our best when the immediate and extended family was close knit. My brother, being the oldest, embraced that atmosphere like no other. With a brain and memory that could compete with any man, he could recall happy family events long after others had forgotten.

He was proud to be from the city of Chicago, and in many ways a reflection of the city and its families in post-World War II. He grew up in a neighborhood, commuted on the train to go to Loyola University and lived in the city his entire life. Sometimes life is not fair, as the saying goes. He is a person who deserved to be recognized and respected. But, as even Bill Gates would tell you, a little luck helps. My brother was blessed with a sense of humor and the rare quality of being free from jealousy, but no luck ever came his way. However, he never lamented his fate and was the same good man to the end. So maybe his luck came in reflection because so few are remembered as "good and decent." In my mind, that qualifies as the "last laugh." *I miss him greatly.*

Summary – Chapter 4

Social Relationships

There is a perception, with time being so important to Baby Boomers, that focus is key. So thus, the further perception is that social relationships take away from the more important aspects of life. Perhaps, Baby Boomers are not good managers of time. Perhaps they do not believe that you can "have at it all." What does this mean? Well, it plays out every day. "No, Sally, I would love to meet for coffee, but I have been so busy at work and as it is, I am already not spending enough time with Jim." "No, Carl, I would love to be your guest for the game, but I have been so tired lately. Can I take a rain check?" Or, you know, "we did not get a card from Jan this year, I hope she is OK." Or, "Bob, I am busy today, what are you going to do at home all alone today?" Or, a Baby Boomer looks in the mirror, and says, "Why do I have this lonesome feeling?" "Why is the existence of my life between these four walls?" "What seemed to happen? It was not always like this."

It is very interesting when you talk to Baby Boomers and, universally, they will talk openly about elderly parents, the happiness of marriage and family, or even their favorite vacation spot. But this aspect of social relationships is hidden, hard to get at. The ones who have rich friendships sometimes think that it is at the expense of others and other things. On the other hand, the ones without the social relationships question why they feel empty, because of lack of social relationships. They further do not know what to do to change the situation. It is not exactly a problem, but more a feeling of "there should be more to my life."

I once asked my grandmother why she thought my dad was right for my mother. She surprisingly said that it was because he had a lot of friends, and was a good friend. She went on to speculate that if my father was capable of being a good and loyal friend, he was likely to treat my mother with caring, thoughtfulness, and devotion. Sometimes the simple logic of generations past serves as a beacon of light.

The person that I most respect is my Uncle Joe. When I was a young man growing up, my father and mother would emphasize to my brothers and I that we should follow his lead. My two brothers and I did follow my parents' advice and it has served us well, for my uncle represents so much to us, both as an uncle and as a role model. This seems fitting to mention in this chapter, for beyond being a respected doctor, beyond he and my Aunt Fran having a wonderful marriage and raising a beautiful family, he has always maintained good friendships. He has friends from high school, as well as friends from medical school, who he still keeps up with on a regular basis. His family life has always been his priority, but like my father, my uncle recognizes the richness of life through social relationships.

Baby Boomers, as is my thesis, can learn a great deal from relationships that came before. Recall, won't you, how your parents would have friends over for dinner on a Saturday night. Recall how they would laugh and enjoy each other's company. Recall how, when your parents needed something, they could call upon a friend for help and guidance. Baby Boomers need a bit of "the days gone by." We claim that technology, the fast pace of life, and mountains of things to do keep us from the life that our parents had. Some of that may be true, and times do change. Life was different in your parents' days. But one can also point out that the basics of life are time honored. A call to your brother, respecting an aunt, checking on a nephew, or congratulating a cousin on a promotion are all parts of the social relationships needed in one's life. This completeness will make you a better spouse and father.

The sun is shining in Santa Barbara, California, the Dodger game is on television, and one of the great people, a Baby Boomer named Dave sits. He is a great husband, a loyal father, and was a respected son to his parents. He is good at his work and has managed his finances well. He was a standout athlete in his high school days. He was popular and had a multitude of friends. He did charity work before he married. I think of him when I think of Baby Boomers who have lived a good life. He and his wife make a standout couple. However, he is also an example of Baby Boomers who have worked hard at supporting their married life and dealt with issues related to parents, but have had social relationships suffer as a consequence. He is the kind of person who you would want as friend. He defines the term loyalty. His laughter would light up a room. His willingness to help others is second to none. He is like many Baby Boomers who have lost something though, that one component, that is needed to make life complete. He longs for a richer day when the phone rings, and his buddy is on the other end of the phone.

We, as Baby Boomers, have made sacrifices to get ahead and support our life style. Our parents valued the two week vacation, while Baby Boomers wanted to see the world. A wonderful woman, whom I met in my travels, said that she was a product of the women's movement and once bought into the slogan that you could "have it all." She concluded, in an astute fashion, that you could "have it all," just not all at once. I met her while she was attending a program called "Elder Hostel." She was there for enrichment, education, and to see San Francisco. She was also there for companionship of peers, to interact with individuals of her own age and stage. To share a joint history of purpose, is how I would describe it. She was articulate, had much to share, and had a personal existence that was engaging. She, by all accounts, must be a good friend to have, and most importantly, she understood the meaning of social relationships.

Chapter 5

Retro – A Longing for the Past

The world that we live in seems to operate at the speed of light. There is too little time, too much to do, and a complexity that makes our existence overwhelming. Baby Boomers, while impressed with what technology and the advances in the world have brought us, find themselves longing for the past. This is what a great many Baby Boomers feel when they have that little bit of down time, which is so precious. Their mind wanders, they daydream, and they think back to a simpler time. In every person's life, there are memories that are indelible. In the psyche of the Baby Boomer, there is a concentration on the present, but many memories linger from their past. They may coincide with events that happened in the world, significant aspects that made an impact on their life, or the simple times with family. Baby Boomers love to recall the family vacation of their youth. They enjoy sitting back and thinking about something interesting, like a room in their house when they were small, or perhaps, some sentimental thought that involved family and friends.

For certain, Baby Boomers have been a generation where events have impacted their lives. Many Baby Boomers grew up having to answer the question, "Where were you the day President Kennedy was shot?" We are a generation that watched the Vietnam War play out in our living rooms. But most of our memories involve family moments that give us a sense of calm, bringing back another day and time. As a little boy, I can still remember sitting around the kitchen table with my brothers, talking with my Mom and Dad. It seemed every happy moment occurred during those times. Born in Chicago, I lived there until the fifth grade, in what was sometimes referred to as "the old neighborhood." It was on the South side of Chicago. It was a three story brick building, with character, that my parents worked hard to buy and fix up. My parents were very proud of that building. We lived on the second floor, and my grandparents, my mother's parents, lived on the third floor. It was the definition of a "close knit family."

My grandfather, a kind man and a true gentleman, worked at G.D. Searle, the Pharmaceutical company. His hours were long, so he rose early to go to work. Because of that, when the weekend came, he was conditioned to rise early. On Saturday morning, I would get up early and go upstairs, and the two of us would have oatmeal together, a memory that stays with me today. It was about that time that My Uncle Joe got married. He had met a nice nurse while starting his medical practice. I remember going to her family home with my parents and grandparents, as the two families got to know each other. What a wonderful custom, when two families joined in harmony. I, like my brothers, stood up for that wedding, a proud day in our family folklore. Although I was a very young boy at that time, I still have fond memories of feeling so important in my role as the ring bearer on that happy day.

It was a time when families were doing well as Americans. They were buying new Chevrolet Impalas or an RCA Color television. It was a time when families were members of a club or church group, and as a result, attended a summer picnic. Our happy memories were going to the "CHI - Armour" summer picnic. This was part club, part athletic organization, and was a local institution. My Dad was the President of this club for 33 years.

My Dad was a hard-working man, and like a lot of men of the era, he was only able to take two weeks off for vacation. It is something that we looked forward to every year. Like many Baby Boomers who look back on childhood, a car trip was the two week vacation. It was not as much the destination that mattered, but the journey. What Baby Boomer does not recall the family vacation with fond thoughts of the past? You set out on the road, traveled Highway 41, and stopped at motels.

These were the days of little league baseball, grammar school, and change. The Baby Boomer generation was part of the expansion from city to suburbia. We, like many, moved to greener pastures. I remember my father sitting the family down and talking of the move from the South side of Chicago to the North side. We all agreed that it would be good for our family, and the excitement of those days is still felt within me today. We would move to Lincolnwood, a suburb in the North shore. It would be our family home starting in the '60s, and would remain so until my parents' death in the 21st century. It was there that grammar school, the choice of high school, and the childhood friends would be a cornerstone of the foundation of life. It was a time when you could walk to the park, play sports all day with friends, and do it free of the worry so prevalent in today's times.

I remember walking into my new school in the fifth grade, the famed Queen of All Saints, and feeling the nervous tingling of being the new kid at a new school. Now I think back, though, and realize how valuable attending such a school was to my life. Baby Boomers seem to get great enjoyment from thinking back and remembering those times and their childhood. When you think back to growing up, you think of it as a different time. You think of family, friends, childhood experiences, and most of all, when your life turned from black and white to color.

Sometimes when you turn back the clock, you do so with a revisionist history. Many Baby Boomers would confess that when they think back to childhood, "and the times of our life," as the Paul Anka song describes it, they tend to glorify the experience. But the fact remains that memories of sitting on one's front step, with neighbors walking by and saying "hello," and the feeling that your whole life was still ahead of you, does give Baby Boomers "a longing for the past."

Saturday, April 16, 2011

Do You Remember?

Years ago, there was an award winning advertising campaign for Kodak. It featured a television commercial with a Paul Anka song playing in the background. The song lyrics ask you, "Do You Remember...," and there are pictures on the screen, as the song continues to ask you, "Do You Remember the times of your life?" Baby Boomers, do you remember the times of your life? Do you remember your first day of school, or your first crush? How about Saturday morning television, with shows such as "Rin Tin Tin," or "Roy Rogers," or "Sky King"? How about evenings with "The Untouchables," "Biography," with Mike Wallace, followed by "Perry Mason"? Many Baby Boomers can recite chapter and verse when recalling the Beatles on "The Ed Sullivan Show."

What do you recall about high school? Did you remain friends with anyone from your class? Do you remember why you selected the college that you went to? Some Baby Boomers will tell you that their college days were among their happiest. Some are curious about how the lives of their classmates turned out, and some even have an overwhelming feeling of wanting to reconnect with old college friends that they have lost touch with. Can you recall the person in college that you thought was "the one," and what it would be like to see them now at a reunion? Baby Boomers who are happily married also like to talk about the first date that led to the beginning of the relationship. Do you remember the times of your life?

Thursday, May 19, 2011

Baby Boomers Remember the Family Vacation

There was a time in this country when a two week vacation for the family that centered on a car trip was very typical. Certainly for Baby Boomers the memory of your Dad gathering everyone in the new automobile with the map from AAA is vivid. It is a good bet that you started out early, drove a number of miles and then stopped for breakfast. Further on down the road, your Mom might pick out a place along the road where a picnic table might exist, and having packed a lunch, everyone could sit out in the fresh air. Before progressing further, it would have been time to stop for gas, at the outrageous price of 35 cents a gallon, unless you could find a Clark station for the discount price of 29 cents.

In the early 1960s, all roads were not interstate, so there was a good chance that you would go through towns and see other walks of life. For a family from Chicago driving to Florida, you might get to see an entirely different country as you proceeded through the Deep South. Remember the first time you saw those fresh peaches on the trees in Georgia, or the first time that the Northern plates attracted attention? Remember going through the countryside and seeing people sitting out on the porch? When it was time to stop at night, you stayed in a motel. You would pass several on the road, and your Dad would ask, how does that one look? You might stop and Dad would see if it was clean, and maybe with a little luck, it would have a pool. Those motels were usually family run, and the experience of getting to know the proprietor was fun onto itself. But the next morning, you would be up early and leave behind your new friends. However, the town in which you stopped would be fixed in your mind. Sometimes, getting to the destination of the vacation was irrelevant, because it was the ride, the trip itself, that was the vacation.

Your vacation was the drive to California. The vacation was the trip on the Kings Highway across Canada. Maybe you would drive to Niagara Falls, but the hidden agenda was seeing family who had moved away.

Those family members that did move away were so rare in the close knit families of the 1960s, when all extended family seemed to live in the same metro area. How great was it to go and stay at Uncle Jack's in Buffalo? How quickly the vacation would pass, and the anticipation for next year's started from the moment that you arrived home. Come September when the leaves were beginning to change, Dad was getting up at 5am to go to work, and you were back at school, the vacation would be recalled with fond memory. It would come into focus again when the teacher said, "your assignment for tonight is to write about what you did on your family vacation this past summer."

Saturday, June 11, 2011

The Family Story

They say that every person has a story. Well, what Baby Boomers are finding out is that every family has a story. Baby Boomers have become increasingly interested in their family history. They are starting to tell their grandchildren the stories that their grandfather told them, and stories that were passed down from their father. Baby Boomers whose families originally came from Europe report an interest in going to the town that their ancestors come from, to learn the foundation on which their family house was built. Years ago, families sat around the dining room table and recalled their history. There were vivid descriptions of the family's hometown in "Old Country," and the young people were captivated by the elders' poignant stories about how the family came to America. There was laughter as tales were told about the escapades of their aunts and uncles in their youth. What Baby Boomers are increasingly interested in is documenting those stories for the generations that come long after. Baby Boomers are sending notes to extended family on a variety of topics, from the creation of a family cookbook to the creation of a family web site.

They are asking older relatives at Christmas to gather the youngsters around the tree and share with them family stories that will stick with them, and which they hope will be passed down to future generations. Mark Twain was one of the great story tellers; he believed that family history was best learned through the telling of stories. Why are Baby Boomers taking such an interest? As one Baby Boomer put it, "as you get older, you look back on your life and you recognize what is important, and secondly, you become concerned about both your own legacy and your family legacy." Many Baby Boomers report that as they have gotten older they have become more proud of their family's achievements and want to make sure they are preserved. Baby Boomers have come to the belief that history indeed is a great teacher. With that said, how are Baby Boomers and their families going about the documentation process? Some preserve the family history by recording videos of family members telling the stories. Sometimes videos are made of family members being specifically interviewed about the family history. Other Baby Boomers have taken simple steps, like writing down the stories in a family notebook. One approach that seems to resonate with Baby Boomers is to encourage family members to share the stories with the extended family whenever they come up naturally in the course of conversations. For example, if you happen to tell your daughter an interesting family story one day, write that story in an email soon afterwards to share with other family members. Even if some members of the extended family do not use email, they will often hear family news or stories through other close family members who do. This way it also gets recorded in writing (assuming that at least one family member prints or at least saves the email in some form). Recording the stories this way, as they come up, can often seem less overwhelming than trying to take on a bigger project, like putting together a complete collection of family history and stories. Furthermore, as one Baby Boomer put it, "you can never go wrong with family sharing, no matter what the form." One thing is for sure: families, stories, history, and family closeness have become paramount to Baby Boomers.

Saturday, June 25, 2011

1969 in Lincolnwood

Lincolnwood, Illinois is approximately 16 miles North of downtown Chicago. In 1969, it was said by many that it was the nicest suburb close to Chicago. Even to this day, Lincolnwood remains a desirable place to live. By 1969, there was already a diverse population living there. For example, Catholics had moved there to be close to one of the best parishes in the archdiocese of Chicago. It had a private school that resembled those in the East, with an austere feel. This of course, was Queen of All Saints.

Those who went to the public school in Lincolnwood felt like they were actually at a private school. Some of the wealthiest people in the Chicago area lived in the towers section of Lincolnwood, but any part was at least upper-middle class. All of the services – fire, police, and town government – were exceptional. It was a place that, although democratic in its voting habits, in reality more resembled what Richard Nixon referred to as "the silent majority." In the middle was one of the most beautiful parks anywhere. On the far end was the tennis courts that would produce some of the states better players. On the other end, bordering the park, was the famed Kenilworth Inn, which at that time was an institution in those parts. The restaurant was part local institution and part family routine.

The hallmark of the park, and part of the town's identity, was the baseball program played on the well-manicured fields. In 1969, the team assembled for senior league play was maybe the best ever constructed for that age group. It was called the Lions Club, named after the sponsor. For the most part, the sixties revolution had not yet touched this group. Their hair was not long, and the only protest was with umpires. No team member would have thought to experiment with drugs or alcohol. Some in Lincolnwood, it was rumored, were succumbing to the times, but it was only passing conversation. It was, after all, a great time and place to be between the ages of 13 and 15. It was a time to be with your friends, play ball, and enjoy the fruits provided by the fathers who went to work in the morning and on their way home, stopped at the park to watch the 6 pm games.

It would be this group that in a few years would be on college campuses where they would see demonstrations against the war, fear (if you were a boy) that their number would come up in the draft lottery, and in some cases, embrace the slogan "The Times They Are A-Changin'." By 1973, the Lincolnwood of '69 had changed. Not in structure, or economic development, but in innocence. While most of the Lions Club team would be more conservative than their college friends, the conditions of the day and the peer environment reflected the times. It showed up in their taste for music, interests, and appearance. It was tame compared to what was happening in the rest of the nation, but certainly reflective of the times. That is the Baby Boom generation in a microcosm. There were a lot of Lincolnwoods across the country and each community and the young people within that community went through a similar transition. Look at pictures of yourself in 1969, then 1973, and note the differences. "The Times They Are A-Changin'."

Baby Boomers all remember what took place. It was, in fact, a time for experimentation, discovery, and, in some sense, freedom. A couple of years ago, at a White Sox game, two Baby Boomers from that Lions Club team happened to be sitting in the same section. Through conversation they realized that they were old friends who had shared a special time together and the bond was renewed. They shared a special memory in their recollection of 1969 and that special team. The two Baby Boomers were now both successful businessmen in their 50s, but that night in Sox Park, they were boys again. The conclusion after their meeting could only be that times change, people grow up, but feelings are forever.

Tuesday, February 28, 2012

When I was 17

"When I was 17, it was a very good year," sings Frank Sinatra. The question to you Baby Boomers is this: was it, in fact, a good year? And second, would you want to be 17 now? When I was in college, second semester of my freshman year at the University of Wisconsin, I was indeed 17. I lived in a dormitory surrounded by a great bunch of guys. Wisconsin was still one year removed from co-ed dorms. We did study, but we also played great games of touch football, ordered sandwiches at midnight from Ella's Deli to supplement the dorm food, and went to plenty of movies in big lecture halls on Friday night. Perhaps at no other time in my life do I remember such camaraderie. Groups of young men hung around in each other's rooms, just "shooting the breeze" – remember that expression? There was always somebody around to walk to class with, always somebody to go for a workout with, or to go with to a football game. But, if you were like me, you developed one friend, one pal, one buddy that would in fact hold the promise of the university brochure – that the friends you make in college are the ones for life.

Yes, one best friend, your buddy, is still the case 39 years later. That is really something – a mainstay friend that stays with you for life. When we get together, or talk by phone or e-mail, all of which is done often, we like to recall that first year in the dorm, the year I was 17. It was, in fact, a very good year. The memories are rich, the laughter is free, and the confidence of the pact secure. It was a different time, as we all know. Communication was not done on Facebook, but face-to-face. Streaming was not a computer term, but a flow of experiences that would be the foundation to become a man. You had to engage people to become their friend, you had to talk to them, and then those conversations were part of the growth experience. You shared things, went through the trials of exam period, and went to dances. It was fun.

I do not know that I would want to be 17 now. Life is so fast-paced. There does not seem to be a chance to meet fellow students at the mailbox on the ground floor of the dorm, for no one is receiving mail anymore. And those hovering Baby Boomer parents – don't they understand that their child is busy at school? Stop the texting, the cell phone calls, and the daily emailing. Give them some room to breathe, experience, and work things out for themselves. I remember calling my parents every Sunday morning. I would give them the highlights, ask when the care package was coming, and assure them that things were going fine. My parents were supportive before there was such a term, but they understood that you grow up to some degree on your own, that you need to make a couple of mistakes. Somehow, the majority of Baby Boomers made it through college without talking to their moms every hour, on the hour.

Perhaps Baby Boomer parents are so involved because they want to relive their own happy times in college. Perhaps their memories of college are so vivid that they feel protection is in order. For the gang and me at Elm Drive B, in 1972-73, it was a time not to be traded. So, going back to the top, I summarize for you this way: I enjoyed being 17, but I would not want to be 17 now. But more importantly, what do you think?

Friday, July 1, 2011

Yesterday when I was Young

There is no better loved athlete to the Baby Boomer than Mickey Mantle. Baby Boomers admired Sandy Koufax, respected John Unitas, and wanted to be Joe Namath, but Mantle always holds a special spot in the hearts of Baby Boomers. Jane Leavey, in her book about Mickey Mantle, tells the story of Mickey Mantle asking Roy Clark to sing his famous song at his funeral. The line, "Yesterday when I was young" resonated with Mantle and his Baby Boomer followers. Even though, as life went on, we came to realize that Mantle had flaws as he got older, the feelings for Mantle never waned. This story of thinking about "yesterday when I was young" applies to all Baby Boomers, but not for the reasons most think. Contrary to popular belief, most Baby Boomers do not want to be young again, but rather want to be the best that they can be for the age that they are now. Also, most Baby Boomers reflect on their youth with fond memories.

One fun thing that many Baby Boomers like to do is look at pictures of themselves from years ago. It is a way of recalling places from a happier time. Most Baby Boomers report that they have become reflective about the past. They think of their parents, and family gatherings, perhaps a favorite Christmas Eve. They think about that best friend from college and the good times that they had during their years on campus. How much enjoyment is felt in those reunions, formal or informal, when you get together with friends of your youth and laugh out loud recalling some small incident that you both can identify. And, there is one further thing about yesterday. Baby Boomers can look back at a set of accomplishments. Their history, and the history of their lives, play as a film in the form of a retrospective featuring the days of one's past. "Yesterday when I was young, so very very young, oh yesterday" – meaningful to Mickey Mantle, and meaningful to Baby Boomers.

Thursday, December 1, 2011

Keeper of the Flame

The late Senator Ted Kennedy was often associated with being "the keeper of the flame" for the Kennedy Family. As the youngest child of the famous family, he was said to be a chronicler of his family. It is said that he could tell stories with vivid detail, of the happy days, the cherished memories. The target audience of his reflections was the next generation within the Kennedy Family, in hopes that they too would understand what growing up Kennedy was all about. But maybe more importantly, he just simply wanted them to understand why his family history meant so much to him.

Baby Boomers should understand this concept well, for they are becoming the "keeper of the flame" within their own families. They are starting to buy into the concept of Mark Twain, who thought family history was important, and best passed down through stories, stories like Baby Boomers are starting to tell. Baby Boomers are looking at the past with a bit of nostalgia. They are remembering the quiet time spent with their grandfather. They remember the excitement of holidays with the extended family, when laughter was the only calling card. They remember crucial times in the family history, when decisions were made with character that enhanced the family legacy.

Now Baby Boomers want to tell those stories. How are they doing that? How are they passing down the family gems? How are they capturing the imagination of a new generation? Here are some examples. As discussed in this space, with the help of technology, Baby Boomers are reaching out to family. They are emailing a favorite aunt, or making the uncle that they admire more aware of their activities. From time to time, they are sending family communication notes. They are using Facebook as a tool. You see the technology has become important, because life today is different than the memories and the times that they hold so dear. Families are spread out, see each other less frequently, and do not have the face to face contact of years past. So Baby Boomers engage in the tools of the day, and they tell stories and paint pictures of "once upon a time." Rather than just send a note that says "Happy Thanksgiving," Baby Boomers are taking the next step, and including a memory of a cherished Thanksgiving of the past. They speak of relatives no longer with them, so they are not forgotten.

They write cousins with a note that triggers a laugh, a thought that they can both relate to, sometimes receiving a note back saying that they told the story to their daughter. Sometimes, they just unburden themselves of things that they want others to know, such as why a dead brother was important to the family. They may relate history that few in the family know, but want to know. For example, how their family made it to this country, sacrifices made by those who came before, and efforts made by family elders to educate and better the lives of their children. They say that every person has a story, and thus every family has a story. Let us applaud the Baby Boomers amongst us who are the keepers of their family flame.

Thursday, December 29, 2011

New Year's Eve – 1972

At the University of Wisconsin in 1972, there was a dorm known as "Elm Drive B." It was considered part of the set of dorms on campus called the Lake Shore Residence Halls. This is because behind this group of buildings was Lake Mendota. Looking back, it was quite beautiful, especially as students arrived in late August. The second floor would become the place to be, with a mixture of athletes, out of state freshman, and a smattering of older students. This group was joined by a set of in-state individuals, all trying to make a way for themselves.

One boy from Chicago was dropped off by his Dad and older brother. The older brother was wondering if all the long hair he was seeing was a sign of the times. The father just shook the young freshman's hand and said, "You are entering here a boy, I expect you to come out of here a man." With that, the boy proceeded to room 215. Across the hall and down a door, a second year student was getting settled. He had been in his room for a while. He was the son of a famous professor on the Madison campus. But he chose to live in the dorm, not at home. This, though, was his first year on campus because the previous year his father had taught at the University of Hawaii for one year, as a part of his work in his field. His son took classes in Hawaii, as a freshman.

Well, as luck would have it, these two young men would meet, and become fast friends. Soon, they operated as if they had known each other for an eternity. Soon, when Sunday dinner came along, the Chicagoan was going home with his local friend for dinner at his parents' house. Soon, when the parents of the boy from Chicago came for parents' day, they too became acquainted with the wonderful family of their son's friend. Soon, the professor and the businessman from Chicago realized that, like the sons, they too had a great deal in common. The mothers of the two boys also got along famously.

So it was, with that as a backdrop, that Christmas would come, and then it was time for New Years. While home in Chicago, the boy called his buddy, and said that his mom and dad had been invited to a New Year's Eve party of some special friends of his parents. The kicker to the story is that these friends had two daughters around the same age. The party was to be held at their summer home up in Wisconsin. It was to be mainly an adult party, so when the hostess asked if the boy from Chicago would like to come, his parents not only answered yes, but suggested perhaps, his friend from college would enjoy coming as well. The people giving the party could not be happier, for they feared that their daughters would be bored without friends their own age.

In 2011, the two friends from college emailed each other recalling the night. For you see these two, now Baby Boomer men, are still best friends. The boy from Chicago became a businessman like his father; the boy from Madison became a professor like his father. They grew up, matured, and saw each other through life all of these years. The man, who was once "the boy" from Chicago, is now godfather to his buddy's oldest child. They went to the party in 1972, and they had a great time. They watched, with the two daughters, as the New Year come in. Dick Clark was early in his run at the time. They enjoyed the company of the two daughters, by 1972 standards, in a wholesome way. They all talked, laughed, and ate together. They enjoyed the innocence of the evening, when just the excitement of being with pretty girls, who were fun to be with, was enough. Looking back, what could have been an uncomfortable evening, a set up by parents, would be remembered for years as the wonderful New Year's Eve of 1972. This was when two good friends, would become friends for life, when the passing of time, would enhance the night of what would later be called the best double date ever. When just the thought of liking a girl, who you just met, and being with a like-minded friend, is worth all the memories in the world.

You see, in 1972, the daughter of a family friend, spending time in a home, and just having a nice night – well, those were good things. Years later, when the father of the boy from Chicago passed away, the hostess of that famed party, came to the wake. Those are always difficult for both the one paying respects, and the family of the one with the loss. You just don't know what to say. After the formalities, and before leaving, the woman looked back and said, to the boy from Chicago, "My daughters thought that New Year's Eve, with you and your friend, was a night to remember." New Year's Eve – 1972.

Thursday, February 2, 2012

One Bathroom

On the South side of Chicago in the early 1960s, in an area known as Bridgeport, families lived in harmony before they pursued the suburbs. On Wells street across from Armour Square Park, and in the immediate shadow of Comiskey Park, buildings known as "three flats" dawned the landscape. Armour Square Park was a place for the community to gather; Comiskey Park was home to the Chicago White Sox, the major league team that the people in this close knit neighborhood rooted for, and followed religiously. This area was part of the eleventh ward, made famous by its most prominent resident, Mayor of Chicago, Richard J. Daley. In fact, many of the people who lived in the community worked for the city, in "the city that worked." This phrase, "the city that worked," meant to Chicagoans that the garbage got picked up, the streets were plowed when it snowed, and a climate to do business existed.

People all knew each other in what they called "the neighborhood." They helped one another. They went to the same church on Sunday, and they brought homemade food to a friend, not because they thought they needed it, but because they would enjoy the treat. On warm summer nights, people sat outside on the steps and people from down the block would come over and visit. It was social, the cultures were similar, and enjoyment was derived from a cadre of people. The group included not just those in your own circle or your club, but a nice mix of people from different backgrounds, with a camaraderie that resulted from the shared experience. A key ingredient that played into the harmony was that many of the residents were of the same heritage. When people came from Europe and settled here, they moved into areas where they knew people and there was a comfort zone. On Wells Street, for example, were the Italians and part of Santa Lucia church. The blocks over by St David's, where the Daleys lived, were mostly occupied by Irish people. People in this time frame were fans of Sinatra, but were excited when this new group from England, The Beatles, played "Sox Park," as Comiskey Park was referred to.

At 3247 South Wells street there was a three story building, which was owned by the family living on the second floor. This was a couple who were raising three sons, with the wife's parents living just above them, on the third floor. Close friends of the family with their own two daughters lived on the first floor of the building. Each of the three apartments had just one bathroom. Somehow, everyone survived. In fact, the better term is that everyone thrived. Of the five children just mentioned, only one, the youngest, born in 1955, is an actual Baby Boomer. He was one of the three sons. He was like a mascot to the older brothers, and a novelty to the two girls on the first floor. This Baby Boomer had a ring side seat to the times. That one bathroom was where his middle brother got ready for a dance at St. Rita High school by taking the longest shower one could imagine. During the shower you could hear the music of Connie Francis, Nat King Cole and The Lettermen blasting from the radio in the bathroom. These were easy times, and happy times, when getting a pizza from Ricobene's after midnight on Friday was a must. You see, as Catholics, you could not eat meat on Friday. Those were the days when you went to David's at 31st and Halsted for a cheeseburger, or a piece of custard pie. It was an institution for the people of Bridgeport, who of course, just called it "Dave's."

Many who lived in the neighborhood had children who stayed in the area after they grew up and started their own families. Thus families would remain part of the fabric of the community from one generation to the next. That was America before suburbia, when people just lived in the neighborhood. But by 1965, like much of America, many families sought bigger homes, grass, a yard, new schools, and multiple bathrooms, perhaps in a nice brick ranch home in the suburbs. It is interesting many Baby Boomers remember childhood as described above. They remember when they moved and started at a new school. Many families can trace higher level education to the move to the suburbs. But it is very romantic, somehow, to think of the early 1960s and think about a different life, vinyl records, Dick Clark, Mickey Mouse, and more specifically, the Mickey Mouse Club. These were the Ozzie and Harriet days, where many named Richard became "Ricky" because of Rick Nelson. Thinking back to the early 1960s brings back memories of living life with one bathroom, and being content.

Wednesday, March 7, 2012

Burger To Burger

The first time I heard the song "(I Can't Get No) Satisfaction" by the Rolling Stones, I was sitting in Bobby's Snack Shop in 1965. This was a wonderful place from my youth. It was at the corner of 31st and Wells on the South Side of Chicago. It was down the block from my first grade school, Santa Lucia. Santa Lucia church was a staple of our neighborhood. With the help of other concerned parishioners, my mother and father built the school that went with the church. Each day for lunch, with many of my classmates, we would venture to Bobby's Snack Shop, sit down in a booth, and inevitably order a hamburger. I remember it like it was yesterday. It was a cheeseburger, actually, with crispy French fries and, of course, a coke. What was it about the way those burgers were grilled that made them so memorable?

They came served in a little red basket, burger off to the side with the complement of fries. What made Bobby's so much fun was that they had a juke box that you could access from your table. You remember the kind that I am talking about. It was contained in a little glass case, the rows of titles of the songs, and the ivory keys you pressed for your selection. One day, while sitting in a booth by the window with Frank – my good childhood friend - and his sister Carol, a song came on that captured our attention. The new young group singing this "rocking" song would later just be referred to as "The Stones." On this day in the 1960s, it was just a song, but one that would stay with you for a lifetime.

This past Friday, while sitting in Habit Burger, a hamburger franchise of merit, with this particular location being in Orange County, the song came over the sound system. I was eating with two dear friends – the Frank and Carol of my adult life. In this case, Roland and Patty were sitting with me as we enjoyed the same menu items of times gone by. Cheeseburgers, fries and a coke – and do not let me forget the Onion Rings – oh, so tasty.

When "Satisfaction" came on, it was like a turn-back-the-clock moment: the Rolling Stones, Satisfaction, burgers, and friends – it was like nothing changed but the years in time. I looked at my dear friends and told them of my memory. We sat in a booth, in a burger restaurant, listening to iconic music and perhaps all recalling our youth, as Baby Boomers are prone to do these days. Isn't it interesting about the music of the Baby Boomer era? It can just take us back. So, in some sort of way, this story is about book ends – recalling an experience from the past ,and a present day lunch, both built around burgers – or, as I would like you to think about it as, "Burger to Burger."

Friday, February 24, 2012

10 Events That Shaped the Lives of Baby Boomers

On a cold day in Washington D.C., members of the armed forces symbolized the end of World War II. It would close a chapter of American History and begin the dawning of a new day. The world was saved by the brave young people who would preserve the values of America. They would become known as "the Greatest Generation." They would then bring about the creation of many new babies beginning in 1946 and stretching through 1964. It was the first key event, the start of the Baby Boomer generation, which would grow to what some estimate is 77 to 79 million strong. As the Post-World War II climate in America began to take shape, young couples now raising children looked for a better life. They discovered that there was life beyond the urban setting. Many called this "living out in the country," which America would later term "Suburbia." With this second big event, the move to the outskirts, came the building of new schools, children playing in cul-de-sacs, and the growth of new programs for children – Boy Scouts, Girl Scouts, and Little League Baseball, just to cite a few.

Life was pretty comfortable, unemployment was low, Americans felt good about themselves, and the country was riding the wave of companies like General Motors. "So goes General Motors, so goes the country" – this tagline is to emphasize the might of the post war economy. America, well, it was an upbeat place. There was no better display of the vigor in the country than that represented by the Camelot-like appeal of the Kennedys. President Kennedy was inspiring Americans by telling us we will go to the moon. Americans believed in the country's unlimited capacity.

Then, in November of 1963, that would all change with event number three. Where were you the day President Kennedy was shot? It was like America's innocence died with the fallen President. The funeral was etched into our childhood memory, a black cloud to accompany the black veil of the woman who Americans liked to call "Jackie." President Johnson deserves a great deal of credit, though. He held the country together, went on to complete the mission of the Kennedy Administration, passed unprecedented legislation, and he had the vision for what would be termed, "the Great Society," which represents event number four. Many today forget that our country was once segregated. How we can forget that is beyond me, but we do. The Great Society gave us Civil Rights legislation and paved the way for one day electing a man named Barak

Obama for President. This Great Society also built on the philosophy of FDR, so programs were developed for education, welfare, and Medicare.

President Johnson, though, is really the tale of two Presidents. In fact, the mere mention of President Johnson immediately brings to mind significant event number five: the Vietnam War. Baby Boomers were shaped by the events in Vietnam. It was not just the protest movement, or the lottery system for the draft; the events surrounding the Vietnam War led us into a period of Civil Disobedience in America, exemplified by what took place at Kent State, Berkeley, and Sterling Hall at the University of Wisconsin. We like to look back at that time with a romantic slant, conjuring up images of the flower children, pot smoking in the dorm, and the freedom of society. But it was also a time when there was a distinct Generation Gap, with views of the past colliding with the modern world. The epicenter may have been the 1968 Democratic National Convention in Chicago, where Police and young people showed the nation on the evening news that society was out of control.

But leave it to Baby Boomers to find silver lining in the midst of turmoil. This brings us to event number six, Woodstock. Not just the actual festival, but Woodstock being the cover band for a generation that created great music that is still being played by the young people of today. So, the category of music during the time of Baby Boomers is a key event, with Woodstock as the metaphor.

Event number seven, best described by the phrase "the breaking of the glass ceiling," was the fight for Woman's Rights. Women today have options. Back in the early 1970s, that was not the case. Today, a woman can be CEO of the corporation or CEO of the home. Today, thanks to Title IX, a woman can have the same advantages in sports as a man. These were significant advances to society that came under the watch of Baby Boomers.

Ever heard the term "corporate life"? Well, it is event number eight. You see, there came a day when Baby Boomers needed to make a living.

In the 1980s, with new technology, a business revolution, and the button down atmosphere of the Reagan White House, business life as we know it was created. Maybe even a bit overboard. Remember the phrase "Greed is Good"? That was the beginning of a slippery road. Much was good, some not so good. There were new companies, new industries, new ways of doing things, and change that would rival any generation. Think back, Baby Boomers, to the dawning of the personal computer, software, and portable computers. But you also have to think of the beginning of what would become cut throat business, stock market scams, and the entrance to event number nine, living with debt service. This meant credit cards, big mortgages, fast cars, second homes, and living beyond your means. The stock market goes up all the time, right? Home values always rise. Second mortgage to provide the cash for the vacation in the Hamptons, no problem. Buy your coffee, break out the plastic. Hit the new restaurants, break out the plastic. Adjustable mortgage – what a novel concept.

And then, one day, event number ten, the unthinkable. President Bush says that, without emergency action, our banks will collapse. Without emergency action, the county will look like it did in the 1930s. At first, we did not believe it. Didn't the stock market plummet after 9/11 only to recover? Didn't we have a little bump in the road that was eased by stimulus checks to Americans as we moved into the 21st Century? Well, this time it was different. It was systematic, and Baby Boomers' lives would be changed forever. They're calling it the "Great Recession" now. Baby Boomers will forever call it "unforgettable."

Yes, Baby Boomers, you have lived in interesting times – times of true change. What will the history books say one hundred years from now? Will the generation that encompasses Baby Boomers be applauded or vilified? Will it be said of Baby Boomers that we were spoiled children of hard working Americans who saved the world? Or will we be the generation that gave the country innovation and a new moral compass with which to navigate the waters? The jury may be still out, for Baby Boomers have a lot more to contribute to society.

Summary – Chapter 5

Retro – A Longing for the Past

As a Baby Boomer, I was born during the Eisenhower Administration. It was a homogeneous time, in the culture of America. It was a time, when Baby Boomers went to pre-school, long before elected officials thought of such things as "Head Start" programs. When we went to kindergarten, many of us cried as our mothers turned us over to the teacher. We sat there in our classroom when the Principal, with a crack in their voice, uttered the words that President Kennedy was shot. I remember running home, and trying to find my older brother Bob, to make sense of what was going on. That was the same brother who would take me to movies at the "Ramova" theater. But, then again, all my formative experiences seemed to involve my older brothers. That is what happens when kid brothers are thought of as something special. Like when my brother Ray went off to college, and I would just pick up and go stay with him there, and he would welcome that.

My brother Ray and I once looked out from our back window, and saw the Dan Ryun expressway being built, a major project in Chicago at the time. Normally, this would be not something that would qualify as interesting reading until you find out that we drove on the "Dan Ryun," prior to it being finished. My father was not too happy to hear about such hijinks. I remember as a Catholic family, as a child, not being able to eat meat on Friday, and going with my brothers to Ricobene's right before midnight, to get pizza and Italian Beef sandwiches. Anyone who is from Chicago, or has visited, knows what a treat an Italian Beef Sandwich truly is.

On Holy Thursday, Uncle Hank would come over. He was really a good friend of my father's, for whom we used the Uncle moniker. He had a tradition with my Dad to come for dinner, usually "raviolis," and we would go make the rounds, visiting the local churches. I do not know how this tradition started, and today, I must confess that I am not very religious, but those outings were for the ages. I last saw Uncle Hank at my parents' 50th Anniversary. When my Dad spoke, he asked Uncle Hank to stand, for he was the oldest one in attendance, and for me a reminder of my youth.

Baby Boomers report that when they are out with couples of similar age and like-minded, they often engage in discussions that center around their youth. They discuss a different time and place, when life was slower, experiences richer, and memories were made that will stay with them forever. Baby Boomers report that, before they got married, they wanted to show the person who they were to spend their life with where they came from, and share a little of what made them the person who they are today. Many, when they share their childhood experiences, share a great deal about the people who made up their youth. Baby Boomers also enjoy the "where were you then" moments. Today, Baby Boomers will tune into PBS, for it will sometimes profile the history of our youth, or play a concert from a band of those days that gives you a special feeling, much like an old song on the radio.

Baby Boomers recently gathered at a Christmas function. Older brothers and sisters, all Baby Boomers, along with friends, were at their parents' home to help welcome their sister's fiancée to the family. As the conversation progressed, the woman's sister-in-law suggested getting the year book out from the old high school attended by the family. The evening of laughter, fun, and memories will forever be irreplaceable. The spontaneous recommendation set off a walk down memory lane that anyone interested in the Baby Boomer Generation would have enjoyed immensely. The woman's parents, so happy seeing the smiles on everyone's faces, watched with significant pride, as their family was reliving the past, looking at the pictures, and telling stories of when the family was at its apex.

That is what memories are to Baby Boomers, a time to look back and recall what sometimes was a better day, or maybe more accurately, a day to remember. Marketers seeking to reach Baby Boomers have gotten the message. By helping to trigger memories and using a retro feel, they can appeal to the heart strings of the Baby Boomer. That is probably just fine, for sometimes a little bit of retro, a longing for the past, is good for the Baby Boomer soul.

Chapter 6

TV Shows – Movies – Music – Sports

In October of 1962, my friends and I, just little boys at the time, walked from school to the corner grocery store. There, the nice elderly lady had the World Series playing loudly on the radio. I was captivated by the Yankees playing the Giants. The game and the World Series ended, when Willie McCovey hit a line drive, with the game on the line, to Bobby Richardson to preserve the Yankee win, and the 1962 World Series Championship. By this time, even at my young age, baseball was in my blood. To many Baby Boomers of the time, it was their sport. We would grow up following the teams, its players, and its history. It would become part of my make up as a person. This chapter is about such areas of interest that for many years have driven the soul of Baby Boomers. By the time Baby Boomers have reached this stage in their lives, they have formed some relationship with certain television shows, movies, music and/or sports. These forms of entertainment have become part of the fabric of Baby Boomers.

One reason these entertainment vehicles hold such a special place for Baby Boomers is that they help you to recall where you were when you saw a particular movie, or heard a special song. It helps you to identify with the life that you have led, and the moments that have contributed to making you who you are today. There is a history there. For example, the Baby Boomer Generation did grow up on television. They watched with their very own eyes as television became a major source of influence on American society. Many Baby Boomers so identify with shows from their childhood, as if they were a friend from the past. Baby Boomers of a certain age can tell you where they were and the circumstances surrounding that special Sunday night, when The Beatles appeared on the "Ed Sullivan Show." For my cousin Kathy, there are many great memories associated with that show. It was around that time that Kathy became pen pals with another young girl in England through a magazine about "The Beatles." Kathy also remembers how she and her local friends, each with the nickname of their favorite "Beatle," would go to Beatles concerts together whenever they were playing in Chicago. For my cousin and this group of friends, that Ed Sullivan show is a memory for life.

Most Baby Boomers can recall their favorite night of television and the shows that made such a mark. Many Baby Boomers would rush home from school for the afternoon television line up, and certainly, for most, Saturday morning television was part of the routine. From "Leave it to Beaver" to "The Brady Bunch," television was your companion. Television was a sign of the times; shows, such as ''Father Knows Best" reflected the family values and sentiment of the country. In my case, we got our first color television just in time for the "Rose Bowl." Most Baby Boomers probably remember that familiar phrase: "Brought to you in "Living Color." I remember how it was such a big deal for families to first anticipate, and then to actually get their first color television. It was one of those moments in time that stick with a Baby Boomer.

What Baby Boomers also grew up with and love to this day is the movies. As a family, you might have watched "The Sound of Music," and as a college student, you may recall seeing "The Godfather" when it came out in the theatre. Baby Boomers can chart their development, the passing of time and their generation, by the movies that span their lifetime. Baby

Boomers report that today, when they have movie night with that special someone, they often get a DVD that reflects some moment in time, or something they want to share about the movie they watch. Some movies reflect emergence, such as "The Graduate." With its combination of a complex story line and the music of the Baby Boomer generation from "Simon and Garfunkel," it resonates with the generation. Some movies reflect what Baby Boomers have always looked for as if they were chasing the Holy Grail, and that is "Love." May it be "Sleepless in Seattle" or "When Harry met Sally," Meg Ryan seemed to reflect the hopes and dreams of Baby Boomers in the characters she portrayed in these movies.

The Baby Boomer generation is often best identified with its music. Ask most Baby Boomers, and they can tell you what was playing down the halls of their dorm. Bill Walton, the great basketball player, starred at UCLA then went on to a legendary career in the NBA, but he may be just as well known for his passion for the music of the "Grateful Dead." Even Jerry Garcia himself recognized Bill Walton as a "Dead Head."

Many Baby Boomers started by watching "American Bandstand," made popular by Dick Clark, and graduated from college listening to "Emerson, Lake, and Palmer." One of my own most memorable experiences in college, though, occurred when we stood in line, not to see one of our own times, but one that came before. We somehow got there at 3 am, even though this was prior to me being a coffee drinker. Looking back, I probably could have really used some coffee at that time, for we had to get up so early to get into our spot in that line to obtain the "Elvis Presley" tickets. He was going to perform at the Dane County Coliseum, and no University of Wisconsin student wanted to miss out on the experience. But that is what it is like for Baby Boomers. Even today, music continues to play an important role in the lives of Baby Boomers. A friend of mine and his wife, two of the great Baby Boomers, recently saw James Taylor, and they are still talking about it with such delight.

But in the end, may it be a TV Show from your youth, a movie that you experienced while dating your current wife, a concert with your friends where the music rocked, or that great game you saw with your buddy, you have fond memories of the entertainment of the times. Many of you have to call it something different than "entertainment," for the programs, films, and games were so much more – they became a fundamental part of your history.

I finally got to go to the World Series. I sat in Fenway Park, with a good friend. We were there for Game 5, of the 1986 World Series. To this day, it can best be described as a "once in a lifetime experience."

Friday, March 9, 2012

March Madness

Well, it is getting to be that time of year when brackets are being filled out, where College Basketball takes center stage, and perhaps one of the greatest sporting events takes place: the NCAA College Basketball tournament – affectionately known as "March Madness." This tournament has so grown over the years that even the casual fan follows it now, although sometimes it is just to win the office pool. For example, through a unique partnership between CBS and TBS and their sister stations, every game will be available live. This is now a billion dollar enterprise, but despite the money involved, the viewing public still sees it as a wonderful display of amateur sports.

For Baby Boomers who have grown up on this tournament, and who have seen it expand into what it is today, it holds a special attachment. The first final game that I saw was in 1963, as a young boy growing up in Chicago. Our city team and the alma mater of many family members, Loyola (known as the Ramblers), played and beat Cincinnati, a basketball powerhouse of the day. That preceded one of the greatest runs in sports history, the dynasty that was the UCLA Bruins under the direction of legendary coach, John Wooden. As Baby Boomers went from grade school to high school to college, they watched UCLA go on winning steaks and win multiple titles year after year. It was rare for them to lose a game. We watched as Gail Goodrich started the party and Lew Alcindor (later Kareem Abdul-Jabbar) and Bill Walton dominated the college basketball landscape. In 1973, Baby Boomers watched Bill Walton have perhaps the greatest game by any player to grace the floor, leading UCLA over Memphis State. Many Baby Boomers watched this game as college students with their friends.

The last team to go undefeated for an entire season also occurred while many Baby Boomers were in college – that team being the Indiana Hoosiers under the direction of famed iconic coach, Bob Knight. The team, led by Quinn Buckner and Scott May, was representative of all that was great about Indiana University basketball. It was where great basketball was coupled with students getting an education and graduating, and a program void of ethics violations. We see that today in Duke Basketball under the leadership of "Coach K," who is a disciple of Coach Knight – and isn't it interesting that these are the two of "winning-est" coaches in Division 1 history? So maybe it can be done the right way.

So, Baby Boomers, how about we mention a few players of the past to get you excited for this year's tournament? The greatest college basketball player that I ever saw was Pete Maravich. He could do things with a basketball similar to what Yo-Yo Ma can do with a cello. The first college basketball player to be, in my mind, the definition of a true student athlete was Bill Bradley for Princeton. Bradley went on to be a Rhodes Scholar, a star with the Knicks, a respected Senator, and Presidential Candidate. And finally, in 1979, the country was treated to Magic Johnson and Larry Bird. This was not just a game, but a pre-cursor to these two college boys then going on to compete as men, as they saved the NBA. However, it all started with that famous final as Magic and Michigan State overwhelmed the upstarts from Indiana State.

So, Baby Boomers, enjoy this year's tournament, celebrate the winner, celebrate the little schools that get in and compete, and remember the players and teams that came before. Enjoy "March Madness."

Saturday, February 18, 2012

The Television of our Youth

Baby Boomers, what comes to mind when the following is mentioned: "The Wonderful World of Disney," followed by "Bonanza"? Does the NBC Peacock, "brought to you in living color," and Sunday night ring a bell? How about "the Lawrence Welk Show" or "the Hollywood Palace"? Does Saturday night at your grandmother's with peanut brittle and ice cream register?

Imagine now that it is a Tuesday night in the world of black and white. Do you remember "The Untouchables" with Robert Stack as Elliot Ness? Did you next watch history come to life as you learned about the likes of Babe Ruth and FDR on the great "Biography" series, featuring a young Mike Wallace? Then perhaps your night come to a close as Raymond Burr won another case as Perry Mason? What was your favorite form of TV? Was it after school with "the Mickey Mouse Club"? Or, was it after dinner with the doctors, maybe Ben Casey or Dr. Kildare? Did you watch Rod Serling introduce "the Twilight Zone"? Or, perhaps you were one of the early Baby Boomers. That is a kind way of saying "an older Baby Boomer who was brought up on the picture perfect families of television." These were the families depicted in shows like "Ozzie and Harriet," "Father Knows Best," "Leave It to Beaver," "The Donna Reed Show," and "the Patty Duke Show."

"Ozzie and Harriet" was the staple show for our generation. When David Nelson died, his obituary carried a reference to the Baby Boomer generation. When Robert Young spoke in "Father Knows Best," he perfectly depicted the men of the times. Jerry Mathers, the Beaver, still marvels at how popular "Leave It to Beaver" is after all of these years. When Beaver's mother, June Cleaver (the late Barbara Billingsley), passed away, it was noted that "America's mother" had died. What this says is that television and Baby Boomers were coupled like no other. While the Greatest Generation got their news, laughter, and sports from the radio,

Baby Boomers grew up with TV. As television grew up, so did the Baby Boomer. In the early days of Baby Boomer youth, everyone tuned into "I Love Lucy." As Baby Boomers came of age, they watched the "Ed Sullivan Show." In college, many Baby Boomer women found Mary Tyler Moore to be a role model. And, interestingly enough, the biggest audience for the widely popular drama, "Mad Men," are in fact Baby Boomers, now mature adults going retro to the early sixties, a time gone by.

Sitting in a forum recently, Baby Boomers began to chat about one of their favorite topics – TV, the Baby Boomer companion of childhood. Some mentioned having a Gunsmoke lunch box because James Arness, as Marshall Dillion, was amongst their favorite characters. One woman mentioned her goal was to acquire the complete box set of "Bewitched." This program, with Elizabeth Montgomery as Samantha and the two Darrens, was listed amongst her favorite shows. Some male Baby Boomers spoke of watching "Wide World of Sports" with Jim McKay every Saturday. They recalled seeing Cassius Clay transform into Muhammad Ali and watching him fight against the likes of Floyd Patterson. Many women of the group also loved Saturday television, but preferred the earlier part of the day, when Dick Clark and "American Bandstand" were on.

A Baby Boomer, 56, said the first World Series that he saw was in 1963 when Sandy Koufax and the Dodgers swept the Yankees. That same Baby Boomer recalled being glued to the snow of his television screen on Sundays as he watched Vince Lombardi and the Green Bay Packers play in the snow. One woman mentioned how every September, for one night, she was "Miss America" as Bert Parks sang to the young girl recently crowned. We saw history through the men of the news. I can still picture David Brinkley saying good night to Chet Huntley on NBC, and Walter Cronkite walking us through the Kennedy Assassination, and then showing pride when Neil Armstrong walked on the moon. We saw President Johnson tell the nation that he would not seek re-election when he spoke to the nation under the weight of Vietnam. We also saw Richard Nixon walk from the White House, diminished by the weight of lies and cover up. Our life, our memories, and the experience of our youth was so influenced by television. Television gave us a barometer of the world. We saw change through "the Mod Squad," and The Generation Gap through Archie Bunker.

History will record someday that once upon a time, a generation grew up on a product that came along as they did – the coupling of television and Baby Boomers. What Baby Boomer cannot sit and recall their youth by the memory of a TV show?

Wednesday, February 1, 2012

Reflections of the first Super Bowl

It was not yet called the Super Bowl. It was a game that, in some ways, was being treated like an exhibition. But to some, it was the foundation of a grand scheme – that being a merger, to create a grand National Football League and a television outlet. To say that countless riches were at the end of the rainbow would be an understatement. This great vision was the brainchild of the late NFL Commissioner, Pete Rozelle. In fact, every NFL owner of today should send a residual check to the beneficiaries of the Pete Rozelle Estate, for without him, players and owners this past summer would not have been dickering over how to divide $9 billion.

But, in January of 1967, it was a game, and just a game, between the established old line NFL and the upstart AFL. The AFL played an interesting brand of football, a lot of passing. But nobody thought that the new league could compete, especially against teams like the Bears or the Browns, or the Colts. These were teams with names like "the Monsters of the Midway," the Chicago Bears, with the legend George Halas at the helm (you know, the man who practically formed Pro Football). The Colts had the great John Unitas. The Browns were famous for the early retirement of the greatest running back to walk on a field, Jim Brown. But, of course, these teams, as great as they were, played second fiddle to the Packers Dynasty under the legendary coach, Vince Lombardi. Yes, for the younger Baby Boomers in our midst, that is the same person the trophy is named after. The best team of the 1966 season in the AFL was the Kansas City Chiefs, owned by Lamar Hunt, who was a key player in the eventual merging of the two Leagues. Their quarterback was the classy Len Dawson, who played his college ball at Purdue, and who was now engineering the offense of the charismatic Head Coach, Hank Stram. They were, in retrospect, an outstanding team. In fact, they would go on to win the Super Bowl, beating the Vikings, the year after Joe Namath's miracle. But, in that first game, they were up against the Green Bay Packers, who were out to prove superiority. They did so.

It was so interesting that first year. Two networks covered the game and the L.A. Coliseum, host to the first game, was not sold out; but even the casual observer thought that they were witnessing something special. Baby Boomers will remember that the old AFL games were covered on NBC, while CBS had the established NFL. So there were two leagues, and two networks in a world that had three stations. The Green Bay Packers sort of chuckled as they left the field. It was an easy game, like a vacation in the sun. But the Chiefs were not embarrassed, so the real smiles were on the faces of Football executives hoping to bring about a merger. Now, on this first Super Sunday, that was not as far-fetched as once thought. Could teams from Buffalo, Denver, and San Diego someday find themselves in the same enterprise as the New York Football Giants? You betcha.

On a cold snow driven day in Chicago, my parents prepared dinner for relatives from the Upper Peninsula of Michigan, big Packer fans, who were coming over to watch. We flicked back and forth from channel to channel on the RCA Television, a color TV in a white cabinet. First to CBS, then back to NBC – this, during a pre-game that looked a lot like what you would see on Fox or CBS today, with its studio coverage. On NBC, they had this quarterback from the Buffalo Bills as a guest commentator. Not a bad field general, but maybe more remembered for his work in government, that being Jack Kemp.

When the game was complete and dinner concluded, you sort of felt like you had witnessed something out of the ordinary. Like, maybe this would be fun to continue. Who would have ever guessed that it would become the National holiday that it is: Super Bowl Sunday. Perhaps, I take that back, one person knew: his name was Pete Rozelle.

Monday, December 19, 2011

Christmas Movies for Baby Boomers

Do you have family visiting this Christmas? Perhaps you live on the West Coast and your family has come out to see you, and they are going to be with you for some time. Well, make sure you have a few movies on hand to enjoy together. Perhaps you want to stay up late and enjoy the company of a brother who you do not often get to see. Perhaps your mother and father want to sit by the tree and view one of the old favorites. Perhaps you are going to have movie night for the family. Well, here are some suggestions for Baby Boomers that will enhance the family togetherness.

The list has the staple, the Bing Crosby classic "White Christmas." No matter how many times you have seen it, once more will help the holiday be merry. A Baby Boomer favorite, especially for families that are involved in step-family situations, is the classic "Miracle on 34th Street." Make sure it is the original, with Natalie Wood. Some of the remakes are very good, but the original is the best.

An underrated Christmas movie that all ages will enjoy for its content, actors, and music is "Love Actually." Hugh Grant is part of an ensemble cast that also includes Kiera Knightly, amongst others. You will come away feeling good upon seeing this movie, which takes place in England.

If you, as a Baby Boomer, are lucky enough to have your parents still in your life, or even an elderly beloved Aunt or Uncle, then sit and enjoy these other two Bing Crosby films with them: "Going My Way," and

"Bells of St. Mary's." Yes, Bing Crosby plays a priest, who makes parish life worth watching. Let me warn you ahead of time, if it has been a while since you have seen these two films, they will tug at your heart.

Finally, for family night, go with the movie for all seasons, the movie that the whole family can participate in. Perhaps this is the perfect complement to leftovers: "The Sound of Music."

This will get you started, and you will have others to add to the list. Now, I know that some will write in and ask about "It's a Wonderful Life," but it is on every year, shown by NBC. It is a good guess that your family will have just seen it on television, so consider it back-up. Also, waiting in the bull pen, can be George C. Scott in the Dickens legendary story "A Christmas Carol." Another backup can be, "Gremlins," the 80s movie, based around Christmas, and especially enjoyed with younger members of the family. So keep that in mind for the young, as opposed to the young at heart. Of course, to add a bit of laughter, you can count on "Elf," with Saturday Night Live Alum, Will Ferrell. That might be the one for when extended family, or neighbors drop by, or a substitute for lack of better plans.

One can say, in conclusion, that movies bring families together and Christmas is the ultimate family time, so call upon some of the movies in this list during the Holiday Season.

Wednesday, November 9, 2011

Down Goes Frazier

Any Baby Boomer of a certain age remembers the life and times of Joe Frazier. He was a boxer in the true sense of the word. From the moment the bell rang until the end of the round, he advanced, he did not back down, he kept coming. Born as the son of a share cropper from South Carolina, he became the son of Philadelphia. Where Rocky is the fiction, Joe Frazier was the non-fiction. After winning the Olympic Gold medal in 1964, he turned professional. He became champion after beating Buster Mathis and Jimmy Ellis. This occurred when Cassius Clay, turned Muhammad Ali, vacated the belt for refusal to join the service on religious grounds. If you lived through this time, it was amazing, and hard for the current generation to understand. First, Boxing was very popular. Ali dominated the landscape, and the times were turbulent. When Ali, now released from prison and back on the scene, sought to re-claim his title, it became a fight that was not just about boxing. In 1971, when Ali fought Frazier, it was for the championship and it was about values. It was about your stance on the Vietnam War. In a titanic battle, Frazier beat Ali, to make his title fully legitimate. Ali, always popular, would remain on the scene. To Ali's detractors, part of Nixon's "silent majority," Frazier was a hero for defeating the draft dodger. This is the way the thinking and the country divide played out back then. It was the days of Archie Bunker. It was the days of "the generation gap." It was long hair versus button down. Boxing, like all that happened in the world, was part of the times that were changing.

Some boxing experts believe that Frazier was never the same after that historic fight with Ali. When he took on George Foreman, and was beaten, he was pummeled. Foreman would later lose to Ali in one of the most strategic fights of all time, known then as the "rope-a-dope." This set up two more historic fights between Ali and Frazier, which would live in the history books. These men were true rivals. In the second fight won by Ali, and then the third and final, Ali got the better of Frazier. In the 14th round of the third fight, the legendary trainer, Eddie Fuch, stopped the "fight" (or was it a "war?").

Joe Frazier has always lived in the shadow of the Great Ali, but for anyone who saw him fight, he gained your respect. He was a great fighter. The other figure that enhanced the two protagonists during these times was Howard Cosell. He probably did more to shape the image of Ali than any other person. He was an iconic figure of the time, and the mouthpiece of the boxing game. He knew greatness, and Ali was that, but he also knew when there was a great story abound. Frazier – Ali was the story of its time. If you ever heard a recording of Howard Cosell today, most likely, you would hear his most famous call, "down goes Frazier, down goes Frazier." So many years later, it is hard to put into context the magnitude of the three men being described. Time has a way of forgetting, but there was a time in this country, when "Wide World of Sports" dominated the news story of sports, when boxing was not about "pay-per-view," and warriors put everything on the line.

Joe Frazier was 67 at the time of his death. He lost his battle with liver cancer after his short stay in hospice. To Baby Boomers, this question must be asked: Do you remember what it was like - Ali versus Frazier?

Wednesday, October 26, 2011

The Bill Buckner Play

As of this writing, The World Series is about to enter the sixth game. The Texas Rangers lead the St. Louis Cardinals, 3 games to 2. 25 years ago in game six between the Boston Red Sox and the New York Mets, a ball went through the legs of Bill Buckner, cementing his name into the history of baseball.

The year was 1986. The Red Sox fans, seemingly always suffering through some kind of misery to keep them from winning it all, thought perhaps that this might be their year. They had rallied over The Angels to get to The World Series, and in game six, seemed to have everything going their way. The starter, Roger Clemens, the ace, was pitching. The group sitting at the bar at the Front Page Restaurant in Charlestown, Massachusetts, could hardly contain themselves. The Front Page, in its time, was one great place to go eat and watch a game. It was located in historic Charlestown. The battle of Bunker Hill was fought there, and perhaps on October 25, 1986, once again history could be made. The place was very popular with The Celtics and The Bruins, for it was situated just across the bridge from the legendary Boston Garden. Upon parking your car, you would enter and see the restaurant to the right and the bar area to the left. That night, every stool was taken, food in front, a drink to the side, and head up to the screen as the early innings provided a Red Sox lead. Late in the game, it appeared fate would be on the side of The Red Sox.

Three things happened: bartenders were putting champagne on ice, town elders were saying how they wished their father had lived to see this moment, and a young business executive, born and raised in North Andover, Massachusetts, noted for his cool demeanor, looked like he was going to have a heart attack from excitement. Perhaps aided by Bushmills, the Irish whiskey, he counted down to ending what they knew in Boston as "The Curse of the Bambino." The "curse," as it was known, signified the fact that The Red Sox had not won since trading Babe Ruth. Dan Shaughnessy, the great sportswriter for The Boston Globe, also helped to identify the history of the Red Sox losing. Many in Boston believe that "The Curse of the Bambino" was popularized by his book. On this night, the curse was about to be broken.

When 25 years pass, sometimes folklore gets in the way of facts. The dribbler as described, by Vin Scully, that went through Buckner's legs did not cost the Red Sox the Championship. The events in game six started by an improbable two-out come back by the Mets, when Mookie Wilson hit the ball that ended the game. There was still one more game to play that occurred two nights later due to a rain out. In game seven, the Red Sox also lost a lead, and then the Series. Yet, Bill Buckner has never lived down his mistake.

History will record that, in 2004, the Red Sox finally broke through. Interestingly enough, they won again in 2007. Perhaps a bit of the pain has been forgotten, after all these years. Bill Buckner was a better than most ball player, who had a long and distinguished career. But his name will always be synonymous with that play in 1986. He has had to live with it, hide from it, and attempt humor, participating in the program "Curb Your Enthusiasm."

With the Red Sox success in recent years, he has been received warmly at Fenway Park. But for the patrons, who left The Front Page that awful night in October, it was like the sad wake of a dear relative. Where were you the night the ball went through Buckner's legs?

Wednesday, October 19, 2011

The Godfather Movies

Mike Brown, owner of the Cincinnati Bengals Football team, refused to trade his star quarterback, Carson Palmer. You see, Palmer no longer wanted to play for what he believed to be a dysfunctional organization. So, Palmer decided to retire rather than go back to the Bengals. But like "The Godfather" has been known to say, Oakland, "made him an offer he couldn't refuse." So goes the life lessons of the movies that started with the original film that came out in 1972. Baby Boomers have responded to the three Godfather Movies like no other generation. One reason for this is that the book, by Mario Puzo, and then the movie "The Godfather," came out at the time when most Baby Boomers were either in college or graduating from college.

The character Michael, played brilliantly by Al Pacino, was like us, in a matter of speaking. You are introduced to him as he returns from the army as a war hero, having left college to join the service. He is our age, and is dealing with some of the same sorts of family issues as Baby Boomers, such as trying to balance respect for his father and adherence to his family traditions, with his desire to go his own way. Marlon Brando, one of America's greatest actors of all time, secured an Oscar for his portrayal of Michael's father, Vito (a.k.a., "The Godfather"). In some ways, Michael's father is like your own father; he runs a business, manages to sustain loyalty in friendships, and has a vision for his family, especially his youngest son.

At this point, you, as a reader, are probably commenting, "like my family, but minus the crime." The interesting thing is that most Baby

Boomers never saw The Godfather Trilogy as a "crime" saga. It is a "family" saga, with crime as a backdrop. This is why Baby Boomers consistently will tell you, in interview after interview, that the movies are amongst their favorites. To be specific, The Godfather I and II are amongst the most watched by Baby Boomers, while The Godfather III, taken on its own, is less popular. However, when seen as a Trilogy, The Godfather III complements the first two and rounds out the story. In fact one of the lines from Godfather III, is amongst the most quoted, that being, "I try to get out, and they keep pulling me in," referring to Michael 's life long quest to make the family legitimate. As a sidebar, the line most enjoyed by Baby Boomers comes from the original Godfather Movie, "Drop the gun, take the cannolis." Tom Hanks loves that line as he emails Meg Ryan in the movie "You've Got Mail."

Here are five reasons why Baby Boomers identify with The Godfather Movies: the love between father and son; the story of coming to America, and making it in America; the story of having to do, what you have to do in life; the practice of loyalty, and the desire to remain loyal to friendships; and, the defense of your values, and the ones you care about, at all costs.

Baby Boomers report that they have seen the movies on numerous occasions, and discover something new each time that they see the films. This is due to the genius of Francis Ford Coppola, who has made these movies the cornerstone of his life's work. This is a tremendous accomplishment indeed. Years ago, when renting a movie was a common practice for Baby Boomers, when picking up some food and going to Blockbuster on a Friday night was part of date night, you rented "The Godfather." Now, when AMC or one of the other cable outlets airs all three movies back to back, Baby Boomers have been known to invest a day watching the life of the Al Pacino character play out. The older Baby Boomers get, the more the parallel to Michael's story. You are seeing his life unfold through the prism of your own life. His youth was your youth, his middle age and his choices were your choices. His attempt to recapture family lost as an aging individual is your attempt.

The ending of the three movies, where Michael dies in his old age in Italy, makes you ponder how your own life will end. When Michael reflects on the life that he has lived, the early days with family were happier times. You yourself think of the glory days of your own family, and wish that those days could somehow return. If you spend a day watching all three movies, you will come away reflective, thinking in review of the life that you have led. This is the secret to "The Godfather," the hidden nugget – it is a movie about life.

Thursday, September 1, 2011

Slogans from Our Youth

The calendar has shifted to September, the summer is in the rear view mirror, and children across America are returning to school. Soon, the "Gridiron" will take center stage. Once upon a time, though, there was another tradition that has faded from modern memory. Remember, when you were a young child, how much excitement there was as the new models of cars were announced? Remember the first glimpse of the '64 Chevrolet Impala? That year, they had a black model with red interior. It was the kind of car that was great on the open road. Chevrolet was a popular car back then, a family car. You saw it at the auto show and sometimes your heroes from TV would be in the sales booth to help make your father aware of the new model.

But more than likely Chevrolet was in your brain because of the slogan, "See the U.S.A. in a Chevrolet." Remember the jingle? I bet you can hear it in your mind as you read this. "See the U.S.A. in a Chevrolet." For that was America at the time, an automobile from the great company General Motors, and the chance to drive across America on the ever growing highway system. "See the U.S.A. in a Chevrolet." This would have been about the time when a business professor would ask, "What would you rather be, President of the United States, or President of General Motors?" "So goes GM, so goes the country." "See the U.S.A. in a Chevrolet."

There was a time in this country when people did not rush from their airplane to the rental car shuttle. There was a bit more civility to the rental car business. It was hard to figure out what to make of the business. However, you knew that it was prevalent because you saw this commercial on television. There goes that TV thing again. Television had a sponsor to go with the program. Madison Avenue was helping the good times of the American people find places to dispose of that income. We are reminded of those days as we watch the very popular program of today, "Mad Men," about the advertising of the 1960s. In fact, it is very interesting, as that period seems in vogue. There is no greater evidence for that than the new Banana Republic clothing line, which teams with the fashions of the "Mad Men" program to bring us the style of today. What do they say? "Everything that is old is new again."

So, as we sat in front of the television, a man appeared to come from the sky and land in the front seat of a convertible. The music would be playing, and the jingle would almost sing to you, "Let Hertz put you in the driver seat." To this day, you can sing it: "Let Hertz put you in the driver seat." These slogans are so powerful, so entertaining, that they are part of the lexicon. They are engulfed into our concord that represents the day and time of our youth. "Let Hertz put you in the driver seat." What was it about the early 60s that Dinah Shore could make you love a car, and Jack Benny could make you feel good about Texaco? The products roll off the tongue because of the slogan. Do you remember "Tang, the breakfast of astronauts," "Moms everywhere trust Tang," or "Up, up and away, with TWA"?

Barry Manilow got his start with jingles. Go to one of his shows and let him sing some of his creations, and it will bring you back to a simpler time. There was a time in your family living room when you watched your favorite programs on an RCA, Zenith, or Philco. It was before the days of watching Super Bowl advertisements for sport. You would be watching some variety program, when it would be interrupted and you would hear, "See the U.S.A. in a Chevrolet." All these years later, the slogans from your youth and the memories they invoke are still with you.

Thursday, July 28, 2011

Baby Boomers and Women's Sports

Ever heard of T.J. Simers? He is a sports writer for the Los Angeles Times. In his market, he is very well respected. He has a way to get to the heart of the matter. When he took on the U.S. Women's Soccer team's loss to Japan, the letters to the editor poured in. The ending of the article went like this, "I say treat the gals like athletes and make sure they understand if they choke again, it's off to Nebraska for the whole lot." The picture painted strikes a far contrast to life before Title IX. A sports writer taking a girls' team to the woodshed would have been unheard of back in 1972, when women were fighting for equal opportunity and women's sports played out as a metaphor for society.

So it gives you great appreciation for how far we have come and the people who deserve the credit for getting us here. Although we may not like the harshness of Mr. Simer's tone, and plenty did not, he treated them no differently than he would a men's team. For example, it was no different from the way he would have taken on the Dodgers, Lakers, or, for that matter, the men's soccer team, if they had been in the same position in the men's World Cup. That is a good thing. As Baby Boomers remember the before and after of women's sports, they note the progress and recall the events leading up to this point.

For example, the champion of women in sports, on and off the court, is Billie Jean King. Every woman who competes in sports ought to pay homage to Billie Jean King for her life long effort of bringing women in sports into the public consciousness. Her legacy as a champion athlete is secure, but her contribution to society ranks with the likes of Susan B. Anthony, Eleanor Roosevelt, and Gloria Steinem, as advocates for women and their plight for equal rights. Baby Boomers recall vividly how she beat Bobby Riggs in the Houston Astrodome, in the "Battle of the sexes." She played that match for her gender, for a cause, and to move progress ahead.

Women in corporate America who have broken the glass ceiling can use the example of Billie Jean King and her win over Bobby Riggs, as more than a mere tennis victory. It was, in fact, a seminal moment. Sports does that - it is a metaphor for life. Venus Williams and her sister Serena, upon winning the major championships like Wimbledon, where both men and women receive equal prize money, should place Billie Jean King as a dependent on their tax form. Surely though, even Billie Jean King would look back on Title IX and the landmark decision to insure mandated equal opportunity, as the foundation for the house that now provides for the WNBA, LPGA, and, yes, the U. S. Women's Soccer Team losing to Japan.

Look to any grade school and look for the future Mia Hamm, or Hope Solo – women who are now household names to young girls who love soccer. Or, how about in the High School gym, where women work on their free throws and look up to the great woman basketball player Sue Bird? Or, how about the woman college track star, who trains amidst a great athletic complex, and looks to a NCAA and possible Olympic chance? Recently, Janet Evans, the legend from the pool, was working on a comeback with the hopes of competing at the 2012 Games in London. The fact that she even has this opportunity is more important than the results. Maybe we should take it a little easy on our friend, Mr. Simers, for maybe he has it right when he writes, "they just gave it away, and to make excuses or diminish the magnitude of such a collapse is to treat the gals like women instead of world class athletes." Billie Jean King would be proud because this sports writer was even-handed in criticism, and that is what she has fought for all of her life.

Thursday, July 14, 2011

10 Greatest Sports Stories for Baby Boomers

In every generation, there are sports stories that stand out and in some ways transcend sports. To earlier generations, it might be the great exploits of Babe Ruth, or Jesse Owens staring down Hitler in the 1936 Olympics.

There was the great boxer Joe Louis, and the 1941 baseball season that saw Joe DiMaggio hit in 56 straight games, while Ted Williams batted 406. It is possible that neither of these feats will ever happen again. For previous generations it was Jackie Robinson breaking the color barrier and Bobby Thompson's home run, known as "the shot heard around the world." For the game of golf, Bobby Jones is still talked about for achieving the grand slam, which was a great moment in golf history.

While all of these are known to Baby Boomers who are sports fans, and though the significance of the achievements are without question, they are not Baby Boomer moments. Bruce Weber, the speech writer, not the Basketball coach, asked a Baby Boomer, "What were your greatest sports stories?" Mr. Weber, being 76 years young, remembered or mentioned most of the ones cited above. The Baby Boomer responded with the following list. See how it matches up to the ones you might have selected:

1. If you are an older Baby Boomer, you would list the 1958 NFL Championship overtime game between the Giants and the Colts, the game that ushered in the NFL as we know it.

2. The 1960 World Series highlighted by Bill Mazeroski's walk off homerun in the 7th game.

3. The Maris – Mantle chase for 61 homers to break Babe Ruth's record.

4. The famed ice bowl between the Packers and the Cowboys, a (-)15 F temperature and a dramatic finish.

5. In 1969, Joe Namath first making the prediction, then leading the Jets over the Colts, thus cementing, for all time, the Super Bowl.

6. Ali – Frazier, the three dramatic fights; (post) Ali being released from prison for refusing to serve in Vietnam on the grounds of religious beliefs.

7. Al Michael's "Do you believe in miracles? YES!" when the USA beat the Soviet Union in 1980, in what became known as "The Miracle on Ice." This one, if these were ranked as opposed to listed, would probably be number one.

8. The 1986 World Series: the Red Sox were poised to win, the ball goes through Bill Buckner's legs and the Mets come back and win.

9. "Yes, sir" comments Vern Lundquist, as Jack Nicklaus makes a dramatic putt on 16, and then goes on to win the 1986 Masters at 46 years of age.

10. "I don't believe what I just saw" shouts Jack Buck, upon seeing Kirk Gibson's dramatic home run in the 1988 World Series. Gibson could hardly walk, but found a way to win with a dramatic game-ending homerun, hitting it off Hall of Famer Dennis Eckersley.

There were so many great sports happenings in the Baby Boomer conceptual thinking that a few additional honorable mentions would be appropriate. For example, there were two grand slams by Rod Laver in tennis, Arthur Ashe winning Wimbledon, and the Everett-Navratilova rivalry. In golf, the exploits of Tiger Woods are of note, and in basketball, the dominance of the Celtics in the '60s. The "Title Town" of the Lombardi Green Bay Packer teams of the '60s, as well as the dominance of the Montreal Canadians in hockey also come to mind. In conclusion, it was and still is a great time to be a sports fan in the Baby Boomer lifetime.

Tuesday, July 12, 2011

The Fad that was Disco

On Monday July 11, 2011, in the Los Angeles Times, a story appeared titled "A disco inferno." It was a fun review of the disco era, which looking back was relatively short, but indeed memorable. The story was, in large part, a preview to the UCLA Film and Television Archive showcase of the favorites of the genre with its "Reflections in a mirrored Ball" series at the Billy Wilder Theater. It was an interesting time, wasn't it? We were post-Watergate, post-college, post-protest movement. It was a time for Baby Boomers to kick back their shoes and enjoy the music of the Bee Gees and Donna Summer. It was a time to get up and dance, and it was a time to explore.

One Baby Boomer traveled the country with the radio blasting, simply because he could. It was a time before responsibility, before family and children, and before the corporate life that lay ahead. Jimmy Carter was President, there were lines for gasoline, and the job market was not all that good. It was a time to have fun. The interesting thing about that era is that it still resonates with Baby Boomers today. Have you ever noticed at weddings that as soon the music from the disco period starts, the place comes alive? Music has an interesting effect, because in addition to enjoying a song, or making you come alive, it has a "remember when" quality to it.

For Baby Boomers and the disco era, the girl that you took to see "Saturday Night Fever" with (then) 23 year old John Travolta might not have been the one you married, but one whom you do remember. The disco era was a time when Baby Boomers' whole lives were ahead of them, and it felt good. It is easy to think back to that time and think of the clothes and the shoes, or the drugs and freedom. It is easy to think of that time as a fad, but it was a very important time for Baby Boomers who were in search of who they were and what they wanted to be.

In a way, the disco ball was one that was to be juggled, between the college life and the dawn of corporate life. The disco era was over, for all intents and purposes, by the time that Ronald Regan took office. The platform shoes, like the Baby Boomers' party days, were just part of a closet that needed to be cleaned and refreshed. Soon the leisure suit would be traded in for a Brooks Brothers suit. With 1980, the Baby Boomer became a part of the workforce, and the "Car Wash" (movie and song) was in some cases now just a place to get your Volvo washed on the way to work. But, like all bridges in life, when we go from one thing to the next, the time in the middle is something that stays with us. So, while we never want to dress like you did then, you would give a great deal to have the feeling of enjoyment of one of those "Saturday Night Fever" type of nights.

——

Wednesday, June 29, 2011

The Music of Baby Boomers

Bill Walton is considered one of the great basketball players of the generation. His exploits, for example, at UCLA, make him a legend when it comes to college basketball. But he is also one of the true Grateful Dead fans, or "Dead Heads," as they are known. Baby Boomers are attached to many things, but music may have defined the group we know as Baby Boomers. Take the cab driver in San Diego, who just turned 65. He certainly was one who remembers the statement, "Rock and Roll is here to stay." He loves Buddy Holly and Elvis and will get up and dance at the mere mention of Chubby Checker. Then there is the recently retired teacher, age 62, from Westchester, Illinois just outside Chicago. She was, and still is, everything Beatles, from "A Hard Day's Night" to "Let it Be." Now she probably plays "Yesterday" over and over as she communicates with her long time pen pal in England, a friendship that started when they were both 15, simply because they were both Beatles fans.

Four women from Detroit, all between 58 and 62, took a girls-only trip to Las Vegas last year. They report that their best evening spent was a dinner and Motown show at the Riviera Hotel and Casino. "Nothing gets you up and dancing," they said, "like the sounds of Motown." Or, how about the man from Oregon, 58, who is still mad at Governor Brown of California for dating the girl he had a crush on - that being Linda Ronstadt, of course. The 62 year old hair dresser from the South Side of Chicago became a Rolling Stones fan while, as a young girl, having lunch at Bobby's snack shop, where she would play the song about Satisfaction on the juke box.

The college students at the University of Wisconsin in Madison claim a diverse selection of favorites, ranging from The Carpenters to Loggins & Messina to Emerson, Lake, & Palmer. The Baby Boomer generation has spanned the time from Connie Francis to Whitney Houston. They have continued their love affair with Frank Sinatra and Tony Bennett. They have died with Jim Morrison, Jimi Hendrix, Janis Joplin, and Cass

Elliot. They have loved the Eagles and Chicago. It is Baby Boomers of today who pick up their telephone and pledge to PBS during fund drives because one of their old favorites are performing, and the memory of the music brings them back to a previous time and place.

The breadth of the Song Book is so great for the Baby Boomer that it seems their music will last for all time. Consider some movie song tracks: Simon and Garfunkel from the Graduate, or the Bee Gees from Saturday Night Fever. The other interesting aspect is that many performers at an advanced age are still performing. For example, Paul McCartney is about to launch his latest tour – who could have predicted that from the forever young generation? The bottom line is that this column could go on forever because the era of the Baby Boomers produced some incredible music that still resonates today. Music was truly in the plus column for accomplishments of people living in this lifetime.

Wednesday, June 22, 2011

1986, A Year for Baby Boomers

A Baby Boomer from Boston looks back on his life. He is married now to a wonderful woman and living in the town where he grew up, North Andover, Massachusetts. The business that he started in the early 1980s is now very successful. He is able to support all of his passions: season tickets to the Red Sox, vacations down on the Cape [Cape Cod], and the occasional conventions that turn into expanded travel. But, yet, like most Baby Boomers when asked to try to pinpoint their favorite year, 1986 always seems to jump out. Some believe that it is when they first came into their own in their career. Some think that it is because of the technology revolution that was happening around them and the excitement that it brought to the work place. Some Baby Boomers just remember it as a good wage earner year.

Conditions were favorable for corporate expansion. It was a time when there was an extremely favorable environment for new companies to start.

Because of this, Baby Boomers seemingly could move from position to position and improve their lot in life. For our Baby Boomer in Boston, it was also a great time to be a sports fan. It was, after all, the era of the great Larry Bird. It was a time to follow the Boston Celtics, and your schedule, if you lived in Boston at the time, revolved around when the Celtics played.

1986 was the year that the Red Sox made it to the World Series and seemingly collapsed at the hands of the New York Mets. The heart break for Bostonians was real, but the excitement of that season lives on. The New England Patriots made it to the Super Bowl only to be crushed by maybe one of the best teams of all time, the Chicago Bears, but any Bostonian who traveled to New Orleans for the game that year will never forget their good time. A prominent long time sports talk show host and Baby Boomer notes that going to that Super Bowl, and the good time surrounding the game in 1986, is still his favorite sporting event of all time.

The Baby Boomer three thousand miles away from Boston had similar feelings, although the team of choice was different; for him it was the Los Angeles Lakers and Magic Johnson that brought excitement. "Showtime" is what they called it, and both coasts brought the remainder of the country along for the NBA ride. A book by Jackie McMullen about Bird and Magic is a great resource to relive those basketball times.

A Baby Boomer woman in Southern California speaks for a lot of Baby Boomers in her assessment of what made 1986 such a great year: "We were getting our careers going, we were making money and just beginning to live well - that is why that time resonates with Baby Boomers." Another Baby Boomer from Boston said, "I went to the World Series and I saw Bobby Short at the Carlyle in New York in the same year, 1986 - pretty hard to beat." "It was the same year that I bought my first Brooks Brothers suit, and my first Condo. Pretty hard to beat." "It was the year that I met the love of my life and attended Christmas at Pops, pretty hard to beat." For Baby Boomers, 1986 was a year that was pretty hard to beat.

Wednesday, June 15, 2011

Ten Movies for Baby Boomers

Picture a cold damp weekend in Seattle, when all you want to do is wrap yourself in a blanket. You might want to sit on the couch, perhaps with a cup of something warm right next to you. The forecast is for similar conditions all weekend, so having planned ahead, you have fired up Netflix and settled in with ten movies that Baby Boomers would enjoy. A good start would be "Best Years of our Lives." The Fredric March, Myrna Loy film tells the story of three men who meet by chance and the film follows their assimilation back into society after World War II. This, after all, is where the Baby Boomer generation got its start, but more importantly, it speaks to the transition of a war to civilian life. In the 1950s Frank Sinatra, Doris Day, and Gig Young made the wonderful movie, "Young at Heart." It is a movie about family, finding the right person to marry, and the closeness between sisters. With a little music, this movie is both entertainment and drama.

Paul Newman made a lot of good films, but maybe his best was "The Hustler." Playing fast Eddie Felson, Newman works the pool circuit until he gets the big confrontation with Minnesota Fats, played classically by Jackie Gleason. The movie is about lost dreams, second chances, and love that goes tragically wrong. Sidney Poitier is one of the great actors, and in the 1960s, he made two films that are imperative to be on any Baby Boomer's list. The first one is "To Sir With Love," in which a young man seeking a career in engineering first takes a job teaching in a high school, in London. The students, not exactly Oxford-bound, are molded into shape by a man who teaches manners as a way to reach the students. The movie also contains the classic song, "To Sir With Love," sung by the woman who made it famous, LuLu.

The next selection is "Guess Who's Coming to Dinner," one of the great movies for the times when America was going through the Civil Rights movement. Sidney Poitier plays a black man with all the credentials, who falls in love with a white woman. The parents of the girl are played by Spencer Tracy and Katherine Hepburn. The movie is set in San Francisco, and as it plays out, you begin to realize that it is really a story about values and acceptance.

Most Baby Boomers will tell you that a movie for their generation was "The Graduate." Of course, this was the movie that put Dustin Hoffman on the map. It asks the question: "What were those four years of college all about?" Most Baby Boomers will tell you that this movie was played more often to packed crowds on their campus than any other. The defining moment is when The Graduate finally figures out what he wants, and goes for it, that being the daughter of Mrs. Robinson, played by Katherine Ross. The problem though, is that earlier, while feeling lost, the graduate had engaged in a dalliance with her mother, Mrs. Robinson, played brilliantly by Anne Bancroft.

In surveys of Baby Boomers asking them to list their favorite movie, one that makes all lists is the 1972 Francis Ford Coppola epic "The Godfather." The story of the Corleone Family, based on Mario Puzo's book, traces the direction of this close knit family. It is a movie that made Al Pacino a star. The fascination for Baby Boomers extends to the Godfather Trilogy. They report spending all day watching when AMC sometimes runs all three Godfather movies together. But, for the purpose of this exercise, the original movie stands on its own.

Have you ever seen a bad Gene Hackman movie? Probably not. Some say "The French Connection" was a Baby Boomer classic. But arguably his best performance was in the movie "Hoosiers." This story of a basket-ball coach's redemption in small town Indiana, where basketball is king, has all the elements: friendship, loyalty, values, love, and second chances.

For a romantic story, a Baby Boomer favorite is "Sleepless in Seattle." Any person who has suffered loss, or anyone who is trying to define what it means to find the right person in life, should certainly make sure this one finds its way into the Top 10.

Finally, a cute finish that will leave your weekend on a high note is the Hugh Grant, Julia Roberts film "Notting Hill." It is an almost impossible situation that arises when a famous actress meets the owner of a travel bookstore. The love story plays out amidst friendship and overcoming enormous odds to make a relationship come to life. So, there you have it Baby Boomers, ten movies for Baby Boomers. Did your favorite make the list?

Tuesday, May 10, 2011

Dick Van Dyke, a Baby Boomer presence

Four entertainers who have made an impression on Baby Boomers are Dick Van Dyke, Bobby Short, Donald O'Connar, and Gene Hackman, all of whom happen to be from Danville, IL. They all went to the same high school and all were in the same class, except Hackman, who was younger than the others. We learn this from the new book that Dick Van Dyke has out, called "My Lucky Life In and Out of Show Business." Ask a Baby Boomer to list their favorite TV shows of all time and "The Dick Van Dyke Show" is always mentioned. It ran from 1961 to 1966, but went on long beyond that in syndication. Dick Van Dyke played the likable Rob Petrie, a comedy writer who had two great cohorts in Rose Marie and Morey Amsterdam.

This show is also where we discovered Mary Tyler Moore, who played the wife, Laura. She would reach Baby Boomer icon status with "The Mary Tyler Moore Show," and her role in "Ordinary People." "The Dick Van Dyke Show" was the brain child of Carl Reiner, who, by the way, produced his own Baby Boomer, Rob Reiner (famous for his role as "Meathead" in "All in the Family" and later a successful movie director). Baby Boomers perceive Dick Van Dyke as one of the nicest people in television. He also registered with Baby Boomers in movies. He was classic in "Bye Bye Birdie," and unforgettable in "Mary Poppins." But it is his role as Rob Petrie that will forever be in the zone of Baby Boomers.

"The Dick Van Dyke Show" made you want to go to New Rochelle, New York, because Rob and Laura lived there. The show was smart and witty, and the comedic timing was second to none. It also showed you a slice of Americana. It was suburban life, it was the office, and it was the marriage. The theme song of the show still resides in Baby Boomer's heads. The opening scene of the show, week to week, is a part of television history. It also had its social commentary. Rose Marie was seen as an equal part of the office writing team, which is no small feat for a woman in the work place in the early sixties. You also saw the limits of television and the role of the censor, for the loving couple Rob and Laura were seen in separate beds (twin beds). Contrast that with another Baby Boomer favorite a decade later, "The Bob Newhart Show," which portrayed that married couple in a King Size bed. But then again, that was part of the changing times from the sixties to the seventies that all Baby Boomers recall.

Dick Van Dyke is a classic performer, and his easy going, full smile approach is remembered by Baby Boomers. They loved "The Dick Van Dyke Show." They, liked the character of Rob Petrie, and subsequently, his persona still carries weight with the generation.

Saturday, May 7, 2011

Seve Ballesteros, golfer and Baby Boomer hero

Are you, as a Baby Boomer, a fan of the Ryder Cup? Were you a golf fan during the late 70s and for much of the 1980s? Do you wonder why there are so many European golfers dominating this present generation? The key link is Seve Ballesteros. They called him a "swashbuckler." He had an imagination on a golf course, like Mark Twain had for storytelling. He took difficult or impossible golf shots, and turned lemons into lemonade. Last year, the Captain of the European squad during the Ryder Cup thought his team was a little flat, so he arranged for a conference call with Seve (in the golf world no last name is needed). Although he was very sick, he agreed to call The European Ryder Cup Team and rally the troops. Colin Montgomerie, always a straight shooter, credited Seve with the spark and motivation that his team needed.

A Baby Boomer woman and golf expert from Lynnfield, Massachusetts, followed his career closely. She loved to watch him play, especially in the Ryder Cup. Even though she was loyal to the American side she was riveted by his expertise. It was fun to watch her try specific golf shots on the course that maybe only Seve could execute. She has since passed, leaving her own legacy on the family who loved her and the golf community of Massachusetts. Nick Faldo, the famed English golfer, and major champion, is now a golf commentator. Recently on a broadcast in the midst of a tournament, he remembered Seve's birthday. The affection was obvious in his voice.

Some Baby Boomers, because of Seve, later cheered for other Spanish golfers in tournaments. Baby Boomers who have been lucky enough to attend the Masters in Augusta, Georgia, held each April, report following Olzabal, Jimenez, and Garcia, because of their memories of Seve. The Masters is on a lot of Baby Boomer's bucket lists when they make the pilgrimage to the lush green surroundings of Bobby Jones fame. They admire the history, they relish in the respect for Palmer and Nicklaus, but most of all, they think of their fellow Baby Boomer, the great Seve Ballesteros.

Recently, Seve has been in the news, but for all the wrong reasons. Baby Boomers followed the news closely as the Associated Press reported that his family released a statement detailing that Seve had suffered "severe deterioration" in the recovery from a cancerous brain tumor. There was an outpouring of support for Seve from the golf world, which is not surprising. He is just one of those figures in the Baby Boomer lexicon that has stayed with the generation. Sadly, today, on May 7, 2011, Seve Ballesteros died of brain cancer at the age of 54.

April 14, 2011

The Verdict – a movie for Baby Boomers

Years ago, Paul Newman made a movie called "The Verdict." In the film, he plays Frank Galvin, an attorney. The movie is set in Boston. The movie tells the story of a man who had worked hard, made himself a good lawyer, and seemingly had it all. He married the senior partner's daughter, became wealthy, and became part of Boston society. In Boston, where status, class, and connections count, he had made it. But during a tough case, which was a money maker for the firm, the firm, behind his back, tried to give him a little help and bribed a juror. Distraught upon hearing the news, he decided to go to the authorities because he is a man of integrity. But the firm and their high powered contacts were way ahead of him. He took the fall and lost everything.

The heart of the movie is about trying to survive after your life has been stripped. While everybody else had deserted him, one friend stands by him. His friend tries to help by sending a case his way that could bring redemption. But as the movie plays out, it is hard for him to get back on the horse. Many Baby Boomers have shared with me in interviews that they can relate to this character because losing and starting over again can be painful.

Corporate executives, who were once successful, are now a pariah at the country club. That is painful. The middle manager loses his house – that is painful. It is reality to a generation that seemingly had it all, but now has lost its way. That, to this commentator, is painful. But the silver lining is the many stories of family and friends who stuck by their loved ones. Their support was thick, not thin. I was told by fellow Baby Boomers that support can make all the difference. The "Greatest Generation" knew about support and family; it got them through the Great Depression. That generation was better for those relationships. It is what sustained them and, in some ways, enriched their lives. Baby Boomers are beginning to see the same.

Tuesday, May 3, 2011

Television that defined a Generation

Simply put, television and Baby Boomers will always be linked. Television and Baby Boomers came of age at the same time. Baby Boomers grew up with television and the coupling of the two is without debate. For the Baby Boomers who just this year turned 65, they can tell you about the litany of TV sets that their family might have owned. For example, there was the Philco with the roundish screen. Every Baby Boomer has a story to tell about rabbit ears, and snow on the screen. But no subject gets Baby Boomers talking more as the one regarding when their first color television arrived and what a moment that was for their family. The television that was watched by Baby Boomers defined a generation. TV programming, from its earliest days, reflected society; it rarely lead.

When Baby Boomers were school children and the push was out to suburbia, television was there to document the family with its view of America. The trilogy of "Ozzie and Harriet," "Leave it to Beaver," and "Father Knows Best" hold a special place in the heart of Baby Boomers. As Baby Boomers grew just a little bit older, they watched programs such as the "Wonderful World of Disney," "Bonanza," and "My Three Sons."

Times began to change, Baby Boomers grew up, and television reflected their taste. One show that identifies the shift from "My Three Sons" to the "Age of Aquarius" was Rowan and Martin's "Laugh-In." This show, which made Goldie Hawn a star, was zany and reflective of the changing times. Later the television series "Mash" became all the rage and an even bigger hit than the movie it was based on. Although set as part of the Korean war, it reflected the lack of reverence for the military, so much a part of the Vietnam era. The last episode set a television watching record.

During the early '70s, the fight for women's rights was at the forefront in the country. The quintessential program that spoke to the movement was the "Mary Tyler Moore Show." Women Baby Boomers point to that show, and Billie Jean King playing and beating Bobby Riggs, as watershed moments. Other programs reflected not only women's issues but also civil rights. One example is "Julia" with Diahann Carroll; ground breaking certainly is not an exaggeration. Another true reflection of the times was the program "The Mod Squad." It had three young people as hip cops of the day: one white male, one black male, and a young woman. Peggy Lipton was the woman lead who helped capture the country's mood of young, diverse, and in the know.

Baby Boomers then went into the corporate world. They were witness to the Reagan Revolution. This would be the group that would make "the West Wing" a must watch, and a part of Thursday night's "must see TV." Many Baby Boomers also laughed along with "Seinfeld" as part of the Thursday night lineup. That was the show that felt a lot like someone who had waited to marry and relied on their social life garnered from their group.

For some Baby Boomers, life came full circle when they saw their children watching programs such as "90210," but the families reflected were far different from those of their youth. Today, for Baby Boomers, life and television are so different. There are not three stations but three hundred. Television is segmented, and in fact, you might not even watch the program at the time that it airs. Not to mention the interactive nature of adding the computer to the mix. And as time goes on, as we combine all of the device worlds, TV as we once knew it will be long gone. But meanwhile, "Mad Men," the reflective AMC program built around the early '60s and so popular with Baby Boomers, taps into the longing to look back.

Summary – Chapter 6

TV Shows, Movies, Music, and Sports

In the fall of 1963, my parents and I were going to my Aunt Evie's for dinner. My father and I were focused on Game 4 of the World Series. The Yankees were down, 3-games to 0, and facing Sandy Koufax, the greatest pitcher of his generation. We were American League fans, because we were White Sox fans who played in the American League. We also wanted the Yankees to extend the series, but in the best of seven that is the World Series, it was a daunting task. But on the day of the game and watching Koufax in action, you just knew you were watching something special. My father, an astute baseball fan, pointed out that we were watching one of the greatest left-handers to ever put on a uniform. That same feeling of excellence came over me, as I watched Muhammad Ali step into the ring – he is what boxing is to Baby Boomers. It is sad, in a way, that the present generation cannot witness what it meant to see him step into the ring.

It also interesting that another great athlete, sometimes known as a singer, crooner, or one who could hold an audience in the palm of his hand, also captivated the ring. That, of course is, Frank Sinatra. As an Italian American, growing up, we were made aware of the great Italian singers. Some of the older ladies in the neighborhood used to like to debate who was best, may it be Vic Damon, Perry Como, or the favorite of many ladies, Dean Martin. Frank Sinatra always liked to say his favorite was Tony Bennett. I remember taking my parents to see Frank Sinatra. We sat upfront because, by this time, I was with the Boeing Company and was able to secure VIP Passes from one of the key sponsors. You know one of those special situations, when all the stars are aligned. You see a star, you are with your parents, and the occasion is special.

Some Baby Boomers report having seen Frankie Valli and the Four Seasons while in college and remember the lights at those concerts being dim from the fade of their reputation at that time. Yet, as usual, they still got the place jumping. The Four Seasons would go on to many roller coaster rides of popularity. This was one of their down periods, before their fame would explode after the movie "Grease" reignited the music of the 50s. Frankie Valli and the Four Seasons were reincarnated again later, with the production of "Jersey Boys."

When I went to college in 1972, I still liked listening to Connie Francis. My brothers were older than I, and because I wanted so much to be like them, I gravitated to their music. But I have great respect for the music of our generation. When Baby Boomers look back they look back at Crosby, Stills, Nash, and Young. They look back at the Eagles. They look back at the first time they heard the music of Chicago. May it have been Karen Carpenter or Linda Ronstadt, you remember the sound of their voices.

I look upon all the television options of today and all the opportunity to view programming, and I hasten to tell all that will listen that there was a time when we had only three stations. Although the choices for programming were limited (by today's standards), the quality left its mark. One can recall the CBS news delivered by Walter Cronkite, who many called the most respected man in America.

Many remember when Sunday Night was bought to you by a peacock from NBC, and you lived and died by the plight of the Cartwright Family as seen on the TV show "Bonanza." Doctors were made famous by the fictional representation of "Ben Casey" or "Dr. Kildare." We watched "Perry Mason" win cases in court, and saw the sign of the times, as the "Mod Squad" came to popularity. Mary Tyler Moore thought she was just doing a television show, whereas later, Baby Boomer women like Oprah Winfrey would call her a role model.

TV shows, movies, music, and sports are the entertainment vehicles of Baby Boomers. Talk to Baby Boomers today, and they can recall watching television in their living room. Go to a game with a Baby Boomer today, and they will cite some game in detail from another time. Walk through many libraries today, and see Baby Boomers taking out movies from an era that is different than the present. See Baby Boomers tune into pledge week on PBS because they are featuring a group, like the Moody Blues, and you will come to find out a great deal about the Baby Boomer Generation.

Chapter 7

Second Career for Baby Boomers

When I was at the University of Wisconsin in the 1970s, the furthest thing from my mind was what I would be doing in my career when the 21st century rolled around. In those campus days, I wanted to enjoy the college experience, have fun with my friends, and somehow find a way to graduate. Yes, I took my studies seriously, especially when it came to my major, Communications. But to say I had a life plan would be a stretch. I did have aspirations. I did want to succeed in life, for I wanted to travel and see the world. I wanted to achieve, because I wanted to make my parents proud. Further, I did want to someday have acclaim in the workplace, for as I witnessed the respect that older men of dignity received, such as the way they were called "sir," I realized that it was a term that I hoped could be associated with me.

When I was 19, my friends gave me a surprise birthday party and it was one of the great nights of my life. What I remember is what happened late in the evening, when my core group of friends sat around the table as we all talked about our dreams of the future. Some spoke of having a big house, some talked about meeting a nice girl and raising a family, but they all talked of someday having to get a job. That is what it was called then, "working." It was before the days in which Baby Boomers would get to hear of corporate structure, reorganization, and the term so associated with much of our career experience: corporate life. No, in those simpler days, it was go to class, have a graduation party, and then think about the world. Going to work, working in a company, making a living – well that is what our fathers did. Yes, you read that correctly, fathers. This was before women broke glass ceilings or were considered major factors in the work place. Baby Boomers, for the most part, grew up in a society where the men in the family were the breadwinners, and the mothers were more concerned with the bread in the kitchen. Our generation, the Baby Boomer generation, would bring change to that paradigm.

There were signs pointing to the future, though; there were internships at a company to help with papers being written; and, there was the formulation of a senior thesis. In my case, because I was a tennis player, I also was involved with sponsors and tennis equipment companies, and that did give me some understanding of the working world. When I finished college, my father and mother began talking to me about what many Baby Boomers call the "now what?" moment. That is best described as the time that you begin to realize that the fun days of dorm life, staying up late, and cramming for finals are now a part of your own history. You graduated, you had a field of study, and now it was time to get a job. Baby Boomers remember that first resume process. In my case, I pursued what was available: working in the tennis industry, teaching tennis, and later, the involvement with tennis clubs. I thought that I was on my way, for in the late 1970s tennis was at the apex of its popularity. Teaching tennis also gave me the opportunity to write columns about tennis and provided spots on the radio. The columns and the radio spot were called "Tennis Tips."

One day, though, it was communicated to me that, while this was a great world for a boy in his twenties, this might not be the life that I would want in my forties. As it was for many Baby Boomers, this was the first transition period. It was when some Baby Boomers began the process of selected planning. Some decided on graduate school, some decided that second jobs were more attractive, and some decided that with age came growing up. Some were the first in their families to move away from the towns that they grew up in and find jobs in companies that would provide a future. There was an interesting merger of class structure, company principles, and change, all somehow colliding. You went to work, where company managers had secretaries, where sales people did cold calling, where reports were submitted in writing, and the paper was filed. Jobs were available to sell copy machines, and the new technology was the initial fax machines and using Mag-card systems to do something called word processing.

Then, somehow, thirty years pass like the blink of an eye. You find yourself at the University of Wisconsin, once again, when the last time you set foot in the lecture hall you were presenting to classmates and professors. Now, you were there to review your career, give guidance to a new generation on their future, and offer tips on how to succeed in the workplace. It was a surreal feeling. Suddenly, so many things rushed through your mind. You were not asking for advice, but giving it. You were not starting out, but sending others on their course. And now, your career was in review. It was like a meteor was controlling the proceedings. So, as the large lecture hall filled, and students and university dignitaries gathered, my mind wandered. Here I was, the keynote speaker, the person that they had come to hear. I was now a middle-aged man whom some thought had a pretty good resume, although my job on this day was to help the next generation with theirs.

I was to give advice to the current student body on the here and now. I recall speaking about the importance of technology, the importance of communication, and the need for team work in today's workplace, the 21st century workplace. I spoke of the techniques, so familiar with the corporate world of today, but could not help but process in my mind all that came before. For, as a Baby Boomer, I had witnessed profound change in the work place. Where once the personal computer was a novelty, it was now part of the framework of the work desk. Where outlines were once sent over by courier, meetings were now being conducted online. But beyond technology, there were massive, systemic changes to companies that gave all new meaning to multi-national corporations. But what seemed more pronounced was the speed, the fast pace of the work world, its life, and the 24/7 mentality.

This brings about a self-assessment in Baby Boomers. It brings about a sense of meaning. Baby Boomers start asking questions like, "Am I making a contribution to society?" "Has what I've done in my career been worth more than just a job?" "Did I just earn a paycheck?" "What did I do to make the past thirty years of my career feel like it had meaning?" Some Baby Boomers have to ask other questions, like, "Why am I being downsized?" "Why was I laid off?" But, no matter how you get there, all Baby Boomers are asking, "What will I do with the rest of my life?"

As you talk to Baby Boomers today, many have taken these questions and turned them into the deduction that it is time for a second career. For Baby Boomers still want to feel worthwhile, still want the satisfaction of work, and still want to make a contribution. They still want to use the experience that they have garnered for the future good. Thus, Baby Boomers have made the choice to pursue second careers.

Saturday, April 9, 2011

Boomers and a second work life

AARP, as they so often do, recognized a trend when they created their campaign known as, "What do I want to be when I grow up?" It was directed at Baby Boomers who want to continue to work and make a contribution, but do it in a field different from their longtime careers. Most times, the Boomer chooses some activity in which he has a passion. The choice usually is not driven by financial gain, but by a desire to be involved with something of meaning. Some, in fact, find charitable avenues to peak their interests. Some approach the passion of work because they always wanted to be involved with a certain field. Some start a new business, on a smaller scale, with less fear of failure. In my case, I was interested in chronicling my generation. Like an athlete, I did not want to stay at the corporate game past my usefulness. However, I still wanted to contribute to society. Also, there is a tradition in my family of working into our later years. My grandfather worked into his seventies, as did my father and my uncle, whom I highly respect, as he practiced medicine. Driven by family history, but mindful of what other Baby Boomers are thinking and doing, I too fit the AARP profile, taking on another career as I have grown up and, hopefully, not yet grown too old.

Tuesday, April 12, 2011

Job opportunities for Baby Boomers

The "Great Recession," as it now is known, has been a difficult time in the lives of Baby Boomers. I remember how my late father would talk about the Great Depression. He thought, like most Americans, that we would never see such a crisis again in this country. But, with the collapse of the housing market, the tenuous banking marketplace, and the massive drop in the value of the stock market, it almost seemed like the world was spiraling out of control. When the job collapse followed, panic set in. For Baby Boomers who had retired, their nest egg was gone; for those near retirement, the realization hit them that they would have to work longer. Those who were affected the most, though, were the ones who lost their jobs and have struggled to find work. Even today, when we seem to be rebounding ever so slightly, Baby Boomers continue to struggle. Companies have been slow to add employees to their payroll, especially the high salaries associated with Baby Boomers. Baby Boomers report that it has been difficult to get back into the workforce. To get hired, it seems a multitude of contacts, heavy prospecting, and numerous interviews are part of the equation. Many go back to work at far lower salaries. What this all means for the golden years still needs to play out. Many Baby

Boomers even say that they wished they had lived like their parents. But Baby Boomers and the appetite for consumption will forever be linked. As one Baby Boomer said, almost speaking for a generation, "I always thought my home would always increase in value, and the stock market would always go up."

Friday, April 29, 2011

Baby Boomers regarding Mentoring

When the media, or even historians, speak about and refer to the late sixties and early seventies, one might hear about protests, unrest, and rebellion against the status quo. The Baby Boomer generation is sometimes associated with selfishness and overindulgent behavior as they went from students to adults. First and foremost, like most generations, when people are young, they do things that they do not always tell their children about. Second, there were causes that people fought for that enhanced the world that we live in today. One misconception about that period was that there was a complete breakdown in family life. Young people of that time did not reject the leadership of their parents, grandparents, and extended family. And, as the years have gone on, young people gained a greater appreciation for the guidance of those who came before them. Now, as Baby Boomers begin to age and reflect on their lives, they see what guidance and support can mean to a life. With that, all across America Baby Boomers are attempting to give back. Most are doing it with the intention of mentoring. Some just do it as a part of family life, perhaps through a kind word of encouragement to a younger cousin. Some are trying to guide their adult children in early job searches. Others try to lend advice as caring uncles, similar to the way that they received help from one of their own uncles at a like age.

Most Baby Boomers think that they have something to offer, and most do. It has been said that there is no substitute for experience. Baby Boomers who are practicing the role of mentor report two key things:

first, it is rewarding to help; second, and most importantly, young people appreciate someone who simply listens. A small group of Baby Boomers have taken it a step further, be it teaching or formal programs that now exist to be able to lend a hand. This may include such things as volunteer programs, whereby your work track record lends a hand as the younger generation starts a business. It could be the doctor who goes one day a week to serve as a mentor for students at a teaching hospital. Perhaps, the lawyer goes back in support of the law school that they attended. One very popular outlet is returning to your university, in support of the professors who look for practical discussion to prepare students for the workplace. Baby Boomers are anxious to share. A successful entrepreneur wants to go to the classroom of a college and tell his story.

Yes, it is true that the gratification of helping does play a role, but most Baby Boomers want to help so that they leave behind a contribution to society. Things, in some ways, have come full circle: Baby Boomers once favored service over corporate life; then, they made corporate life their passion, and now, they want to return to a giving and contributing agenda. There are Baby Boomers who now join the Peace Corps to work hand in glove with someone who could be their grandchild. There are Baby Boomers who are assistant coaches on baseball teams in support of the young coach. But, most of all, Baby Boomers are reaching out and talking to the young person at the next table, and sometimes, they both learn.

Friday, May 13, 2011

Baby Boomers in the Workplace

Baby Boomers report a feeling of uncertainty in the workplace. They want to continue to make a contribution to society and feel they have a great deal to offer. This was a topic originally raised on the discussion page of the *Harvard Business Review*, as seen on LinkedIn. Baby Boomers who have already retired feel a sense of relief, while Baby Boomers still in their fifties and in the corporate world soldier on. There is another part of the Baby Boom population that, unfortunately, was a casualty in the crossfire due to the recession. If you are in that group, you have to do a great deal of research to find a company that matches your skill set and appreciates your experience.

Baby Boomers also report a need for patience, for the interview process can be long and arduous. Baby Boomers in the workplace report the need to get along in a multi-generational environment. Some embrace their younger colleagues, especially, their technology skills. Some feel comfortable mentoring without becoming overbearing. Some, though, find it hard when they work for younger managers for the first time. The question of how Baby Boomers are perceived in the workplace is complex. Some are valued for their experience and their skills built over time, but some are under pressure to continue to show their worth. Baby Boomers report that the system works best when they are doing work that they enjoy.

It is interesting: being in your 50s and being in corporate life can sometimes feel like limbo. You are not ready to retire, social security is still far off on the horizon, but there is this feeling that you have been at this a long time. The newest development along these lines is the second work life. Made popular by the AARP campaign, "What do I want to be when I grow up," it takes a Baby Boomer out of the corporation but not out of the workplace. These are individuals who are starting a business, working for a non-profit, or being a self-employed consultant. This works well for some, for instead of staying beyond your time in corporate life, it is a new beginning. Baby Boomers in this role report a sense of newfound energy. But at the end of the day, some Baby Boomers simply have to make a living. It could be because their savings were depleted due to the recession, or because they did not plan properly. Or, perhaps they are still under the weight of a major responsibility, such as aging of parents or children still in school. These Baby Boomers report a need for thick skin. The gray hair does not always equal a distinguished reputation; sometimes Baby Boomers get the sense that fellow employees would feel more comfortable if they just moved on. But, sometimes, this is more perception than reality. The bottom line is the world is an ever-changing place, and, as Baby Boomers have been told their entire careers, the only thing that you can count on is change. Baby Boomers who are managing change are the ones doing best in the workplace.

Monday, January 9, 2012

A Baby Boomer interviews for a job

Chris is a Baby Boomer. She raised a family and now wants to return to the workforce. She adores her six year old grandchild, whom she seems to spend a great deal of time with, but in her heart, she knows that her job is not only to be a grandmother. So, she applied for a job as an executive assistant for a CEO of a mid-size company. The process has been slow, and there is no sure bet that she will get the job. But her experience speaks to many Baby Boomers, no matter the level of the job or the gender of the applicant.

The three things that she has encountered are a slow resume review process, a deliberate interview schedule, and doubt of her technology skills. One can argue that the first two have a great deal to do with the economy. Companies big and small just seem to have a hard time getting candidates in the door and then pulling the trigger on the start date. It is no different if you are an administrator or a CFO. While companies such as Microsoft and Apple stockpile cash, human resource departments stockpile résumés.

Chris finally thought that she had an appointment set with the hiring manager. He canceled at the last minute. Chris, all dressed for success, was prepared, having studied the company and the executive, and having shown some initiative. She asked if there was any time during the course of the day that the hiring manager could work her in. She said that she was ready for the interview on that day and would meet at any time of his choosing. Her fortitude got her in the door; he liked her initiative.

When the interview came to pass, the hiring manager liked her communication skills and her organizational skills, but he questioned her computer skills. To Chris, it came out of left field. She is, by the way, one of the most tech savvy persons that you will come across. But she had a perception problem. The resume told the hiring manager that she was – how do we put this –an older applicant. So, assumptions were made. Chris decided to confront them head on, without being too aggressive. She sidestepped the issue like a figure skater with a bump in the ice. With cool and calm in her corner, she detailed her skills, careful to not give any hint of insecurity. She posed questions in return, on matters such as what skills were most important for the position. What skills would he personally like to see? What skills would best match his comfort zone? She, in a short period of time, was now being taken more seriously. They were past the age issue, and on to how she would function in the position.

As the interview concluded, the hiring manager shook her hand and said he was impressed with what she could bring to the table. As she left the interview, Chris felt good about herself, her performance, and her preparation that led to her good performance. She also showed some closing skills, saying that she would like the job, but more importantly, could do the job. Will she get hired? Will the company go from procrastination to actually making a commitment? Let us hope so, for Chris did her part. Now the company must just say, "Yes." It is not an easy word these days.

Tuesday, February 7, 2012

Starting Over

If you pay attention to social media, plenty of chatter exists about Baby Boomers and a second career. The consultants abound, each ready to step in at a moment's notice to offer advice. Some Baby Boomers are willing customers, for this whole second career thing is difficult. Once upon a time, Baby Boomers interviewed for their first job. Thirty years later, they had a resume. For many, it was impressive, a wonderful story of past accomplishments. The key word is "past." For many Baby Boomers, resting on the record was enough. Many Baby Boomers utter phrases like, "I worked hard, I paid my dues, and now it is time for a new generation." But for a variety of reasons, resting, closing that chapter of life, or moving to retirement is not in the cards.

Baby Boomers are returning to the workplace. It may be with their own businesses, applying for work in a corporation, or even doing non-profit work. The point is that they are returning, starting anew, and it has been a challenge. A Baby Boomer so very successful, but out of the workplace since 2004, is worth looking at. He has traveled the world and scratched off all the action items from his bucket list. Problem is, by 2011, he was bored out of his mind. Even the game of golf, which he loves, had become tedious. For he was not just playing on weekends as a form of relaxation from the stress of his executive position; playing golf now was his position, his only job. Something had to change. He was going to open a small consulting business, to aid start-up companies. Made sense, right? He could walk the new level of companies through the door of success. It would be just like a seminar: "This is what I did – now let me show you how it is done." The concept was a good one, the idea great, but the day-to-day implementation was a nightmare. A lot has changed in the world since 2004.

For one thing, technology has made the world move at rapid pace. His clients, while enamored with our Baby Boomer's background, were frustrated by his inability to use the tools of today. Here is a man who was accustomed to delegating to someone whom he still called a "secretary." Now he is his own administrator, and the task that would have been delegated, he can only delegate to himself. Many of the young companies seeking his advice were small, but run by thirty-somethings with their phone that does everything. Webcasts replaced face-to-face meetings. Skype replaced United Airlines and background checks became Google searches. Profiles were done on Facebook, while connections and networking were done on LinkedIn, and information exchange was about 140 characters on Twitter. The Baby Boomer who was just getting used to Google was now asked, not to join a circle of friends from the club, but to become familiar with the benefits of the circles on Google+.

It is a funny thing — when you are the consultant, the people paying you for your expertise usually do not want to be spending time teaching you technology tools. But that is only one challenge. Those years away from the grind can make you soft. The long hours that it takes to build a business is not what you signed up for. You just want to keep your hand in it, you tell yourself, but quickly you find that pride takes over. That is a good thing until you realize that you are out of shape physically, and your energy is not what it used to be. You need to be fit in order to be prepared to work long hours, to be willing to put the time into networking, and to use the tools of the 21st century. You know that you cannot even volunteer today without understanding the way the world functions. Job applications are online, and you need an e-mail account to become an usher at a ballpark. You need scheduling software in some cases to donate your time.

This is the way of the world, and Baby Boomers are answering the call. Many report a passion for the new business they started, like the dog lover who sells bakery treats for the canine. Or the Baby Boomer who completed his online application with Starbucks, and was so pleased to be called for the interview. Then, there is the human resource person who found out that actually showing an interest in employees was so welcomed by her coworkers that soon employees would request to speak to her, because somehow her answer did not include the phrase "go to the website." I think that one Baby Boomer summed it up best when he pronounced that he is very motivated because there is a new woman in his life, and it is the one he always hoped would come along. Because of that, he will do whatever it takes to learn new skills, go work out, and put in the hours. Baby Boomers, always a "can do" group of people, are taking on the challenges of using lemons to make lemonade, and liking it.

Friday, March 23, 2012

Baby Boomers at a Crossroads

Baby Boomers all across America are at a crossroads. It is the intersection where their past lives meet their future. One foot is in one bucket of sand, while the other is dangling in the water. Some Baby Boomers report that they are holding on for dear life. They stay in a job that is not meaningful; there is sameness to their days. But they will not change because the economics of change are compelling enough to leave passion on the back burner. These are the individuals who are still on the treadmill of restaurants, vacation homes, and all other material concerns. They laugh at their contemporaries who try something new. They say that you should have just stuck with your corporate job, toughed it out, and retired. The defenders of starting a new business can take pride in the new accomplishment, the enjoyment of the work, and the newfound reputation – there are smiles to go around indeed. But sometimes, it does not work out. Life savings are lost. Marriages are put to the test. What seemed like such a good idea turns radically wrong, and then sadness comes. Nobody likes to fail, but at this age and stage, it can be devastating.

It is very hard for the Baby Boomers to get back on the horse. They had successful corporate careers, they used that experience to start a new business, and it did not turn out as planned. So now, with resume in hand, they have to belittle themselves to interview when they are overqualified, but yet they have to act like that would be their dream job. They have to work, don't you see? Oftentimes the reason Baby Boomers fail in new enterprises is that they trust the wrong people. You have great skills, but you need to complement those skills, so you partner with people. Good idea, but check them out. Do not be too trusting. Look into their backgrounds. Do not take people at face value just because they buy you a cheeseburger. If things look too good to be true, they probably are not true. The person with the good heart and caring attitude on the surface can be as selfish as the next guy. Watch it play out.

So, it is time to re-group. What is next? It is okay initially to say, "I don't know." Just do not stay in that condition for very long. Baby Boomers have long known that life is about heartbreak. Things do not always work out. This is life, as they say. So now the Baby Boomer – void of his corporate stripes, business, and just "blowing in the wind" – has to come up with an answer. Here is the good news: most of us will keep trying, for as Baby Boomers, we are a generation of individuals known for being resilient. Let us hope that the Baby Boomer in in this difficult situation meets the crossroads head on and does, in fact, make the right turn.

Summary – Chapter 7

Second Careers for Baby Boomers

They are the Baby Boomers whom you see sitting in your local coffee shops early in the morning, reviewing today's plans. They are the Baby Boomers opening up small offices to start charitable foundations. They are the Baby Boomers whom you see having small meetings in libraries as they pursue their love of literary endeavors. They are the Baby Boomers conducting Skype calls on new business enterprises. They are the Baby Boomers opening up the little chocolate shops in your neighborhood, because they always thought it would be fun to have such an enterprise. These are Baby Boomers doing the right of passage in the Baby Boomer orbit of the "here and now." They are the Baby Boomers of the second career.

These are Baby Boomers who adopted this life by choice. They have found passion again in the workplace. They could be described as people who had successful careers, generally worked hard, and raised families, but do not want to retire. It is important to them to make a contribution to society and to make a difference. Perhaps they spent entire careers working for somebody else, and now want the satisfaction of being their own bosses. Perhaps they have been successful and want to give back through charity, through volunteer work, or through helping others. Perhaps as Baby Boomers, they feel – and this is important – that their time has not passed. They still feel that they have gas in the tank, and they want to do more to add to their life's résumé.

These are conversations that go on every day, in real life, with friends and family, and in social media about Baby Boomers desire to work, to do more. This is a complex issue. Some of these decisions are not about choice, but about necessity. It is no secret that many Baby Boomers are unprepared for retirement. So many Baby Boomers have no other choice but to work. For many in this situation it is very hard, as the job interview process is sometimes brutal. All of a sudden, the years of work are not seen as experience, but as being too old for today's work. Sometimes, the person interviewing you is young enough to be your son or daughter. Sometimes, there is the feeling of starting over, and that can be overwhelming. These Baby Boomers are struggling with the thought pattern of staying relevant, even though in the majority of cases, they have so much to offer an employer.

Some Baby Boomers are just cut of a certain kind of cloth, where getting up in the morning and going to work is in their DNA. For this group, no amount of golf, travel, services, and activities within an over-55 community will satisfy, for these Baby Boomers simply want to work. The questions become what to do, and how to do it. This becomes the subject matter for the choice to work, or be active in an occupation, has already been made. There is a whole consulting industry that is starting up to serve the need of these Baby Boomers; they are the people seeking to help other Baby Boomers start on this path of a second career. You see this in the press, discussed on social media, and it may even show up in a note in your computer's inbox. It is referred to as an encore career. Some chatter on social media also mentions parents who help their children in business. There is conversation about the accountant who donates his time at a start-up company run by young people. There is satisfaction gained by helping and contributing.

I, myself, after years of corporate life, where I took pride in my work at Fortune 500 companies, and even starting and running my own firm, sought the world of "something more." After my parents passed away, work and my career did not have the same meaning. I had once been so driven by the thought of making my parents proud and giving them things that they did not have, because they had sacrificed so much for my brothers and for me. One day, you wake up and you do not want to do "it" anymore; Baby Boomers know what the "it" means. That feeling that corporate life and the meetings have no more meaning. There must be more, or something different, or life has evolved and other paths need to be taken. My own path led me to a study of my generation, to travel and talk to Baby Boomers, to research, study, and then report on the behavior of my peers. It has become the fulfillment of the second career, my encore in career life, that will be my contribution to society.

Chapter 8

Long Term Financial Planning – Are you prepared for Retirement?

When you speak to the majority of Baby Boomers, they are amazed as to how well their parents managed their money. For the most part, as the "Greatest Generation" reached their golden years, they did so with peace of mind. Largely, at the time of their death, they were debt free. Perhaps that generation was short on extravaganza, thrills, or the accumulation of "stuff." They were better prepared for retirement than Baby Boomers. Most Baby Boomers are still trying to figure out what the next twenty years will bring. Some will work longer than they anticipated. Some will carry credit card balances to their grave. Some will just experience hardship beyond their wildest imagination.

How did this happen? Part of it is that, mentally, Baby Boomers never thought that they would get old. Retirement always seemed in the far distant future. There always would be time to plan for retirement, if it ever came. Baby Boomers, as college students, dreamed of experiencing things. There was a restlessness to the Baby Boomer generation. They were, and still are, a generation that did not like the status quo. They questioned institutions, were cynical on structure, and certainly rejected the lifestyle of their parents. It was a generation that grew up on the family two week vacation, but saw their adulthood trade car trips for frequent flier miles. They were the generation who sat at the dinner table each night, at home with mom and dad, and as adults, made eating out a spectator sport. Dad seemed to fix everything, and Mom did all the house work; Baby Boomers thought others should do the work, and hired, instead of did.

But that is only part of the story; Baby Boomers became spoiled on the good times. The technology revolution created widespread opportunity for the Baby Boomer generation. In Boston, in the 1980s, it was not uncommon for Baby Boomers to change jobs every 18 months, and each time add to their salary. All of a sudden things such as stock options and revenue bonus, were part of the equation. Baby Boomers grew accustomed to a higher standard of living.

In the 1990s, trading stock for gain became part of one's lifestyle. Having a broker on speed dial created an explosion. Suddenly you did your job at a tech company, and traded stock as a further generator of profits. It was a never ending carousel. The talk amongst couples of the time was built around four star hotels, four star restaurants, and the word "exclusive." When four star became too mundane, you upgraded to five star.

Soon, the conversation centered on which Country Club you were a member of, or when you were taking your trip to Augusta or Wimbledon. There was the need for "the best": the best cruise, the best hotels, the best seats. There was a Social Climber feel to the generation, the race to the top, the race to impress. Suddenly, your worth was measured by the things that you could buy, such as the cars, or the size of the house. Whatever it was, you had to have it. Membership to a club, to rub elbows, was an example; going to New York for the weekend was an example. It was all to achieve a certain kind of status. It was part insecurity, part that you wanted what you did not have as a child (so you thought), part just the mad dash to, as the movie "Wall Street" says it, "Greed is Good."

The lifestyle described did catch up to Baby Boomers – too much living, not enough saving. But there are other things at play, like the subculture of Baby Boomers, Vietnam veterans who are homeless, couples who have divorced, and Baby Boomers who now have to rely on children to help them out to make ends meet. There are women who have lost husbands, who are unprepared for being alone, and living alone. There are family expenses, due to three generations colliding, where Baby Boomers are helping their parents, while still supporting their children. Then, of course, the big fly in the ointment: the "Great Recession." Do not underestimate what impact this has had on Baby Boomers.

It has been devastating, and the jury is still out as to whether Baby Boomers will ever recover. The years, starting at the end of 2007 continuing to the present, have done to Baby Boomers what the Depression did to their parents. Here is the story in a nutshell: the 401ks were depleted, excessive borrowing put Baby Boomers in debt, and the loss of work led to losing the house. But it was also a crisis of faith, for bank foreclosure was now a reality. You see, Americans have short memories; they simply forget the crisis that existed in the financial world that had its impact on the life of every American.

So now, Baby Boomers have to do what they have done throughout their life, adjust to change. Live within their means, find second careers, and try to catch up on the lost years of saving. Each and every Baby Boomer now has to ask, "am I prepared for retirement?" They have to assess, plan, and try to make the best of the years ahead. Baby Boomers are a resilient lot. You do not want to bet against them; they have a will like no other generation. Baby Boomers are using Social Media, finding new ways to network, and finding a silver lining in starting businesses. They have gotten over the fear of starting over, are starting again, and have embraced the challenge.

One last group of Baby Boomers does need to be addressed here in this section. It is what is called the non-flashy Baby Boomer. It is the husband

and wife, who have saved, who have invested smartly, who did not buy designer clothes, and whose car is 10 years old. They enjoyed their life, educated their children, and had one credit card that they paid off every month. They were the ones not talked about during the dot.com boom, or profiled on American Express Magazines. They lived more conservatively, respected the values passed down to them from their parents, and did not care how big their house was, as long as it was all their own. These Baby Boomers are out there and they should be respected, for they did have it all, and it was called "peace of mind."

Tuesday, March 27, 2012

Five Critical Things Facing Baby Boomers Today

Having traveled the country interviewing Baby Boomers and talking to my peers on a regular basis, a trend has developed. The symmetry is undeniable. The issue is too much the same not to highlight. One word of caution as you read this, there are Baby Boomers not facing these aspects. They should be known as the lucky ones. For the more than many who are, take to heart that you are not alone. With that, let us cover these five critical impact points.

Number 1: Are you caring for an elderly parent? Is your elderly parent's health failing? Does their condition, or not being what they once were, bother you? Then join the millions of Baby Boomers who are in the same situation.

Number 2: Have you suffered loss of a loved one? Perhaps those elderly parents have passed, or perhaps your loss has involved a spouse. Have you lost a beloved brother? Well, Baby Boomers, you are not alone. As we have begun to age, our lives have changed. We may long for what once was, but life is simply different. Baby Boomers across America, perhaps yourself included, are all trying to cope with loss.

Number 3: Is your life not like what it once was? Has your financial condition changed? Do you struggle to find happiness? Do you sort of feel like the treadmill of life has worn you out? Well, welcome to a club of fellow Baby Boomers who say, "I thought life would be different at this age."

Number 4: Are you unprepared for retirement? Has the "Great Recession" taken its toll on your 401k? Are you faced with working longer than you thought? Are plans to retire in that warm weather climate now on hold? Do you get upset with the continued mantra to raise the age for Social Security and Medicare? Does it seem like politicians are working against you as opposed to for you? Then, you are part of the Baby Boomer Nation that wishes that they lived in the times when pensions were part of the landscape.

Number 5: Baby Boomers are very concerned with health and wellness. Baby Boomers want to re-invent aging. They call it "Active Aging." You can find a group on LinkedIn by that name. Baby Boomers refuse to go quietly. They still feel that they are relevant. They still feel that they are the generation by which all generations are measured. So, from walks in the morning to counseling on nutrition, even down to the water that they drink, it is all part of the plan to stem the tide on the age curve. The more affluent are at the tennis clubs and the spas. But even the average Baby Boomer is looking into how they can keep from landing on that rocking chair that looks at them each morning from the porch. Sixty is different today than it used to be, says the Baby Boomer. Yes, that is the same person who once said, "Don't trust anyone over 30." It is all about perspective, I guess.

Good luck, Baby Boomers. Whichever issues you face in your life, remember the educated amongst us know that a life led needs to be judged in totality. Whichever issues you face now cannot take away from the 53 years when it was, as the young people today like to say, "all good."

Tuesday, January 24, 2012

The New Board of Directors

I have no biological children of my own, but that does not mean the story that you are about to read did not touch me. The title, "The New Board of Directors," applies to a growing, unfortunate experience that has been happening to Baby Boomers. That experience is Baby Boomers having to go to their children for shelter, food, clothing, and money. This sad but true turnabout occurs in families that just a few years ago, you could not have imagined this happening to.

It has been widely reported that the economic conditions in our country have resulted in many Baby Boomers taking in grown children and grandchildren. But what I describe here is a real-life example of the opposite end of the spectrum, which is also playing out, and in fairness, needs to be written about. A man from Palm Desert has five children, is going through a divorce, and his business prospects are short. He talks a good game; meet him at a Starbucks and you may think that you have come in contact with an Investment Banker. He has "friends in high places," and he is raising money for "big, big projects." All of his meetings are with "sweet people," as he would like to say. There are $50,000 commission checks just right around the corner. The man is likable, believable, and you want to pull for him.

But one day, he asks you if you can buy him a cup of coffee, and you then realize he is hurting. No shame in that, it is not what this story is about. He went to live with his daughter for about a month, until his ship came in; currently, it is in dry dock. His daughter is very wealthy, living in a 10,000 square foot home that she is adding on to. Her husband's Engineering firm just crossed $100 million in revenue. He had to leave, though, because the nanny's parents were about to visit from Brazil, so he was put out of his room in this wealthy conclave.

His other children run the gamut of equal success, with one of his sons being a senior executive with Bank of America. He reluctantly asked his children for some financial help. It killed him to do so. He is a man of pride. He does believe that he has prospects. He just needs to get over the hump. So, this is his reality: when he needs financial help, as he does now, the children call a meeting. They talk about whether or not they should help, and how much they should provide. They have decided that they all must agree, and share in the output of cash. This Board-of-Director-like operation usually results in gas money, and a little beyond. So this man sits day after day at Starbucks, waiting for the phone to ring, unable to go share a pizza with a friend, for he cannot afford to use the gas.

The story above is just one example of the many Baby Boomers who did not do better than their parents did. These are Baby Boomers with little to show for the hard work of a life time. Yes, the media will say that those Baby Boomers lived an excessive lifestyle, ran up those credit cards and feasted on the appetite of life. Well, many do fit in that category. But some sent those loving children to Stanford, so that as adults, they could live the good life. Baby Boomers who made sacrifices for the children, gave up the dreams they had for themselves, only to encounter a world that long ago put out to pasture company pensions, where the age for Social Security availability continues to rise, and the job market is not excited that Baby Boomers still want to be in the work place.

So, Baby Boomers look to be supported by those children that they sacrificed for, just as previous Generations once did. Many a Baby Boomer remembers that, as a young child, Grandma Mary had her own room in your childhood home. But Baby Boomers are not their grandparent's grandparent. This is for a lot of reasons, one being that Baby Boomers do not see themselves as rocking chair types. But they do want some degree of respect from their adult children.

So often Baby Boomers will tell you that they had hoped, because their adult children had turned out so well, that they would offer a helping hand. Maybe they could even do it with a bit of decorum – perhaps by saying something like, "Hey dad, I just got a raise at the firm, wanted to give you a little gift, to show my appreciation for all you did for me." Maybe that is just too much to ask. But for the father pictured in this story, his Board of Director type children have hinted that the gravy train will come to a halt until the Baby Boomer Dad exhibits some assurance that the hand outs will not become a permanent thing. "Tough Love," they call it. The Banker son calls, not offering how to transfer funds, but to see if Dad has applied for a job at Starbucks rather than just sitting there. He did apply, and he will work at Starbucks if he has to, or to make his children happy. Or maybe he will do it because the indignity of asking for help from his children is just too distasteful. Somehow "on your own" and "independent" take on a different meanings, when gas money is at stake.

January 21, 2012

When I am 64

When you heard the Beatles sing that line for the first time, do you remember what you thought? My guess is: "64 - wow, that is old." Well, now Baby Boomers think a little differently. I recently met a Baby Boomer who just turned 64 this past December. He thought carefully about when he should take his Social Security. Yes, he could have taken it at 62, but he did not need it then; however, he needs it now. He has decided to gut it out for one more year. As difficult as that is for him, he knows the consequences of taking that check early.

Our protagonist's name is Dave. He is a nice man who raised four children, all of whom are successful. He sent them to schools like Stanford. Dave has worked hard all of his life. He "hustled," as he would say. Perhaps, nobody made more insurance calls than this man. Why? Because educating his four children was all that got him up in the morning. Did he want to do it? No, but he had to do it, for tuition does not come cheap. His wife pushed him; they shared the same values, except, perhaps, for one. Security to her was more than a paycheck - it was a second religion.

This is interesting because religion is actually Dave's profession, or "his calling," if you will. He is an ordained minister, who ran a church with all of the pastor type care that a flock could ask for. But, as many Baby Boomers have discovered, your passion does not always fit into the reality of life. At 64, with the kids already grown up, you would think that the pressure is over. Now perhaps Dave can do what many Baby Boomers crave, which is to start a second career. Now perhaps waking up in the morning can be about making a contribution to society.

But some things never change. His wife still talks about security rather than about saving souls. This is ironic, considering her overt Christian values. It is a rub on their marriage to such a point that they are into trial separation. This is not uncommon for Baby Boomers, when one partner just cannot compromise any longer. Dave still has ministry on the mind. His hope was that he could make enough money in business to then spend the remainder of his life helping people. But life can be cruel, even for the fervent. Not much insurance was sold the last couple of years, and saving accounts were depleted. Dave, being Dave, tried to branch out by putting some deals together. He describes trying to "raise capital" and "teach young bucks the ropes." He was attempting to find other streams of income. His ministry is still the goal, but keeping his marriage together is also a key objective.

He is really something to watch in action, trying everything, it seems, to succeed. Each new person he meets is first a conversation, then a prospect, and then a potential deal. Dave wants his wife and children to see him as a winner. Isn't it enough that he is simply a good man? Short term thinking sometimes makes you lose sight of the bigger picture. The church and the sermon are on the back burner now. "I just need that one big one to close," he confides. Do his children love him? Better than most, it seems. Does his wife love him? Yes, by all accounts, she does. They are just not singing out of the same song book these days. Perhaps Dave will be one of the lucky ones. Perhaps his ship will come in, and perhaps his family will see both his success and the man that he is. And maybe one day he will walk to the pulpit with peace of mind.

Saturday, October 1, 2011

I have Already Raised my Children

A Baby Boomer in her mid-50s, from San Diego, California is glued to her cell phone. She waits for the call. Her first grandchild is about to be born, and she can hardly contain her excitement. Another couple of similar age, maybe a bit older, from Eugene, Oregon, looks forward to the drive to Portland. Just down Interstate 5 are their two grandchildren, who are the apple of their eye.

You see, some Baby Boomers are, in fact, now grandparents. Many Baby Boomers find the role to be an extension of life, a natural part of the cycle that is life. It is but one more addition to the general landscape that goes along with retirement, travel, and making your time productive. "Let us go see the grandchildren," might be a popular refrain. With this suggestion, one assumes that a visit to see the grandchildren means taking the little ones for ice cream and then returning home. Oh yes, and by the way, be sure to look at all of those photos of the grandchildren on Facebook. Grandma and Grandpa will also be posting their own pictures of their trip to Italy. It will be easy for them to travel, because in their 55 and over community, all they need to do is just lock the door behind them. These are the Dick and Jane of grandparents, the ones where wealth-management was not just a slogan.

Other Baby Boomers, perhaps from a different economic category, find the role of grandparents not so arms-length. These grandparents are part of the everyday scene. They are the new daycare. They are involved because they have to be. When their daughter calls, the cell phone is not met with excitement, but with the stress of responsibility.

In contrast, for the grandmother-to-be from San Diego, it is like the old ketchup commercial. Remember, you would hear the Carly Simon song "Anticipation" playing in the background, as you waited with, well, "Great Anticipation," as at the ketchup slowly came down from the bottle. It was that "can't wait" feeling.

Our couple from Eugene, Oregon would represent the "manage the time" segment of the Baby Boom population. They might ask the question, "What is the balance between my life that I continue to lead, and the amount of time I spend with my grandchildren?" There is a Baby Boomer grandfather from Indiana who asks that question every day, because his wife seems to live at his son and daughter in-law's house now. She "loves being a grandmother," she shouts, as he sits home, seemingly never able to get around to those plans that he and his wife had for when he retired. He laments, "I already raised my children."

Another example of Baby Boomer grandparents are the couple from Sarasota, Florida. The husband was an executive, and his wife was a marketing professional of note. They have recently retired and feel a sense of guilt. They confess to feeling bad that they live so far away from their four children and their nine grandchildren. But they are, it seems, the exception, not the rule. What once was the middle class is now being squeezed by the pressures of everyday life. Baby Boomers, many of who are still trying to work themselves, now find the pressure is compounded by this additional burden of caring for their children's families, who were hard hit by the economic downturn. For them, life is no fun, and certainly not a trip to Disney World. Baby Boomers used to hear their parents or their grandparents talk about the Great Depression, and how families all lived together in the 30s and 40s. Well, for many, those are the times that they live in now. This begs the question, if Baby Boomers have to step in and help raise their children's children, how much say should they have? If you want to see controversy, take a look at these families in motion. It is amazing how paying the bills can influence who has the say so.

So which is it, Baby Boomers? Is it the AT&T ad where grandparents gleefully talk with little Johnny about his baseball game, from a thousand miles away? Is it Grandma so into being a grandmother that all her hopes and desires take second place to the grandchildren? Is it grandparent slash provider-by-necessity? Maybe it is all of the above. Some grandparents are Baby Boomers who still look into the mirror and see their own life. The

RV is packed, the country awaits, and the grandchildren are on the map. For other Baby Boomers, the Golden Years did not get a parachute, and kids still need to be fed. Didn't I already raise my children?

Tuesday, September 27, 2011

Please Don't Ask Me to Apologize

On a busy day in Boston, a couple from the West coast will explore transportation passage at Boston Logan airport. The international terminal at Logan Airport is expansive, modern, and the final stop in the maze that is Boston. The couple have enjoyed themselves for the past three days. They flew from the West coast, and toured the cradle of the Revolution. They walked the Freedom Trail, shopped on Newbury Street, and somehow got tickets to see the Red Sox. But now their true purpose is about to unfold. They are headed for two-weeks in Italy. The cab driver drops them off, receives a big tip, and soon the couple, in their late 50s, are in front of the Air Italia ticket counter.

They are sometimes referred to as "a professional couple," for they have both worked their entire lives. Although they raised two children, there was never a thought that either would sacrifice their career. This was a couple on equal footing. As a result, they brought in income, invested wisely, and own their home outright. They made few sacrifices, the children went to private schools and attended prestigious universities, and one of their children got married in their expansive back yard.

At this stage of life, their number one priority is travel. They do not play golf and are not extravagant when it comes to material possessions. They, as the old-timers would say, "have a nest egg." So now they wish to explore, see the world, and indulge themselves. They make no apology for doing so. They are the type of couple that you might see in a wealth management advertisement for The Northern Trust Bank. They are part of a group of Baby Boomers who refuse to feel guilty for doing the right thing. Yes, they were fortunate; the couple described came from upper-middle class families. They themselves are highly educated, both with Master's Degrees. Their chosen professions of Education and Computer Science have resulted in steady growth. They retire on solid footing. While they hate to see the gyrations of the stock market, they are a little more settled than most, in that they reduced their portfolio in 2007 and most of their investments reside in safe havens. Yes, they hate low-interest rates on their savings and, sure, they wish their Dividend paying stocks would also increase in value, but the days of chasing the new technology start-up are gone.

This couple, like peers in the same category, did not eat out every Saturday night [over the years] and did not buy Gucci bags; they managed their finances conservatively. They paid as they went, lived in moderation, and took care of their responsibilities. Now, they board the plane in Boston. They cannot wait to see Rome. They are excited about Tuscany. They wonder if Milan is as fashionable as people say. They also wonder why people just cannot be happy for them. They feel as if they have earned the lifestyle that they now seek.

Saturday, September 3, 2011

Social Climber

The American Heritage Dictionary of the English Language notes the following in their fourth variation of the word "climber": "a person who avidly seeks a higher social or professional position." Baby Boomers call such a person a "phony." Our dictionary from above defines that as "not genuine or real." Further description goes on to list words such as "fake, dishonest, deceptive, and hypocritical." Baby Boomers have little respect for such individuals. They see a social climber as the person trying just a bit too hard with someone that they think has status, while giving a snub to one that they believe to be of lesser scale.

Why is this a topic for discussion now? Because of the times we live in, and the need for a "reality check" in the nation. Yesterday, a report was released that showed no job growth in the country last month. In Miami, Baby Boomers waited in line for the chance to fill out an application for a construction job. In a picture in The Wall Street journal today, one Baby Boomer was a man who should be thinking about the golf course, not a new career path. The man, estimated to be 62, looked like he had never seen a hammer in his life. But there he was in line for a possible job. I wonder what he would think, if on his way home, he was knocked over by an overbearing, bombastic social climber, rushing to show his importance to the world.

Let us read into the picture a bit to help articulate the view that Baby Boomers have of social climbers. Is "detest" too strong of a word to describe the Baby Boomer view of the social climber? No, not too strong, maybe too weak. After standing in line, our Baby Boomer thought perhaps he lost some self-esteem. But many Baby Boomers, in looking at this situation, would actually have gained respect for this man.

To continue the examination, let us take actual events and combine them with the greater majority of Baby Boomers' feelings on the subject matter of Baby Boomers as social climbers. Let us imagine what the Baby Boomer in line in Miami did after the trials of standing in that line. As he drives home, he feels like he needs to stop before he has to face his wife, who will be waiting for him at the door. As he continues, he looks to the right and spots a Starbucks. Suddenly, he craves a cup of coffee.

At the Starbucks, he sits with a Grande sized coffee, the bold blend, and wonders about his future. As he looks to his left, he sees the man with the shades, the fast talker. The man was the one who tried to impress the barista, then became rude when his charms failed, as he talked about his car, home, and anything else that would be defined as "the brag." He is the "don't you know who I am" guy. He is the one who never read the book that stated "money and class are not equitable." As we have come to find out over time, however, the social climber never has as much as he projects to have. Like the wise man once told the young teenager, "if you are the real deal, you don't have to talk, people will just know." You see, when your lifestyle is paid with plastic, and manners never enter into the picture, then, of course, you are not the "real deal." Somehow, you are more like the young high school girl, so insecure, that a mean stone face, and "never talk to an unpopular kid," is the mode of operation. If these individuals were not so transparent, or rude, you would try to feel sorry for them. But in these times, who can bother, when so many hard trying individuals are more worth your time, like the man in line to apply for a job, who we described earlier.

Baby Boomers respect knowledge, hard work, true accomplishment, and intellectual prowess. They like their accomplishment mixed with a chaser of modesty. They like Jones as a last name, rather than a "keeping up with" kind of action. They like charity for its giving, not as a social mixer, as if it were a sock hop. They like professional behavior and ethics, rather than insider trading. They respect someone who comports themselves with a positive image as opposed to someone who is in need of an ill-fated consulting project.

There was a time when a pleasant smile, thank you, or a kind word was worth something. That was before the days when "trying to get the edge," or "rude and crude" were in vogue. "Ruthless?" asks the MBA student, "is that what I need to be to get ahead?" What message are we sending when you get ahead not for performance, but because you beat the system? If you live in the North shore of Chicago, the high rent district, are you satisfied with your life, if you did not earn it? Is the Porsche a toy, or is it that one thing I always wanted to get when I felt that I could afford it, based on my effort?

Before anybody gets the wrong idea, wealth is not a bad thing. Just because you have money does not make you a bad person. If you think like that you are in the same ballpark as the social climber. You deserve respect for your accomplishments. You do not get respect because you pound your chest and demand it, but rather, just like with anything else, because you earned it. Then again, that will be something a social climber will never understand.

Saturday, August 27, 2011

The State of Baby Boomer Nation

You know that scene that occurs, by law, based on the Constitution. Every year, the President gives the State of the Union Address. He reports to the people of the nation on the status of the country. His assessment is usually followed by a description of his recommended course of action for the upcoming year.

The following is a small take on that winter ritual. Since this writing is based on Baby Boomers input rather than the hopes and dreams of a country, the Baby Boomer State of the Nation will be shared with far less grandeur.

But make no mistake about it, the Baby Boomers who had input are every bit as concerned, as they evaluate the state of Baby Boomer Nation. It is safe to say that Baby Boomers as a whole are not happy campers. While a small percentage of the generation are content, on solid financial ground, and see a bright retirement future, they represent the minority.

There is also a small percentage, greater than the group described above, who are distraught, distressed, and destitute. Sadly, many described are veterans.

The majority fall in the middle; they are stressed, over-worked, and worried. This would be a synopsis of Baby Boomer Nation. They are the Baby Boomers who have seen and experienced the greatest of highs, and now are trying to cope with the lows. It is a group who thought the Great Depression was a history lesson, and that nothing like it would ever be seen in the Baby Boomer lexicon.

For a very long time, it seemed as if nothing very bad or serious ever happened. The house would increase in value, stocks would be a great investment for the long term, and the technology sector would always be there to provide work. Retirement worries consisted of warm climate, housing, a fitness routine, and travel. This was a generation that was going to redefine the "Golden Years." Well, it has, but with a far different picture.

Those years now are about working longer, if still employed. Those years are about looking for work, and swallowing your pride, and the pay cut that goes with it. It is about trying to get by on meager savings until Social Security kicks in. Now, as if things were not bad enough, politicians talk of the great problem, the close to 79 million Baby Boomers who are going to break the system. You have heard them say, "We need to curb entitlements."

This is the State of Baby Boomer Nation. What is the solution? Here is what your fellow Baby Boomers advocate: Baby Boomers, first and foremost, want some protection or cover when it comes to Social Security and Medicare. They ask, "Where is AARP to advocate on behalf of Baby Boomers?" Baby Boomers also are not fond of the moving target; they are tired of hearing the constant drum beat of raising the age for benefits to kick in. While Baby Boomers are sensitive to fiscal discipline, they also want to point out that they have spent a lifetime working hard and paying into the system.

Baby Boomers are also looking to corporate America to open up the purse strings and start hiring. Major corporations are sitting on a great deal of cash, so perhaps they ought to look at some resumes. Baby Boomers have value and experience. Hey, Microsoft, Baby Boomers could use a job. Hey, Apple, you are sitting on $76 billion - remember those Baby Boomers who bought the Macintosh? They are still ready to contribute. The key word is "contribute." Baby Boomers can add a lot of value to a company. They are not graying employees ready to be put out to pasture, but sharp minds who have "been there, done that." Let them come in and help shape the future; and by the way, let them also mentor the younger employee, just as previous generations once did.

Mort Zuckerman, of U.S. News and World Report, asks, "Where is President Obama's leadership?" He wants AAA leadership for a AAA country. There might be something to that: the leaders of this country need to step up and help make Baby Boomers part of the solution, rather than accusing them of being the problem.

Thursday, April 28, 2011

Baby Boomers – A Profile of a Couple

Three blocks off Hollister in a quiet neighborhood in Santa Barbara, California lives David and Diana. Both are Baby Boomers in their late 50s who look much younger. These two articulate, smart, and most of all, nice people, live a life that most Baby Boomers should want to know about. David, a food service executive who is an expert in supply chain management, and Diana, a medical researcher who works in a lab, have lived in the same home for the past 28 years. They raised two daughters, both accomplished in their own right. Their eldest, a UC-Berkley graduate, works up in the Bay area. Their younger daughter, a Cal-Poly graduate, now studies in England. The couple, by their own admission, each lived their own life before being married when they each were 30.

David, who went to school at University of California Santa Barbara, or UCSB as it is known, grew up in Santa Barbara, was a great local athlete, and enjoyed college life with his friends. After college, he did charity work abroad, which helped give him his sense of purpose. Diana, a brilliant student, gravitated to research from the beginning. They met, fell in love, and got married. They also realized during their courtship that they had a similar idea of how they wanted their future to play out. They were both fiscal conservative with the same ideas of how to spend and handle money. Maybe because they were both mature when they said, "I do," they were savers from the beginning.

As is typical of Baby Boomers, they were a two career family. They have consistently earned well over the years and have been in the same stable work environment for most of their work life. Their home, beautiful and in an excellent area, is not overly ostentatious. They practice what financial experts call "living below your means." Their key expense in life was the education of their daughters, which they did to the fullest extent. Their life today, as it has been, revolves around hard work. They both rise early, David making the coffee while Diana gets ready. Their time in the morning is their communication time. Diana will work until about 7 pm, so she takes a little break in the afternoon to come home, have lunch, and read the newspaper. It is her quiet time. David, who arrives home before Diana, does most of the cooking. He is a great cook, both inside the house and outdoors on the grill. That food preparation time is his quiet time. It is, however, supplemented by watching sports, which is his passion. Once Diana arrives home, they eat together and go over each other's day. On most nights, they will watch a favorite program. But other nights, David might work on the computer where one activity is charting the family finances.

They pay close attention to where their money goes, and attentive detail to their investments. They do most, if not all, transactions online. They also keep up with friends and family with a steady stream of email. When the weekend comes, they enjoy the movies, but rarely go to the movie theatre. They are Netflix fans, who get what they ordered in the mail for their Friday night at home over popcorn. They are not likely to be part of the Santa Barbara restaurant scene, although they do have their favorites which they might enjoy once or twice a month. They share responsibilities around the home, which also takes up their weekend. Diana likes to work in the garden, and David takes care of the cars. They do, twice a month, receive maid service.

Diana has a best girlfriend, Robin, who she goes for coffee with on most Saturdays. The best coffee shop is Goleta Coffee, run by Annie, who will gladly tell you that in Santa Barbara all coffee shops are independent. Robin, a county teacher of the year, and Diana have been best friends for several years. David enjoys talking sports amidst the camaraderie of his work buddies. David and Diana go to church service on Sunday mornings. They have always been respectful of their parents. In recent years, both of their mothers were widowed, and they made a point of visiting them regularly. Diana was also a respectful daughter-in-law. David's mother, who became ill, was helped by his sister, who is a nurse. She came from Denver to help care for their mother in her waning days. After she passed, and after the service, they settled the estate with little problem, due to the respect for their parents and each other.

This couple will easily work until they are 65. They will be well prepared for retirement. They hope to travel and enjoy the fruits of their labor. They will continue to live in Santa Barbara.

Tuesday, April 19, 2011

Three Baby Boomers from the East Coast who "Get It"

Jack spent many years as a real estate developer. He was very good at what he did. Long before the end of his work life, he and his wife began to plan what kind of retirement life they wanted to live. Where did they want to live? What life style was paramount? What was the balance going to be between carrying out their life plans and spending time with grandchildren? Their choice was two-fold: an over 55 community outside of Ocala, Florida, and a summer home on Cape Cod. Their Florida life is complete with active community life, where Jack is on several committees. He is an avid tennis player who competes in the 60 and over category. Last year he and his partner made it to the state mixed doubles semi-finals. His Cape Cod home is quite different. The family spends a great deal of time there. They make frequent trips to Boston and to Providence to enjoy restaurants and cultural activities. Jack is a good example of a person who turned his hard work and planning into the lifestyle of his choice.

Our second subject, George, lives in Sarasota, Florida. He and his wife bought on the beautiful Siesta Key portion of Sarasota some ten years ago while he was still working. Originally from Indiana, this businessman and Purdue graduate wanted the Siesta Key residence to be his retirement place, which it has turned out to be. George has decided to provide for his grandchildren's education. He has also done Estate Planning, complete with communicating his wishes to his children. George is a good example of a Baby Boomer who knows the importance of looking ahead, while also knowing what is important today.

And then, there is Fred. He owns one of the most respected corporate recruitment and placement firms in the country. For the past 25 years, he has launched careers, and aided Fortune 500 companies in dealing with their intricate hiring needs. He has raised a family, contributed to the well-being of the Hartford, Connecticut community, and has done a great job of maintaining friendships. He puts a great deal of emphasis on friendship, both with his close friends and with business associates. He is an example of a Baby Boomer who understands that you do not go through life alone in either work or private time.

These three individuals profiled have several things in common. First and foremost, they are gentlemen in every sense of the word. Yes, they have been successful, but they carry it with a sense of modesty. They do not have to blow their own horn because they are comfortable in their own skin. They have always maintained their priorities, and worked hard for everything that came their way. They, in fact, are fine examples of their generation.

Friday, April 15, 2011

Baby Boomers seek places to live after retirement

It may be time to downsize and think about the future. It may be time to start thinking about how you want to spend the remaining portion of your life, and that surely involves where to live. This topic has become a bit of a cottage industry. Books have been written and magazines exist for that purpose. The process actually begins while you are still working, and you are planning ahead. Let us assume, for the moment, that you have done a lot of the right things, saved to maintain a lifestyle, thought about if you want to have a post retirement life of work or charity, and you have a handle on what might make you happy. You have worked hard all of your life, and now you want to enjoy yourself. But where do you live? For some, this is not much of a choice. A common comment is "my family is here, so why move?" Some are just comfortable with their surroundings. But for others, they seek out places with weather considerations, cost of living, and lifestyle choices. One may want to live where they can just lock the door and go, because they want to travel. Others may want to live near a university to take advantage of the resources. The consensus has weather as a determinant. Many smart Baby Boomers are researching, making a short list, and then visiting those places that they think may suit them, and which they can afford. This has become a focus for Baby Boomers, and just another stage of life key to their current thought process.

Tuesday, April 5, 2011

Baby Boomers turn 65

Recently the news media has brought focus to the fact that the first group of Baby Boomers turned 65 starting in January of 2011. USA Today, in particular, did an outstanding job of highlighting issues facing the generation, as well as bringing some historical perspective. In 1946, when the generation came to be, our country was full of a fresh spirit. With World War II over and the country full of enthusiasm, people were anxious to get on with their lives and that included starting families. By the mid-1950s, expansion to suburbs had begun and school children all over America needed places to go to school. As years would pass, it would become obvious that this generation would be like no other in terms of numbers and future complexity. Thus, when news outlets reported the historic occasion of Boomers turning 65, it was also accompanied by companion stories about issues such as social security, as well as lifestyle issues facing a generation. For the people that I have interviewed, both are paramount. Most Boomers are not flying around the world. Sadly, many have not saved enough and are ill prepared for the "Golden Years." They need that social security safety net, as created by FDR. For those who are prepared, their lifestyle is front and center. How that lifestyle plays out is at the heart of Baby Boomers thought pattern.

Summary – Chapter 8

Long Term Financial Planning – Are you prepared for Retirement

Are you prepared for retirement? Do you have a handle on how you want to live out the remainder of your life? Have you thought about issues such as where you want to live and the affordability of housing? Have you given thought to work? How long do you want to work, and what you will be doing? Do you want to start a second career? Or, are you one of the lucky ones, who have provided for your future, who wants to travel, and maybe start checking off the items on your bucket list? Whatever the case, you are amongst the growing number of Baby Boomers thinking about retirement. Some ask the question, "Am I ready?" Some ask, "Will I ever be ready?" But the commonality is the focus on the retirement years. There is consideration to health. There is consideration to 55 and over communities. There are thoughts about not being your grandfather's grandfather. You ask the question, "What does grand-parenting mean to me?" You contemplate having to juggle your babysitting responsibility with your own goals. You debate telling your children that you have already raised your children.

Yet, the pressures of life make you prisoner to your children, for some simply need their grown children's help. Whatever, as a Baby Boomer, your economic condition or plight is, the challenge is to think ahead. Think like your fellow Baby Boomers who are planning for that next stage of life. Think less about what you have not done, but more on what you will do; for, as Baby Boomers, you have an enthusiastic nature about you. You are willing to try something new and continue to experience something new, which has always been the character of Baby Boomers. The retirement years are the next stage of life for Baby Boomers. Embrace that period of your life, no matter what you choose to do, and how you want to live your life.

My own personal story about retirement began during the year 2008. Tired of corporate life, I began taking interest in the Baby Boomer generation. I began to be fascinated by vacation spots for Baby Boomers, places that Baby Boomers were retiring to, and how my peers had progressed with the stages of life. I also had begun to focus on how I wanted to live out my life. This was made easier by examining who came before and what they did. I began formulating the thesis that my grandfather had worked into his 70s, so did my father, as well as my uncles. I began to think about how I was going to accomplish a similar feat. You see, you tend to do what comes naturally. You seem to inherit much from family members, especially ones that you respect. So my challenge was to carve out a life path that would include work as a part of my lifestyle. I also did not want to have "just a job," but to make a contribution to society. I knew that retirement for me was not sitting on the porch, but to being active and productive. Baby Boomers, it is never too early to reset the table for the vision of your future. And, do not get too hung up on the labels. So many of the Baby Boomers that I have talked to need to somehow change the name to protect the innocent. A second career becomes an "encore," a new enterprise has to be a "long lost passion," and continuous improvement is replaced by a "wellness campaign." I understand this, for even in this writing, after examining Baby Boomers, I have tried to use some of the language of the times. Simply put, my understanding of the future is to work hard, make a contribution to society, let it be a form of income, and to respect the need to take care of myself and my health. This will, I believe, insure a better retirement.

This chapter is about choices, ones that you have made in the past, and the ones you will make in the future. Decision-making regarding the years ahead has three components: 1) Baby Boomers need Social Security; 2) Baby Boomers will have a better chance of succeeding in the years ahead if they have a plan, one that can be started today; and 3) Baby Boomers should not worry about all the things that they did not do to secure their retirement, but should instill a belief that it can be accomplished.

From talking to Baby Boomers, being a Baby Boomer, and delivering this message to the Baby Boomer generation and those who want to study our generation, I have full confidence in the attributes of the Baby Boomer Generation going forward.

Chapter 9

Social Security and Medicare

My father liked to tell the story of when FDR first started to circulate the thought that we as Americans have a responsibility to have a safety net for the seniors in our country, and how he embraced the idea. My father had a vision that when he reached a certain age, he would need this kind of security. My friend's great-aunt is Francis Perkins, the legendary female Cabinet member who helped President Roosevelt usher in what many call the government's best program. Some would even go so far as to say that it was the best Government program ever enacted. My friend is certainly proud of his family being so much a part of history, and my father and mother realized the promise of FDR and benefited from the program that helped the members of the Greatest Generation.

In January of 2011, Baby Boomers began turning 65 in large numbers, and today, 10,000 a day reach the retirement threshold. What once was a program for our parents is now front and center to Baby Boomers. It once was a program that was to be for another day and time. But the time is now. They like to call it an entitlement, an especially popular term of politicians in current times. It is not a gift or a handout, but the money that Baby Boomers worked hard for all their lives and now have coming to them, and that many need. It is part of sustainability. President Roosevelt thought that when you reached a certain age, a protection was needed as a safety net to live out your years. He believed that this was something the country owed to its citizens. People wonder why, in his time, FDR was so popular with the majority in this country. The reason was that in those fireside chats, through the radio to the American public, the average person had the sense and feeling that the President was on his side. The American public thought that he cared, that he had their best interest at heart. Social Security was a pillar of the "New Deal." That was FDR's way of saying to Americans, "I have a handshake with each and every one of you."

This was America at its best, looking out for its people, for that is what defines Social Security. Times were hard during the Great Depression, jobs were scarce, and pensions were not even foreshadowed. Social Security was to be there for you, provided by the government, so that you could live out your years with dignity. The program worked, and it is a rite of passage for people of a certain age to sign up for the benefit that is so much a part of the country's legacy. The problem is that, in the times in which we live, Social Security may become history. For it is under assault, thought of as something that some people believe should be cut, or certainly scaled back. Many Baby Boomers will tell you that this would be a travesty. Further, Baby Boomers would be devastated; for, the fact is, many Baby Boomers are unprepared for retirement.

As I traveled the country talking to Baby Boomers, two glaring topics were talked about over and over: retirement and health care. Baby Boomers spoke of thinking that they would have the same senior lifestyles as those of their parents. They would receive their Social Security checks, and Medicare would cover 80 percent of their healthcare. These were the promises of the "Great Society." The Great Society was President Lyndon Johnson's continuation of FDR's policies, and the realization that America would now reach its full potential. President Johnson, who came to office after President Kennedy was assassinated, had three things going for him.

First, he had the will of the people, who were in shock after President Kennedy met death in Dallas. Second, he was a master legislator who knew how to get things enacted within Congress. And, third, America simply was doing well, and it seemed time to bring services to America.

But as I traveled the country and began commenting on the state of Baby Boomers, it seemed that the promise of the New Deal of FDR, the hopes and dreams of President Kennedy with the New Frontier, and President Johnson's Great Society, were just faded yellow pages in a scrapbook to the Baby Boomer who saw little in his future. Baby Boomers were now unemployed in big numbers, their savings were depleted, and their lifestyles had caught up to their ages. The generation who had lived on credit was now hoping for some dividends from programs that they expected to be there for them in their senior years. The sad reality is that most Baby Boomers will need the safety net that President Roosevelt thought of as protection. Baby Boomers, for all their talk of youth and redefining age, are facing the reality that the Social Security check will matter, and Medicare is essential. Some argue that older Baby Boomers have nothing to fear, that any changes proposed will not affect them, but younger Baby Boomers are not so sure that the status quo will be present when their time for retirement comes.

Baby Boomers who were so paralyzed by President Johnson during the Vietnam era, now long for his policies before the war. The government today is under siege, with its inability to get things done in Washington, its failure to compromise, and its inability to manage factions. There are people in this country who want to turn back the clock and make Americans fend for themselves. While we have to manage our fiscal house, Baby Boomers are feeling increased pressure to solidify their futures. What will housing be like in coming years for Baby Boomers? How will they make it with reduced pensions or an insufficient 401k? No, Baby Boomers are not their grandfathers and grandmothers. Yes, they are trading in the rocking chairs for exercise, good eating habits, and the dreams of active lifestyles. But it is clear, beyond a shadow of a doubt, that the social programs of another time are of key importance for Baby Boomers, in whatever form that their lives constitute.

Yes, Baby Boomers are concerned about their future, are concerned about their finances, and fear that what was available for their parents will not be available to them. It is sad that Baby Boomers are criticized for having been a generation of excess. They themselves know that they chased gratification. They know that they went on vacations that they did not have the money for, or sought out a life of "live now, pay later." But they also worked very hard. They endured changes in corporate structure. They were a part of vast technological change that affected their job security. They were a part of a "me" generation that included cutting jobs for many to impact the wealth of a few. Baby Boomers were a group that had Social Security taken out of paychecks, and now want the benefit to be paid and to help secure the remaining part of their lives – lives that will also hopefully include the benefits of proper healthcare without having to choose between medicine and food. Baby Boomers, no matter their age, feel that they should be able to count on some things, and that list must include Social Security and Medicare.

Thursday, April 21, 2011

Baby Boomers need Social Security

Baby Boomers do not all live in Wellesley, Massachusetts, Lake Forest, Illinois, or Bellevue, Washington. They do not all spend time in Santa Barbara, California, Sarasota, Florida, or Del Mar, California. They do not all drive Bentleys in Palm Desert, California, or vacation on Nantucket, Massachusetts. Perhaps you get the picture. Those are all exceptions and not the rule. For the Baby Boomers who have done well and are living dream lifestyles, one can only be enthusiastic for their circumstances. Unfortunately, the norm is quite the opposite. For the majority of Baby Boomers, the Great Recession has been devastating. Over the last three years, Baby Boomers have lost jobs, and those still working have seen their nest eggs reduced. Baby Boomers are likely to work longer, some by choice, but most out of necessity. Another sad truth is that the vast majority of Baby Boomers are ill prepared for retirement.

One can argue that the present conditions for Baby Boomers are not all that different from when Social Security was created. When FDR instituted Social Security, it was designed as a safety net for the elderly. Baby Boomers may want to grow old gracefully, and they may see themselves as different from their parents, but they do need the same safety net. FDR thought that it was a moral obligation for America to take care of citizens who had reached a certain age. Baby Boomers have worked all their lives and are now owed what they have paid into the system. For many Baby Boomers, it may be their only form of income as they go forward. Baby Boomers who are already 65 are not overly worried that Social Security will disappear in their lifetimes. However, Baby Boomers in their 50s are very concerned.

For some Baby Boomers, there was always tomorrow, but tomorrow has come. Most Baby Boomers can take pride in the fact that they have enjoyed life, some would say to excess. Many have had experiences far beyond imagination. Some say it is now time to pay the piper. What a mistake it would be to abandon the greatest social program the government has ever created. FDR had it right: we have a moral obligation to take care of the aged. That thinking works no matter the era, whether it is the Great Depression, the Great Recession, or whatever is yet to come.

Tuesday, September 13, 2011

Rick Perry and Social Security

Have you been following the saga that is Rick Perry and his position on Social Security? He calls Social Security a Ponzi scheme. This should really make Baby Boomers comfortable going into the next election. While there is no guarantee that he will get the Republican nomination, or even be elected President, for the time being he is the front runner of his party. Last night, facing attack from his fellow office seekers, especially Mitt Romney, he tried to soften his stance, to no avail. For example, he said that if you are close to Social Security in age, you will be okay. What does that mean, coming from a man who wants to eliminate the program? What can you believe from a man who once was the point man for Al Gore's Presidential campaign in Texas? Of course, that was when he was a Democrat. What did he think of Social Security then? Now that he has found religion, being the champion of the right wing of the Republican party, he now thinks all social programs are offensive. He does not believe that government can help people at all. Here is a news flash for Governor Perry: you are running for President. The job description includes running the government. Where do these candidates get these ideas? He says he is not George Bush, because he did not go to Yale. As if going to Yale is a bad thing. Many would give their right arms for that opportunity. He tells us that he was in the Air Force – perhaps that is not part of the government. He went to Texas A & M, the school that is trying to sell its athletic program to the highest bidder. He touts his job creation as Governor of Texas, but what kind of jobs did he create? All of this is second-place thinking, or at least it should be if you are a Baby Boomer, for Social Security has to be the focus.

While all Baby Boomers would agree that Social Security needs to be brought to stability, and we need some tweaks to make it solvent, it remains the most important government program. To suggest, as Mr. Perry does, that it should be eliminated is a travesty. The question becomes, why has he not been called on the carpet? How anyone could think to even say they would vote for this individual, someone with such little regard for history, compassion for the elderly, or the understanding that Social Security is a compact from generation to generation, is beyond Baby Boomer comprehension. This then brings into question the sincerity of the man. Does he change beliefs to fit the climate, and thus advance his personal agenda, or does he believe in public service, a pre-requisite for higher office? In 1992, for example, when Rick Perry said that he was a good Democrat, what was his stance on health care, as President Clinton and Hilary Clinton were trying to advance the debate? A person cannot possibly have such extreme change, as to first be for FDR's politics, and then later on in your career denounce FDR's greatest achievement.

President Obama, in the tradition of Baby Boomers, has not been the greatest defender of Social Security. Remember that he was willing to negotiate benefits away during the debt ceiling crisis? But Baby Boomers have to believe, or must believe, that a Democrat will never give away the most cherished of safety nets. But who knows, given this uncertain political climate, what you can count on. To his credit, Mitt Romney has attacked Perry, almost sounding like Harry Truman as the defender of Social Security, so this is a good thing. But Baby Boomers not only need to hold steadfast to the program, but also have a reasonable opinion on when the benefit takes hold. To say that you believe in Social Security, but we need to raise the age in which you can receive the benefit, is foolhardy. So, as Baby Boomers watch over the next year and chart the positions of the candidates, they must examine closely what they say about Social Security. There is nothing of greater importance now to Baby Boomers.

Thursday, July 21, 2011

The Debt Ceiling impact on Baby Boomers

"I have seen the future and it is now," goes the phrase. Have you been following the debt ceiling talks going on in Washington, or what may better be termed lack of civility within the beltway? Why does this happen? Why do partisan politics polarize the country? What is it about the need to win that makes compromise seems like a term that fails to be understood in the English language? It is an embarrassment to watch our elected officials in action. Of course, what other conclusion is to be drawn? Politics and positioning for the 2012 election are one thing, but the impact on the lives of Americans is an entirely other matter. "I have seen the future, and it is now." The *Wall Street Journal* has a section called

"Letters to the Editor." On page A18 [Opinion Section, 7-20-2011], a headline reads, "Cuts: The President Will Show his Priorities." The readers who wrote in are not Baby Boomers; they are who Baby Boomers will be, our future. John Vuksich: "President Obama's prioritization: he believes that Social Security is not sufficiently important to be paid with funds collected from this month's payroll taxes, but rather is a luxury only affordable if the nation can borrow the money." A. L. Cynton: "A coffee party, millions of Americans telling their elected representatives to wake up and do the people's business now."

FDR must be rolling over in his grave. Social Security is not a negotiation chip, it is not an entitlement, but rather it is the right of every American when they reach a certain age to be assisted. Today, the average Baby Boomer is simply not prepared for retirement. Boomers will need those benefits and the cost of living increases that are part of the package. They need Medicare. How far have we slipped from the days of the Great Society? LBJ would not understand his Democratic party today and its failure to pass legislation and find common ground for the good of the nation. He would not understand the modern day politician who puts his or her own agenda over the country's agenda. Baby Boomers would remind their elected officials, many who are fellow Baby Boomers, that the job is called "public service" for a reason. The decisions made by Congress in the next few weeks will impact how Baby Boomers will live out their "Golden Years." The case already exists that Baby Boomers will be working longer, facing lifestyle adjustments, and will be worse off in their retirement than their parents. They need help from Washington, not crime and punishment.

To be fair, the problem or fault is not the President, nor the conservative Republicans, or even the media. They all probably think that they are on the right side of the issues. Maybe so, but at some point someone has to be an adult and stand up and ask what the impact is of our actions. Surely a deal will get done in Washington, but what will it look like? To some Baby Boomers, tax code relief will help, but estate tax issues and lack of money for services because of a lack of revenue will impact the future. This comes on the heels of Baby Boomers losing their jobs due to the cost-cutting measures of corporations. There are no new jobs available for the aging Baby Boomer, who makes a last run at saving for retirement.

So that brings us back to the core issue: Social Security. Every Democrat who even entertains any change in benefits must have been absent on the day in school when teachers covered what it means to be a Democrat. For Republicans, it is all well and good to fight for a balanced budget, but not on the backs of people who have worked all their lives, and paid into a system that was meant to be a safety net. To the young Congress members who look to Social Security and Medicare as a line item, someone should coach them on the fact that someday, they too will be 65. Every day we pick up the paper and find another politician who makes a misstep with American history. Here is a little advice from the Baby Boomer community: take a look at the Great Depression; the times today are similar. Learn from FDR – do not dismiss him. Those principals were sound and are much needed today.

Tuesday, July 26, 2011

The Other Side of Life

On a warm Sunday morning in the midst of summer, 2011, two Baby Boomers enter a nearby Starbucks. One is on the way to services at the Episcopal church down the street. The other is entering in what appears to be a no plans strategy. For both men this is their regular Starbucks. Baby Boomers use phrases such as "regular Starbucks," because they have been conditioned to do so. For many years, Baby Boomers have been making it a part of their routines to stop for their morning cups of coffee. The person with no plans, so to speak, is ahead in the line by several people. The individual on the way to church is in full observation mode. As he, let's call him person "A," makes his way to the register, he has $1.50 proudly in hand. For many weeks, his order has been, in a polite manner, to ask for some hot water. For you see, he has been stretching the two tea bags that are part of the cup he nurses. But on this day, which would be a day of luxury, he would be able to treat himself to a cup of coffee.

The barista greets him by name because he is nice, a gentleman, always pleasant. She kids with him, "Not the usual today?" No, on this day it would be a tall coffee, double cup. She hands him his drink, and he gladly pays. Who would have thought that this man, with so much pride, had a lifestyle that, up until just a couple of years ago, was mandated by a mode of operation that signaled "anything you want"? No, that person does not exist anymore. Like Baby Boomers all across America, frugal is "in," and excessive indulgence is way outdated. The world has a lot of Baby Boomers just getting by. They hurt inside because they are not the people that they once were. They do not know about the latest restaurant opening, or what is new at the movies. Their cars have multiple miles, the cell phone bills are now a struggle, and just reading the morning newspaper is a pleasure in life.

Somehow the dignity of the man, while a bit tarnished, still allows for the fight to continue, looking for work to hold on to the house at all costs. There is no patience for the social climber who thinks rude behavior is a way of showing that he has made it in life. No, this Baby Boomer is trying and trying and trying, hoping at all costs to just get it back. To just return to the life that was, where people would look at you with respect, and when you smiled, they would smile back. They long for the days when the thrift shop was not their clothing store. They wait with anticipation for when they can return the kindnesses that others have shown them while they have been down on their luck. Will that day ever come? Will they work again? Will they provide again? Will they be able to have a savings account and look to retirement? Will the frustration ever go away?

So, on this morning what others have termed "frugal fatigue" plays out amidst coffee and the newspaper at the regular Starbucks. How shameful it must be for our person "A" to read about the ridiculous glory that the

NFL is taking in proclaiming that they have settled a way to divide up 9.5 billion dollars. How insulting it must be to this studious individual that the President and the Speaker of the House are displaying a partisanship that may bring the country to default. And, how sad it must be for the Baby Boomer whose last hopes are Social Security and Medicare, that these safety nets are referred to as "entitlements" that some claim need to be reformed, or that the age limit needs to rise to make the country solvent. Someone ought to remind Washington that people are hurting, and that there is another world outside of Santa Barbara, the Hamptons, and Vail. The hopelessness is paramount. As person "B" reached the register at his regular Starbucks, dressed in a blue blazer and gray pants with a North Carolina style light blue shirt, it was time for him to order. He said, "Can I please get some hot water?"

Tuesday, August 9, 2011

The Great Compromise

The Great Compromise, the conclusion to the debt ceiling debate. Well, as Baby Boomers, how do you feel about things? The S & P still downgraded the U.S. of A., although its track record for accuracy can be called into question based on its performance during the housing crisis. But, when you look back and review all the back and forth, the back biting in Washington, the need to win talking points, little was accomplished. Neither side could hold its head up high. Vice President Biden did a commendable job early on, even managing to form a relationship with Eric Cantor before the representative and second-in-command of the House Republicans walked out on negotiations. By the way, the initial work by Biden's team ended up being the framework for the final deal. Looking back, a deal could have been completed on May 17, thus creating some degree of stability in the markets. Representative Cantor stands for the same district that was once represented by James Madison. As the saying goes, he is no James Madison. Please, Mr. Cantor, stop saying that you must do something to curb entitlements. First of all, Social Security and Medicare are pacts or safety nets. Social Security is an obligation, as FDR put it, to individuals who paid into the system all their lives. The program should not be harmed, but protected, as well as the cost of living increases that go with it.

If you are so bent on curbing entitlements, how about reducing your House pension? When President Johnson built upon FDR's legacy with Medicare, he never intended for it to be taken off the table in political wrangling. Quite frankly, the President opened the door with his feeble attempt to get a grand deal done with House Speaker Boehner. Please, Mr. President, listen to your base. Social Security and Medicare are not bargaining chips to use in your re-election campaign. That might explain the tepid response that you got from your party.

As has been written in this space, Baby Boomers need Social Security; they should not be held hostage to events in the world, to defense policy, or to younger politicians who do not know their history. As for the raising of the age for Social Security, this is a slippery slope in a never-ending process. Yes, people are living longer; yes, the Baby Boomer generation, because of its sheer numbers, presents a problem. But a benefit that is always out of reach is vastly unfair.

Once the Baby Boomer generation clears through its population, the average numbers originally created by the government as part of the generational planning during the Depression, will then meet calculations. So, in effect, this is a one-generation issue, a Baby Boomer generation issue. Partisan politics are out of hand. The citizens of America want Washington to work, and to have both parties work together.

For example, the political world lost a great statesman this week when former Senator Mark Hatfield from Oregon passed away. He was a moderate Republican, and we sure could use some of those. He headed up appropriations in his day and worked with Democrats to get legislation passed. He was a "do the right thing for the country" kind of statesman, an attitude that permeated his time in office and was shared by his colleagues.

In the end, the country needs to work. As of this writing, the markets plunge, the reputation of the country to the world has been marred, and the elected officials in Washington are at a loss. All of this while Baby Boomers across America worry about their futures.

Tuesday, June 28, 2011

A Look at Lyndon Johnson

Ask Baby Boomers about Lyndon Johnson, and the response is immediate: Vietnam. It is natural in some respects, because a Baby Boomer's formative years took place during the military escalation of the Johnson administration. But, as the years have passed, we need to take a fresh look at the man and his career. While the Kennedy assassination was a defining moment to Baby Boomers – you probably remember where you were when you heard the news – and the Nixon years were associated with Watergate, Johnson is a bit more complex. For example, how many Baby Boomers know that his career started during the FDR years, or that he may be one of the greatest majority leaders in this country's history? How many Baby Boomers remember the "Great Society," or, for that matter, the care and feeding of our mourning country from the time that he took office? His record on civil rights and the push to help the aged with the passing of Medicare is a hallmark to his dedication.

The historians often ask, "What could he have accomplished if it were not for Vietnam?" Johnson did things when he took office that we can only long for in the present day. He avoided gridlock in Congress, achieved bipartisanship, got legislation through the Congress and turned ideas into laws. Most likely shaped by the influence of FDR, as were the majority of his generation, he believed that America was a great country. He believed that government could help people, and that our wealth should benefit all citizens. He believed that by making sure black people were afforded the ballot box, we would one day have a black president. He believed in opportunity for all, be it through education, through trade schools, or by way of small businesses. He believed that the capacity to help and deliver services was important to everyday life. The Great Society was the promise and the vehicle to achieve his goals. Oh, if only it were not for Vietnam. Of course, no one likes revisionist history. He did not get it right when it came to the war. The oldest of Baby Boomers today either were sent to fight or spent a good deal of effort trying to avoid being drafted. The protester at age 19 does not remember Johnson for Medicare, which he will soon take advantage of, but more for the distrust Johnson garnered from the war. The war destroyed everything that initially was accomplished by Johnson, to the point that it brought riots to the streets and the loss of lives abroad.

By 1968, when he chose not to run for reelection, he was a beaten man. But, over 40 years after his death, we need to look at the man in totality. We need to garner some of his strengths for present day politics, such as the art of compromise, bargaining with the other party, and not being so rigid in thought that the system is paralyzed by dogma. Johnson, up until the last two years of his career, could teach us all lessons about the way the political system is supposed to work, and that winning at all costs does not benefit the country as a whole. It would be great if there were a more congenial nature in Washington, or, at the very least, the ability to see the other person's point of view. Many elected officials today are Baby Boomers, but rather than simply remembering Johnson in one vein, maybe they could look at some of the man's positive aspects to pass some meaningful legislation.

Summary: Chapter 9

Social Security and Medicare

The year was 1955, and a Baby Boomer was born in Chicago, Illinois. That Baby Boomer, like many Baby Boomers, heard stories from his parents about life during the Depression. He heard stories about family members and friends helping each other to get through the difficult times. My father was one of the lucky ones; he worked during the Depression. Born to a Catholic, Italian family, it was the custom when a child was born to pick godparents for the new baby. My parents, in their time, would have 33 such godchildren. My parents were popular, had many friends, and were active in the community, which accounted for the many opportunities to be asked to take on this role. During tough times, people make decisions based on finances. The Depression era is what accounted for decisions of all kinds, perhaps even appointing a godparent for your child because that person had a job. President Roosevelt, who himself was born to great wealth, somehow had his pulse on the plight of the less fortunate. Maybe his own health issues accounted for his empathy toward the less fortunate. Regardless, it is clear that his policies were designed to improve the lives of Americans.

President Roosevelt had great respect for elder Americans; he thought it was the responsibility of the government to provide for Americans as they grew old. The people who voted for FDR, who listened to his message, supported his short-term and long-term visions for the country. The vast majority of Americans trusted him by all accounts during his time. He is the only President to serve more than two terms. He was a president whom the country supported, as spouses do in marriage, through the good times and the bad. Roosevelt believed in Social Security and its ability to pay for itself by Americans who supported the elders in exchange for the promise that, when their times came, they would be supported in the same time-honored tradition. Baby Boomers, along with their many other accomplishments, have changed all the rules. When

Social Security was started, the population, the age expectancy, and the years an individual would need Social Security, were far different. Baby Boomers have always been a boom population; from the time World War II ended, there was a growth in the population base. People are also living longer now, and Baby Boomers have longer life expectancies than those of the generations that came before.

This presents a crisis of proportion in our country. There are Baby Boomers who need the services and programs that Social Security and Medicare offer, but the fiscal issues are putting these programs in jeopardy. Baby Boomers want to live long lives, they want security, and they need help. There is a loneliness that falls over Baby Boomers sometimes, the feeling that nobody cares about their well-being, that they are a punching bag for breaking the country's budget. We need thinkers in Washington more than ever, and we need congressmen who take the job of serving the country seriously. We do not need ideologues, but problem solvers. We do not need separate agendas, but compromise for the greater good.

In the years of the Great Recession, what some term as the greatest crisis in this country since the Great Depression, I traveled this country. In the years 2009 through 2012, I spoke with, interviewed, and took the pulse of the Baby Boomer generation. As of this writing in 2013, the issues are the same as they were when I first found them. Baby Boomers are aging and are in a new realm of their lives. While they are holding on tightly to the ideas and ideals of their youth, they see the future. While they search for youth in a bottle or reach for their dreams, they also see reality. Baby Boomers have become practical, sensible, knowledgeable, and most of all, fundamental. The basics now rule the roost, and issues such as Social Security and Medicare are paramount. AARP lobbies for this: Baby Boomers follow the issues closely in the news, elections are fought over what we do with services versus fiscal management. This debate is healthy, and the resolve of the debate is necessary.

One thing is crystal clear: Social Security is not an entitlement that is talked about for Baby Boomers' futures, but part of the "here and now."

Overwhelmingly, Baby Boomers need Social Security and Medicare to be solidified for their generation, and for generations to come. President Roosevelt knew that Social Security was imperative and the right thing to do, President Johnson had a balanced vision of Medicare, and the future leaders of this country will benefit from that history lesson for the betterment of this country's future.

Chapter 10

Estate Planning

The discussion is a hard one, the moment Baby Boomers approach their children and tell them they would like to sit down, and talk to them about the plans for when they are gone. Most Baby Boomers report a reluctance to have the conversation, and an almost phobic reaction from the children. Somehow, it is hard for Baby Boomers to believe that they have reached that point in life. Baby Boomers are forever young. But the time has come on a great many scores in the game regarding this subject. Baby Boomers still recall how difficult it was for them when their parents began talking to them on the subject. The reaction was swift, a resounding "no," to the parents' attempt. This was because you wanted your parents to live forever. Their solid rock was needed in your life, and the mere mention of what would happen in the future was troubling to the soul.

My own experience started when I was in college. My parents called me while I was away at school and told me that I needed to come home. My father explained that my parents wanted to add my name to their bank account, just in case of an emergency. That was the first step. As the years would progress, they began talking to me about their plans regarding how they wanted things when they were gone. I remember being so upset, resisting the suggestion, and fighting my parents tooth and nail. I simply wanted to always recall my parents as they were and never think about what might be the alternative. Many Baby Boomers report that they have said to friends, "I don't know what I will do when my parents die, I won't be able to handle it." But as parents of Baby Boomers, the previous generation is steadfast on the subject.

My grandparents once took me to what they termed "Silent City" to help them pick their grave plots. It was a day that I would recall for the remainder of my life. My grandfather, through a family friend, had helped me obtain my first car, a blue Mustang, and while my parents were away, my grandmother, sometimes known in our family as "the Chief," called and said that she and my grandfather wanted to take me on an outing (and I would be driving). My Grandparents wanted their arrangements to be in order when their time came. My grandfather, a true gentleman, patiently explained that they thought it was "just the right thing to do," so as not to leave my parents, aunts, and uncles with anything to sort out once they were gone. On that day at the cemetery, I saw the plots that they picked out for themselves, watched them select a stone for their grave, and most importantly, heard their philosophy on Estate planning.

The basics of my grandparents became the mantra of my parents, for that is what families do – they learn from generation to generation, by family members watching what the others do as an example to follow with their own immediate families. Sisters learn from sisters, brothers from brothers, and the impact is felt on cousins. When my grandfather died in 1982, my grandmother tried living on her own at first, but quickly gave up her apartment and, upon the urging of my parents, uncle, and aunt, divided her time between three households. For about four months at a time, my grandmother alternated between living in my parents' home, my aunt's home, and my uncle's home. In each case, this decision of support was not made by any one individual, but was the consensus of an entire family. That is the key idea, for a family to have a good plan. The thing that I remember most about that situation is that there was no friction, no arguments, and no trouble. There were no fights within the family, or one sibling complaining that they were bearing the burden, while others in the family got off free of responsibility. Like a family should operate, there was cooperation.

When my grandmother passed away, my Uncle Joe, as executor, smoothly navigated the issues of dividing my grandmother's estate. Although my parents never specifically said so, the feeling that I always got was that they had learned from that experience. Assessing what went on with their parents' estate and the interaction with their siblings, they made decisions accordingly for their own estate. With a lawyer friend as an adviser, they worked through the issues and specified the way they wanted their estate to be divided. They sorted out the medical questions and the medical power of attorney, in case they were to become incapacitated. These are the kind of decisions that all parents of Baby Boomers go through. Most Baby Boomers have been witness to these proceedings. Looking back on it, in my case, the steps to planning my parent's estate and settling the estate were significant. It took me three months, working on it full time, to settle my parents estate. It was a major event in my life.

When I first learned that I was even the executor, I was puzzled. I had two older and accomplished brothers, who were very capable. My brothers lived in Chicago, with proximity to my parents, whereas I spent my entire adult life living away. But when I was younger, I had spent a considerable time living alone with my parents at home. My older brothers were already out of the house, educated, and married before I finished high school. Maybe as my parents aged, they were just comfortable because of the amount of time that I spent with them. After they retired, my parents would come and stay with me, a sort of vacation from Chicago. First in Boston and then in Seattle, they would come stay, enjoy the surroundings, and it is where we would have rich family discussion. It is also where they began to articulate their plans for their estate. There is something very interesting about the parents of Baby Boomers. They have a commonality about them: the need to have their affairs in order. It gives them a settled feeling. As a couple, my parents worked as a team, discussed matters of importance, and yes, planned their estate.

Although I miss my parents terribly, their organization and well thought out plans for their estate made it easier for me to step in when the time came to settle the estate. My parents, being my parents, put the added precaution to have my Uncle Joe guide my brothers and I, so that in death, there would be the same family harmony that existed when they were alive. My experience is the experience of many Baby Boomers. Many have had to plan and settle their parents' affairs. It is a tough job. Now though, the job is made more difficult because they have to take the same prescription that was once the cure for their parents, and use it to guide them as they lay out their own plans for their children. It is, as Baby Boomers confide, not easy.

Friday, April 15, 2011

Baby Boomers pursue Estate Planning

As Baby Boomers begin to age, they begin to think about leaving behind a legacy for their family. They want to make sure that the life that they have lived counted for something. Those who have been more fortunate might increase their exposure to charitable gift giving to a favorite school, hospital, or library. Many successful Baby Boomers have, in fact, turned to philanthropic endeavors. Most, though, are just concerned about providing for those left behind. It might begin with a living trust or putting a child's name on the bank account. It may continue with a complete listing of all assets. It may also include lists of important possessions within the home. Some seek guidance from an Estate planning professional, seek out a class, or the resources of organizations such as AARP. At some point in the process, one involves their accountant and lawyer. It is of utmost importance to have a will in testament. It is surprising how late to the party Baby Boomers have been to something so necessary, but that is changing. Experts advise to also communicate with your children what your intentions are. This is commonly referred to as having "the talk." It should be explicit, covering everything from the medical power of attorney to who gets the dishes. If a Baby Boomer chooses, as time goes on, to give things to those of their choosing while they are living, it should be recorded. Some Baby Boomers in these hard times are helping their children and that is a good thing that should not be forgotten. Also, some seek to help provide assistance for grandchildren's education, which is great, but do it while living or be explicit in the will. Sometimes, in families with multiple siblings, all financial conditions may not be the same. In these cases, if a parent seeks to aid a particular child, the intentions should be known and supported by the other siblings. As may also happen, one particular child may want something for sentimental purposes. That should be communicated to the parent while they are living, and the Baby Boomer may deal with the request presently or as part of the will. In the end, communication and sensitivity can go a long way to help the process.

Thursday, April 14, 2011

Baby Boomers and settling the Estate of a Parent

In most cases, when a couple has been married for a long time, as is the situation with the majority of Baby Boomers' parents, after the first parent dies the surviving parent becomes one. This is when two lives become a single entity. When the second parent passes, an estate then needs to be settled. Most people from the generation that preceded Baby Boomers are surprisingly diligent with their affairs and instructions on how they want things carried out after they have passed. For the most part, they have little debt because they came from a generation of hardship, so they paid as they went along. They, for the most part, leave a paid house, paid car, etc. If a parent had already sold those assets to live in a retirement community, those proceeds then are usually in cash or some form of a safe investment. Some choose to have a lawyer or family friend as an executor, but most turn that duty over to a child. When there is more than one sibling involved, and one child is designated, it can sometimes cause a rub. One brother or sister will wonder why one sibling was chosen over the other. Even in the best of families, and even with a clear cut "Will," tension can be created.

The executor has an important job to do, and that is to carry out the wishes of the parent. There must be an understanding and a great deal of communication to make sure that things get carried out without long-term ill effects amongst the siblings. It is a time when a family must come together, avoid self-interest, and remember the loving family that they were raised in. Above all, the wishes of the parents need to be respected. Most Baby Boomers learn from this situation and embark on Estate planning in their own lives, which is a very good idea. Some Baby Boomers report that families become stronger, and through the shared process, siblings use the occasion to realize that what is left of their family is each other. Sadly though, a rift, usually involving grandchildren, can sometimes have the reverse effect. As a senior citizen once told me, I have tried to do the right thing by leaving everything evenly amongst my children. It is my child's responsibility to provide for their children. In the end, family should count for something, and fighting between siblings who are the age of Baby Boomers over the wishes of their parents has serious consequences. It is so interesting, when you talk to Baby Boomers, that they all tell you how important family is, but yet very few have a good story to report on settling the Estate of parents. Let us hope that the Baby Boomers who are still lucky enough to have their parents, and who maintain a relationship with their siblings, will learn from their generational peers.

Thursday, February 23, 2012

Excerpts from: Heard On the Street

John W. just retired as a school teacher in Chicago. He and his wife raised one daughter in the Western suburb of Naperville, IL. Here is what he had to say: "I considered myself a blue collar, roll-up-the-sleeves teacher. That is all I ever wanted to be. I taught school on the West side, not in a good neighborhood. I loved the students. They were eighth graders; you can make an impact on them at that age. I was tough but fair. I insisted on interaction with the parents. I miss teaching. Retirement comes upon you," he went on to say. "One day, you are caring for your parents, the next day you see your daughter treating you like what you remember you did with your own parents."

John's memory of being the dutiful son remains etched in his conscious. He finds the symmetry of his daughter now caring for him as part of the family tree. Listening to John speak, one can gather that his example of caring for his parents was a positive example for his daughter. Perhaps that is why she picks up the flag.

John is also acutely aware of the fact that it is now the Baby Boomer's time to be concerned about the issues of Estate planning, following the example set by their own parents. That is why John and his wife have recently sat down with their daughter to outline their wishes for how they would like their estate settled when the time comes.

Summary – Chapter 10

Estate planning

In late June of 2004, and in the midst of wrapping up my assignment of settling my parent's estate, I made a trip to Savannah, Georgia. My best friend's parents had retired there. They are like family to me. They thought that it would be a good idea if we were together during this difficult time. My buddy and his wife came from Oregon, and we all stayed at his parents' house. I had made the trip from Chicago where I had been staying at my parents' home in suburban Chicago. I was on the last lap, the selling of the house. By this time, my parents' home had been broken up, their wishes accomplished, and together, my brothers and I were making sense of life with both my parents gone, buried, and their affairs settled.

While in Georgia, especially on the first night, we spoke about my parents, the kind of people they were, and the brilliance of their estate planning. What I discovered, from discussing the situation, was how much I had learned about the process. I learned what was involved and the importance of why my parents wanted to get their estate affairs in order. The experience of working on my parents' estate paid further dividends when I began traveling and talking to other Baby Boomers about this topic. I learned also, that this had become a major focus for organizations, like AARP, who were trying to give advice to seniors on estate planning. I began to learn about Baby Boomers meeting with lawyers, insurance companies, and financial planners, about their own estates. They were beginning the process of getting their own house in order. It is interesting that, when your parents pass away, you seem to cross over into a new dimension. It was like when I was starting my first day of college, and my dad and older brother had brought me to campus, we had unloaded my belongings in the dorm room, and I had walked them to the car. My dad then gave me the familiar speech that many Baby Boomer men have also heard. He said, "I drop you off as a boy, when you finish, I expect you to finish as a man." Sobering words, at the time, but like all other words of wisdom, it stays with you. Just like settling the estate when your remaining parent passes. The mere facts of the case are indisputable.

What I believe happens is that once Baby Boomers experience this realization, they begin to focus more on their own planning process. They hear stories from friends, who are lucky enough to still have their parents. They talk of their parents being focused on the end game. They start to examine their own situation, and begin the process of the ultimate plan. A Baby Boomer lawyer, who I recently spoke to, thinks that this process is essential. Baby Boomers are being encouraged to put wills and trusts in order. They are encouraged to think about the remainder of their lives, their families, and leaving things in order for when they are gone. It is an interesting dichotomy. Baby Boomers are so involved with health and wellness, so involved with finding the fountain of youth, and yet, meanwhile, they have to take on the task of leaving clear instructions for something they hope is in the far distant future – the settling of their estate. It is true that many Baby Boomers are very focused on the caring for elderly parents and others are grieving for the loss of their parents. We examine both of those topics in other chapters of this book. This chapter focused on two aspects that are extensions of what happens when the estate of the parents needs to be settled, and the process Baby Boomers go through to then make the transference from their parents' affairs to their own.

I feel for Baby Boomers who have, in a heartfelt way, discussed the pain that they have when they are going through their parents' clothes, having an estate sale, or attending the closing on the sale of what was once your family home. It is a sad gut wrenching feeling, when you look up one day, and know that things will never be the same. Life as you always knew it has forever changed. That life is now different, that call to your parents, is no more. It is also interesting when you talk to parents of Baby Boomers, and see the process of their thought pattern. They are focused on the organization of their affairs, which they hope will someday bring about the settling of "The Will." Parents of Baby Boomers, for the most part, I have found, want to do the right thing, by their Baby Boomer Children. While all families are different, and the wishes of Baby Boomer parents are all different, there is common ground. There is a need to be fair and open, and a true desire that after they are gone, the family will continue with a sense of togetherness. They want very much that their final wishes contribute to that end result.

My father died in April of 2004, and I remember it as if it were yesterday. I had just finished an important meeting and I checked my voice mail, only to hear the words of my very sad brother, delivering the news that my father had passed away. My mother had preceded my dad in death. My father was lost after her death. He, at best, had just survived, until he failed himself. The procedure is what a great many of Baby Boomers experience, and we explore the grief aspect in another part of this book. But, after the funeral, I returned to Boston, where I was living, and made arrangements to spend an extended period of time in Chicago, doing what would become the most important job and task that I ever faced – settling my parent's estate. In May, I arrived in Chicago and stayed until July. When the time was completed and the legal process ended, the memory of that experience was lasting. While my example is just one story, it is the saga of a great many Baby Boomers, who have to do the same. It is not easy; the all-encompassing and procedurally complex agenda is exhausting. As the years have passed, and my journey with my own family turned into council to other Baby Boomers, I've thought about three things: the preparation that my parents did, the research that I did to become an effective executor of their estate, and the cooperation needed in a family to bring your parents affairs to closure.

In retrospect, when I finished the settling of my parents' estate, I was not ready to face my own affairs, and quite frankly, my own day-to-day life. That is why I so admire Baby Boomers who have turned their parents' example into something workable for their own lives and the lives of their children. Baby Boomers have shown the willingness to plan for the future. Baby Boomers would universally agree that it is time for them to be thinking about and planning their own estate while they remember the wishes of their parents.

Chapter 11

Marriage, Family, and Baby Boomers Dating

When my parents celebrated their 50th Wedding Anniversary, it was a celebration. It was a party that, at the heart of renewed vows, was everything that we stood for and respected. It was about family coming together, longtime friends gathering, and most of all, the symbol of what commitment can mean to a couple. My grandparents also had a 50th Anniversary party, and at my Aunt Evie and Uncle Herb's 50th, my Uncle Joe highlighted in his speech to the crowd the long tradition that they were following. Since that party, my Uncle Joe and Aunt Fran have shared the celebration of their own 50th Anniversary.

Having stood up, as a young man, for my brother Ray's wedding when he married my sister-in-law Sandy, I will see some day in the not too distant future, another generation following that same tradition. Baby Boomers in many families have been witness to such moments as described in my family. They wear their formal clothes to such events, admire the contract of time, and do some degree of soul searching. Some, like my best friends, reflected on the success of their own marriage and their wonderful two boys while they sat in the church in Savannah, Georgia, watching the minister lead a celebration of my friends's parents' 50 happy years together. I was sitting next to them at the time, and I was going through my own reflections, some of which mirror another perspective of Baby Boomers, the feeling that "this may never happen to me." This thought pattern in the minds of Baby Boomers comes about from a segment of the Baby Boomer generation, who either did not find their "one and only," or have lived through divorce. What it brings about in today's Baby Boomer population is a memory of their parents' generation, when more couples stayed together and marriage was thought of as an institution. Another thing this brings to mind is the contrast between Baby Boomers whose long marriages resemble those of their parents, and Baby Boomers who are still looking for that special person.

This makes for an interesting dichotomy on the social contract. You have a friend calling another friend, and these two Baby Boomers, who are the best of friends, are having a discussion centered on marriage. One friend details the marriage of his 28 year old son; the second friend talks of the special woman whom he is engaged to and who finally completes his life. Baby Boomers are a hopeful lot – most Baby Boomers who are single still believe, and rightly so, that there is a special someone out there for them. Marketers have seen the trend, and every day on television, you will see a commercial about an online dating program, targeted at Baby Boomers.

Baby Boomers, who as a group are trying to redefine age, display some interesting patterns when it comes to finding that special someone. In some ways, Baby Boomers have not aged and are conducting themselves as if they are in high school, even experiencing that tingling feeling that goes with the prospect of "the date." But, in another way, there are some major differences. For Baby Boomers, dating at this stage of life is influenced by a lifetime of experiences that are packaged into who they are at this point. Many Baby Boomers report a sense of enthusiasm for dating at this stage of life; as individuals, they feel that they know themselves better and are aware of their priorities, which translates to better communication with a future spouse. That is also of key importance because most Baby Boomers who are dating seek long-term companionship. This is because they are not in high school anymore and they are very focused on aging, the years ahead, and living a quality life. Ideally, that includes a spouse.

Baby Boomers dream of the "fairy tale." They do not want to go to their grave with regrets. They want a partner in life. They want to travel and have someone to enjoy the time and places with. They simply want a special person to share their life with, for being alone, according to some Baby Boomers, is "hard to do." But make no mistake, Baby Boomers don't want just anybody. This is not a quest for a warm body. They want a "love that is forever after." Some would denote it as the difference between "always" and "sometimes."

I remember talking to a Baby Boomer a couple of years back on this subject. It was a woman who used to come to the Starbucks in Del Mar, California each night. She was a nice woman, an intelligent woman. She was a woman of substance, who had started a prosperous business after the break up with her husband. She was quick to say that she had her priorities in order. First, the relationship with her 20-something daughter was at the top of the list. Second, the care and feeding of her business enterprise had meaning. She had started the business, was proud of it, and it meant something to her. Third, she wanted to be a good friend, especially to those special girl friends who stuck by her during the time that she was going through her divorce. She had no hard feelings toward her former husband, but because she was a woman with perspective, she shared that she now realizes, in retrospect, that he was not the right person for her to have been married to.

She also revealed some further perspective on how being a member of the Baby Boomer generation influenced her situation. She commented that, when she was in college, she was not as interested in finding "the one" as in being "the one." She was more focused on making sure she would have all the same work opportunities as men. Looking back, she felt that perhaps it kept her from finding a "nice guy" because her ideas were about work success and not about, as her mother would say, "being taken care of by a man." She was, by all accounts, someone who dated, but "Cinderella" was not the goal; instead, "Working Girl" was the objective. But she has come to a conclusion that at this stage of life, "what is life, if you don't have someone to share it with?" This is the thought pattern of many Baby Boomers.

Today there are many Baby Boomers who have experienced the joy of marriage, and perhaps have raised children and are now navigating being grandparents. There are the Baby Boomers who have experienced a second marriage, and for whom blended families and step-children are in the equation. Another group consists of the Baby Boomers who are seeking that special person to bring a wonderful addition to their life.

The dynamic is so much fun to observe. Whereas thirty years ago, a "couples' party" hosted in a home would consist of several married couples, today's party with people of a similar age includes an eclectic group. Couples coming to such a party today run the gamut of types of relationships, from long-time married couples, to couples who are just starting to date, mixed in with married couples who are making step-families work. Baby Boomers who over the years have been, like no other generation, so hard to predict, and whose constant was change, have once again started again.

The generation that gave new meaning to dating, experimentation, seeing other people, and going to singles bars, has traded "Annie Hall" for the "Sound of Music." Baby Boomers have found the meaning of words, like "partnership," "team," and "being a unit." Baby Boomers now are practicing what their parents did, which they previously did not want to be a part of. Moreover, they have now embraced the sanctity of "home life."

Thursday, January 5, 2012

An Affair of the Heart

Baby Boomers, do you remember the movie "An Affair to Remember," with Cary Grant and Deborah Kerr? It is sometimes remembered by Baby Boomers because of its mention in the movie "Sleepless in Seattle." The premise of the movie is that a couple meets and falls in love, but complications exist such that they cannot act upon their feelings. Thus, they agree to meet six months later at the top of the Empire State building if the feelings were real and the entanglements released. If you have not seen it in a while, or ever, do rent it, especially if you have a significant other in your life.

Why does this come up today in the world of Baby Boomers? Well, simply because Baby Boomers are indeed, according to data, finding love late in life. The spark, the feelings, and the desire is not reserved for 18 – 49 year olds as the demographic experts would like you to believe. Why is this happening? The simple answer is that a lot of Baby Boomers are single at this stage of life. The more complicated reason is that it has taken a long time for Baby Boomers to figure out who they are, and now they are in a better position to be more sharing, caring, and giving.

Take John, a professor from Lake Tahoe. He is, for all practical purposes, a fine man. He is smart, and successful in his profession, but he is also painfully shy. He masks it with intelligent conversation, and a remoteness that adds mystery. He is a wonderful single father of a well-adjusted teenage boy. He is ready for a relationship in his life, whereas during his first marriage, he was a bit uncomfortable. This was not only due to being self-conscious, but also perhaps because he did not have the right partner. You see, many of our generation married the wrong people, and before you knew it, children came along and years passed. This is typical of the now single Baby Boomers. But there are other factors as well; for example, it is easier to date when you have resources. When you are twenty one, you can get by, but at fifty five, resources can give you a bit more confidence. When you are young and starting out, things such as building careers and having children sometimes take the place of romance. As many Baby Boomers feel deep down, there was a stage of life, when getting ahead was everything. But now, a little older and a little wiser, the new mantra is "can I find happiness before it is too late?" To many Baby Boomers, the credo is "happiness is still in reach."

So when John met Pat, introduction courtesy of a friend, he liked her immediately. As it turns out, she likes him too. His qualities, such as a quiet reserve, a pleasant smile, and a caring soul, agree with Pat. She asked him to call her. He did so, and his friend was supportive, no different from your old college roommate cheering for you back in college. The excitement of the dating process agrees with John, he is happier for it; the anticipation of life is in his corner. The people around him notice the excitement in his voice when he speaks of Pat. Even total strangers just observing him and his friend talk about Pat can see the importance of this dating process.

John is but one example of stories that could be told. Baby Boomers, as has been written many times in this space, just see life differently than their parents and grandparents did at this same age. It is like Baby Boomers have not grown up, in the best sense of the subject matter. This is not about being mature or "all grown up." It is about defying the pundit who cries out "you can't have that anymore." This certainly comes into play when it comes to "An Affair of the Heart." Some Baby Boomers will tell you they never have been happier. Some will tell you that it is not about being young again, but about having enough courage to believe that happiness still awaits you. This is not a story about the 55 year old rich old guy with a Bentley, seeking the young blond for a trophy wife. This is a story about the 55 year old who believes love has eluded him thus far, and who hopes to find it before it is too late. It is a story about the feeling one still gets on a date that reminds you that you are alive. It is a story about what you feel when his or her name shows up in your email inbox. It is the story like in the movie, "An Affair to Remember," of the experience of that relationship, the meeting, the transition to friendship, and then to more than a friend, to – well, you know the rest. It is out there for all of us, even when you are the age of Baby Boomers. Some may read this and think the story that has been related is just simply about relationships at a later stage of life. While that is a major part of the theme, the greater thesis is that when it comes to relationships, there is a diverse set of possible situations facing Baby Boomers in the 21st Century.

March 29, 2012

The Meaning of Being a Couple

For two years, I traveled the country interviewing Baby Boomers – hundreds of formal sessions and many more informal conversations. It was a fun experience, but a great learning one as well. Of all the subjects discussed, everything from the television of our youth, or starting a second career, to caring for an elderly parent, no topic received more air time than the one that we will cover now. There was a great deal communicated about the meaning of being a couple. There was the woman who has been with a partner for many years but never walked down the church steps. There was the husband who has been married since 1978. There was the Baby Boomer man finding love late in life. These are just three of many examples representing different types of Baby Boomer couples that I encountered during my travels.

Let me share three major categories that came up in all conversations. The first is that many couples wish they had talked more before they said, "I do." They wish that they would have talked about the shared vision of the lives that they wanted to live. They wish that they would have discussed the basics, like money, politics, and religion. Sometimes, when the passion fades into the background, couples need to be on the same page to live as a team. It is amazing how many couples even reported not talking about children, career paths, and roles.

Second, many couples do not know, or have not defined, what a couple means. They have a view in their own mind, but somehow have failed to communicate it to the other person. One husband related that his wife, who he said he loves more than anything, shares more about their relationship with her best girlfriend than she does with him. Another man shared that the woman that he loves just assumes he should know things. A woman said, "My husband doesn't seem to do anything sweet for me anymore." Another couple, a professional couple, complained separately that the other person is so busy with their work that neither seems to have time for the other. A bad sign is when you need to schedule time together.

Ask Baby Boomers to define the ideal, and the term "team work" comes up over and over – sharing in thoughts, actions, and responsibilities. This could include a Baby Boomer woman asking her mate about how to handle critical issues within her family. It could be about the shared responsibility of doing things around the house, so one or the other does not seem overwhelmed. It could mean doing what the other person is interested in, just to be together. A man who loves baseball can go to the symphony, and his wife can sit next to her "favorite guy" and watch a few innings of the World Series, and perhaps make a few snacks.

So, that brings us to the third major point, and that is making sure that the person in your life knows that they are important to you. Men will tell their buddies in the tennis locker room, "I wish she would let me know that I am important to her." You see, a person in a relationship feels vulnerable and insecure. Why? Because they care so much. A woman, excited about something new that she has started that may result in extra income for her family, cannot understand why the husband resents her excitement. Why? Because he has not been made a part of it. The thinking of "we" versus the thinking of "I" should always be the default position.

Baby Boomers, maybe more than any other generation, are romantics at heart. The Greatest Generation tended to be more stoic in their relationship actions. One could say that "the meaning of being a couple" has to do with the thought pattern that the one that you love is so important to you, that you think of that other person before yourself.

Sunday, February 26, 2012

In Sickness and In Health

Baby Boomers, this is a personal story and it deserves your consideration. Let me begin with a question: as a Baby Boomer, do you have uncles and aunts that you respect? Well, your faithful scribe does. It is sad to say that my parents have passed and I miss them greatly. One of the reasons that I can identify with Baby Boomers who are caring for elderly parents, dealing with the loss of their parents, and having to settle an Estate is because I have lived it myself. What I have learned as a result is to never forget the ones who have been lost, and never lose sight of the loved ones you still have. That is why I take to this space to write about an aunt and uncle who are standing by the side of a spouse of more than 50 years. My aunt is very accomplished in her own right with a musical resume of performance and classical training, and is now doing charity work to raise funds so the next generation of young people studying music will have opportunities. Amidst all of this, she has managed a 55-year marriage of love and understanding. Her husband was one of the most successful attorneys in the country, a brilliant man, who also gave lectures and wrote books. He was known for having a steel trap mind. Well, now the trap door has begun to close, as her husband has early stages of Alzheimer's. There is no complaining or "woe is me" involved. No, it is a time of support, standing by your man, in sickness and in health.

There is a similar story going on with another uncle, the above described aunt's brother. He spent his entire life as a leading doctor. He never rested on his laurels. He always attended medical conferences to stay up-to-date and his patients always knew he cared, including his newest patient, his wife of fifty years. He has been by her side through operations, pathology reports, and America's heartbreak, cancer. For years, he walked the halls of hospitals comforting families in pain. Now, he does that with his sons and daughters, remaining strong, and being by the side of his wife. He knew what the vow "in sickness and in health" meant.

The common theme of the above stories applies to the families of many Baby Boomers. As Baby Boomers age, they will notice a change in their extended family. The smiles will still be there. The excitement to see you will still be pronounced, but Baby Boomers will indeed see change and have to adjust. These aunts and uncles become the priority. Your exciting news will have to take a back seat to the life decisions being made for the good of extending the quality of life. But there is something else going on here as well. You have the opportunity to observe and learn from real life examples, where the actions of family members reflect the values with which you were raised. When life is going well, when people have their health, and when security is never in doubt, the vows of matrimony are a bit easier. But when the trouble starts, and the health issues and the care giving begin, will the vow be just words, or will it include actions?

Well, for one aunt and one uncle of one Baby Boomer, "in sickness and in health" is playing out in living color in the program of life.

Saturday, March 17, 2012

Love Letters

Many Baby Boomers are fans of American history. One of their favorite books in recent years was by David McCullough on John Adams. Later, PBS did a mini-series based on the book. While Mr. McCullough did exhaustive research for the book, his main source was the letters between John Adams and his dear wife, Abigail. Over the years through the Revolution, and later while he was representing our country in Europe, John Adams had to be away from the person that he loved most, his wife Abigail. It is one of the great love stories in history. Here is evidence: she saved every one of his letters. What man would not want to have a partner in life like that? Further, she saved the ones that she sent to him, just in case they never reached him. She would later be able to share her love with him. Some historians argue that, because Abigail was so brilliant, and because the letters included communication about the events of the time, she probably also had in mind that she was also recording history. David McCullough understood this, which is one reason why he is so respected both as an author and a historian. The romantic can read his book for the love story, the historian can read his book for an accurate portrayal of our county's development, and the biography buff can gain new appreciation for one of the great historical figures in this country's history.

No greater authority than Thomas Jefferson recognized the value of John Adams. Jefferson and Adams rekindled their friendship and wrote each other repeatedly until they both came to death, ironically, on the same day. But many who love Jefferson, myself included, respect his recognition that this country is what it is thanks largely to the contributions of this man from Massachusetts, John Adams. The late Senator Ted Kennedy also did his part to make John Adams visible in our psyche. Senator Kennedy would often lament how someone like John Adams could do so much, and yet receive so little credit.

There is a comedian, George Baker, who travels the country now and does a wonderful one-man John Adams play. He begins by asking the audience how many have been to Washington D.C., our nation's Capital. Many raise their hands. He then asks, "Did you see the Washington Monument?" They all nod. He then asks, "Did you see the Jefferson Memorial?" They again nod. Then he asks, "Did you like the Adam's Memorial?" Of course, the crowd looks puzzled and embarrassed. The comedian then laughs and says, "They haven't built it yet, but I am still hoping." In that same show, George Baker, portraying John Adams, begins by mentioning that Abigail sends her best. He speaks of her with such pride, just like the real John Adams must have done about the love of his life.

The readers of this column are likely wondering why this topic was taken up today. Well, a Baby Boomer man recently found out that his own Abigail Adams has saved every one of his emails. Like John and Abigail Adams, our Baby Boomer couple has to spend time apart, so they email, share, talk, and have conversations electronically. They share their hopes and dreams. They always speak of missing each other. Perhaps one could say that the emails saved, printed out, stapled together and placed in a folder, has the same romance of those letters of the 18th and 19th century. The Baby Boomer man is every bit as "in love" as John Adams was with Abigail. The woman Baby Boomer, it can be argued, is every bit as smart as Abigail Adams was. So let us conclude, love letters are good in any century.

Sunday, February 12, 2012

Fruit and Donuts

Oh, those cute Baby Boomer couples, "courting proper" and all that. This is a fun way of introducing you to a Baby Boomer couple who met last summer, and who have become serious recently. This story will be interesting for three reasons: one, it is the story of love, and with Valentine's Day coming up, you can never get enough romance. Second, the story is unusual in this respect: neither party has been married. Third, it is a turn-back-the-clock courtship. If one would not know better, the year is 1962 instead of 2012.

How did this come about that two people could arrive at this stage, free of a past? Well, that might not be the right characterization, in retrospect. They had dated people in their lives - after all, they have not each been living in a monastery. Truth be told, this couple that we are calling for this writing "fruit and donuts" (and will explain) never had, up to this point in time, met the right person. Many Baby Boomers can relate to that. But why fruit and donuts? She (fruit) is a distance runner, a health conscious woman. He (donut), although a former athlete, being fit and working out regularly, loves to eat. His family culture growing up where food, family, and Sunday dinner was part of a lifestyle… well, let's just say he would prefer a donut to an apple. They are a fun couple to watch ordering dinner out on Friday night, date night.

They have a lot in common, these two. They are both highly educated and come from good and loving families. They both have had successful careers. Both see those careers continuing and being a high priority. Neither feels guilty about not having children, although they did not make a decision in life not to have them. Chalk it up to "circumstances." What is most important, though, is that timing is this couples' ally. They are both ready in life to embark on a serious relationship. They would often see each other early in the mornings when she would make her morning run. This is how they met. He of the same body clock, would go for his walk, then sit on a bench overlooking the Pacific Ocean, where he would read his newspaper. Soon, he would discover the "fruit" of his discovery. Soon, it went from a wave, to a "hello," to a conversation, to a walk, to coffee on the weekend. You get to know someone pretty well, seeing them every day. The conversations were rich, thoughtful and both people seemed to have a kindness and consideration about them.

Both began to look forward to the new day. In fact, for our man, who – to show a bit of play on words, could be called Dunkin (come on, Baby Boomers! Wake up! You know, like Dunkin Donuts, the coffee and donut chain) – well, he began to believe that this was the girl for him. This is not a couple that will think living together is equal to marriage. This is a couple where family and friends are important, so they will make the rounds to visit before the ultimate course of action is served. These are two proper individuals who are "courting proper" as the old timers would say. It is refreshing, really. Dates are something to look forward to. Time together is savored. Communication and compassion are not buzz words. Telling their loved ones about this new person in their life does not come with caution signs. And the loved ones, the family and best friends, who have stood by these two people all these years, could not be happier. So on Valentine's Day, this couple will go for coffee – she will have fruit with her coffee and her favorite guy... well, let us just say, he will not be having fruit. Yes, maybe a donut.

January 26, 2012

The Woman from Columbus

I received an interesting email from a reader the other day. He wanted to know about the woman from Columbus, who was mentioned toward the end of the Christmas Post-Script story. For readers unfamiliar, the line about her from the Baby Boomer was, "All I want for Christmas is you." This was a part of a description of a Baby Boomer who had found love upon turning 56 years of age. Well that couple is going strong, navigating the waters of an adult relationship. The man, before meeting this wonderful woman, had lost his way. Loss of important people in his life, had given him the blues, if not bordering on depression. Life was an existence, a chore, when every step is like walking in cement. The thirst for life had long since left our Baby Boomer, but then one day, as she ran by on her morning run, it was like a candle was lit in the dark dreary room.

This is the story of not just romance, or a kindle of the spirit. It is not just the story of renewal or redemption. But further, it is the story of brick and mortar of a man rebuilding his life because he is motivated to do so. It is in him, as our Baby Boomer is highly educated, with a successful resume. His skills are second to none, albeit rusty, but easily recalled. The wine still flows from the smoothness of the intellect. What was missing was motivation – the reason to get up in the morning. But now he wants to make good again. When he is presented to his female companion's family, he wants to show that he is worthy of her. She is bright and well respected in her field. The old timers would say, "She is no fly by night girl." She comes from a family of acumen. Her father is a highly decorated professor, and her mother a well-respected researcher. Her family is from Columbus, hence the title. But the title is also a metaphor for the objective. You see, in this relationship, all the man can do is control what he can control. So he needs to work hard and make something of himself. Living on past glory is out of the question. And as it has been known, a relationship does not survive on romance forever. So at 56, a Baby Boomer acts as if he is 26, building that career again, building a business in fact, because he has an incentive: "a woman from Columbus."

Tuesday, November 22, 2011

Communication between Men and Women

The inspiration for this column comes from a book titled "Keys to the Kingdom," by Alison A. Armstrong. Ms. Armstrong is the creator of the workshop "Celebrating Men, Satisfying Women." The book is an outgrowth of the many hours of seminar work, and seeks to help men and women communicate better with each other. She is credited with a study of the behavior of men, and has helped women to benefit from the understanding.

Do men and women communicate differently? Does communication affect a relationship? Are there ways that effective communication can have a positive impact on the way men and women function in the world together? Is lack of communication the cause of Baby Boomer couples breaking up after years of marriage? Is communication between men and women holding Baby Boomers back from relationships at this stage of life? These are the questions on the minds of Baby Boomers, regarding this subject matter.

What was your reaction when Al Gore and his longtime wife and political advocate Tipper Gore called it quits? This was a couple who seemed to have it all and had been through so much together. We were led to believe that they were soul mates and that their love resulted in the raising of a wonderful family. Their teamwork was instrumental in Al Gore's career. They were destined for a lifelong partnership. They even, we were told, survived the heartbreak of the 2000 election. Yet, there was the news report that the couple seemed to have grown apart. How and why does this happen? Most communication experts say the couple stopped being a partnership.

The Gores, like The Clintons, are Baby Boomers. In 1992, when the two couples raised their hands in the air at the Democratic convention in anticipation of Bill Clinton's run for President and Gore's for Vice President, who, if they were betting, would have thought that in 2011, Bill and Hillary would still be married while Al and Tipper would be divorced? Further, who would have thought that the Gore's would become emblematic of relationship problems that fellow Baby Boomers face, such as growing apart, loss of partnership, and communication issues. But this is what happened, for after the Gores went public, the story of the issue amongst Baby Boomers became a news item. According to Ms. Armstrong, men and women are wired differently. They come at things from opposite directions. Her book is very interesting, for instead of sounding like a textbook, it reads more like a story with two women having a conversation with their husbands. It becomes clear that she is an advocate of men and women operating like partners. She believes that it is important for men and women to try to understand each other, and work at communicating their points of view, while listening to each other.

They must work at nonverbal as well as verbal signals. Each must understand where the other one is in their life and what is important to them. They must both also understand the value of compromise. Ms. Armstrong sometimes goes as far to suggest that a man can become the enemy when the man fails to communicate with a woman properly. With that mindset, it is hard for men and women to find common ground. She is a proponent of women taking the time to understand men, the stages of life that they go through, and the changes that happen with age and circumstances. A man must, above all, be an effective listener, ask good questions, and be very good at follow-up, based on what he is told. While Alison Armstrong is most adept at dealing with married couples, a great many of her tools can work for Baby Boomers, who for whatever reason, find themselves single. The art of asking good questions, listening closely, observing body language, and watching for facial expressions are crucial to relationships. These simple basics can go a long way toward the art of becoming a couple, or staying a couple.

One further note, men and women give off signals of what is important to them, and the key is to recognize the cue the opposite sex is giving you. Most relationship experts, communication experts, or the man on the street will tell you the secret to men and women in relationships, or in everyday life, is communication. Why, armed with that knowledge, do so few put it into practice?

Friday, November 4, 2011

Baby Boomers and Step-children

Baby Boomers, more than any generation past or present, have step-children as a part of the mix. For many reasons not to be articulated in this column, Baby Boomers married and some later divorced. While step-children have come about in a limited sense through a parent remarrying after the death of their spouse, in most cases stepchildren are the result of parents divorcing and later entering new marriages. What makes this topic relevant for today's Baby Boomer environment is that with age, comes evaluation. Second, if you were a Baby Boomer who happened to fall in love with someone who already had children, and you and your spouse do not have additional children together, the step-children in fact represent "the children" at this age and stage. What does that mean? As Baby Boomers get older, they think about such things as, "Who might care for me down the road?" They think about grandchildren that perhaps could supply love and caring in coming years. But most importantly, all Baby Boomers want to think that their life counted for something, and what could be a better representation of that than people you had an impact on when they were growing up, and who have now grown into adults.

Further complications to the subject arise when, for example, your wife dies, and she was the mother to the girls who you first got to know as children. What makes this situation difficult is that when the bond is gone, you wonder what sort of relationship will continue with those girls. You feel love for them, their life has meaning to you, but they are not technically your children, even though they may feel that way to you. What the step-children do not understand is that, as an aging Baby Boomer, you need them more than ever. You need the connection, you need to review the memories, you need to feel loved, no different than a biological parent would. But if you think raising those children was a challenge, wait until you try to convince them to feel something for you at this stage if it was never in their hearts in the first place.

Here is the issue – you are 30 and you meet someone who becomes the love of your life. For a time, there is bliss, but then comes the time when you have to meet the children. So it begins the life of unorthodox, children are thrust upon you, domestic life becomes the norm, and a lifestyle all so foreign is now part of the routine. Time passes, and you learn to love them, while sometimes not liking them. They are the source of your changed dreams. They are the source of changed plans. They are the ones that remind you, maybe not with words, but actions, that you are not their father. But you love their mother, there will be no other person in your life, and you are committed to a woman with two daughters. The mother spends a lifetime convincing you that the girls love and care for you, but in your heart, you know better. But you endure and you find a way to make your life work, complex as it may be. You have career ambition that you must satisfy and your well-being calls for not being all consumed by the step-family. While you may consult the head of the Step-Family Association of America, you know that for your life to be a success, there are times you must be away from the day to day actions of the environment. Surprisingly, the woman who loves you understands.

There is also another factor that plays out in the dynamic. That is resentment. That time when you got that big promotion and it was a chance to move to another city, with the opportunity for a better life, only to have the people in control, the kids, say "no," not to mention the resentment caused by the influence of the biological father. The list can grow from there, but you see when step-children look at you, even today, they see from the prism of what they remember as a little girl. They do not grow up and say, "I am sorry you did not become the CEO of the Fortune 500 Company because we would not move to xyz city"; they only look at the Red Sox game that you failed to take them to because of the hurt you had inside, as both experiences happened the same week. They saw absence, while you saw reaching your goals. So you can imagine now, with all that baggage, how seemingly impossible it is to make it work in 2011. They constitute children to you, you need them, and they do not need you. To further complicate matters, the love of your life is gone, she understood you, and she knew how to make it work between you. She knew how to balance the children as the number one priority, and love you too.

Baby Boomers want it all to work out. They want on occasion to visit their children, see the grandchildren, and biology has nothing to do with it. The step-children must understand, after all, who else have they known like this person for 25 years? Who else has played such a role that has helped them turn out as they have? Who else was in their mother's ear and had a vision for their education and life? The mother herself even acknowledged the contribution. This composite story is the story of a lot of Baby Boomers. But there are some Baby Boomers who report that their relationship with their step-children is excellent. Some step-children even show the proper respect. But sadly, most Baby Boomers report that they have never even gotten a card, not once in their life, for Father's Day.

When it concerns the present day Baby Boomer step-parent with stepchildren who have grown into adults by now, it sometimes helps to adopt the attitude of "expect little and hope to be surprised." Follow them on Facebook, enjoy the pictures posted. Write often via email, but do not check your inbox every 20 minutes expecting a response. Let the step-children know that you love them, but do not make them feel obligated to come visit. Wish them a Happy Thanksgiving, but do not ever expect an invitation from them. You, as a Baby Boomer, need to just worry about doing the right thing yourself, keep an eye on them, and comment when you think they are off track, even at risk of them not liking you. Remember it is just like it once was, and your responsibility is for their well-being, for that is what being a parent is all about.

Always hold out hope for the day they call, write, or invite you to their home. Sometimes, it does happen.

Wednesday, October 5, 2011

Second Time Around

There are so many reasons to visit the Palm Springs Area. There is golf and tennis. There are the resorts, the restaurants, and the Arts. People who retire there also have the benefit of outstanding health care. One key example is the Eisenhower Medical Center. While the Betty Ford Clinic gets the headlines, a little known fact is that Eisenhower is also host to a world class Bereavement Center. While on a smaller scale than its other treatment areas at the hospital, nonetheless, it helps numerous people cope with loss. Its key attribute is the group session, where you find out, if you attend, that the feelings you are going through are shared by others. This is especially true when it comes to losing a spouse.

A woman originally from Oregon sought the council of the Director of the Program when she lost her husband. After a time, she would go once a week, sitting in a room with like-minded people. She will tell you that it made a significance difference in her life. Like others who have lost a spouse, you never forget your mate, but for Baby Boomers, this type of counseling does help you to move forward. Baby Boomers having loved and lost is an ever growing dynamic in the Baby Boomers' world.

What is also part of the case study is the starting over process, which then includes the possibility of meeting someone new. For some Baby Boomers, there has been the experience of finding love the second time around. Baby Boomers report, that when the bolt of lightning hits the second time, it is initially a complex feeling. On the one hand, it is filled with a rush of adrenaline – that feeling that only attraction can provide. But also there is guilt, because one wonders if they are being disloyal to the spouse that is gone. Certainly this is a worthy topic for Baby Boomers, for if you lose your spouse in your 50s or 60s, for example, the typical Baby Boomer still feels young enough to contemplate a future with the assumption that they have many years of life ahead of them. Many would prefer to not live out those years alone.

Some Baby Boomers speak of actually seeking avenues in which to meet possible mates. But for some, it just happens, and those cases may be the most interesting. It is rather significant to hear a Baby Boomer of 55 talk about butterflies on a date, buying flowers, or that "can't wait to see her" feeling. Baby Boomers, as a generation, are young at heart. They look in the mirror and see what they want to see. They are not their grandparents, or for that matter, their parents. They expect to be active until late in life, and expect the Golden Years to be productive. A Baby Boomer will tell you people are living longer, and living differently. So, it makes sense then that approaching love the second time around would fit into that thinking. A Baby Boomer who likes to read and has found attraction to a librarian finds himself taking out a lot of books. A Baby Boomer who runs into someone the same time each morning in the coffee shop cannot wait for tomorrow morning to come. It is the adult version of college. You see them, you hope to meet them, you in fact get to know them, and you tell your friends about it.

Your married friends might think that you are unique, or that you have found your second wind when it comes to adolescent behavior, but for Baby Boomers this is part of the new stage of life. Perhaps in a another column, we might deal with the dating as it affects divorced Baby Boomers, certainly that has its own menu, but for now let us stick to the situation as it affects the remaining spouse. The reason why the two are different is because, many times, the second love happens without the individual who has lost their spouse knowing it is happening.

There is the Baby Boomer who every morning goes for a walk, sits on a park bench, and reads the paper. One day, a woman runs by, and soon as days go on, you talk to her, you like her, and find that she has the qualities that you admire. The best example of what is being discussed here is that which is depicted in the movie "Sleepless in Seattle." Baby Boomers love that movie. Tom Hanks finds love the second time around, after losing a woman that he loved, when he through Hollywood magic he meets Meg Ryan. What Nora Ephron created, and Rob Reiner brought to screen, was a Baby Boomer story, just a bit ahead of its time. For what Tom Hanks comes to feel for Meg Ryan's character is what many Baby Boomers report happening to them while loving the second time around.

Saturday, July 9, 2011

Family and Divorce

In the Review section of The Wall Street Journal, covering Saturday and Sunday [7/9-7/10-2011] a story appeared titled "The Divorce Generation." It was written by Susan Gregory Thomas. It was advanced from "In Spite of Everything A Memoir " by Susan Gregory Thomas, to be published by Random House. The piece looks at Generation Xers who are determined to keep their marriages together. The reason that this is so paramount to them is because their generation survived their own family splits. Of course, the reason that this is so germane to Baby Boomers is because they were the parents doing the separation. Ms. Thomas, in the article, does a great job of taking the reader through the generational differences in marriages and families, highlighting, for example that the Greatest Generation married earlier in life than later generations. The Baby Boomer generation, meanwhile experienced a higher divorce rate, which unfortunately resulted in many Generation Xers growing up in "broken homes." She details the pain and suffering that many Generation Xers endured as result of their Baby Boomer parents' split, and how these Generation Xers, now married themselves, are determined that it will be different for them. From the perspective of the Baby Boomer generation as parents, the mistakes they made are serving as lessons for their own children.

Baby Boomers, for the most part, rejected their parent's lifestyle, for good and for bad. The good was the changing roles for women, career opportunities, sports equality, and equal footing in a marriage. But there were some bad changes along the way as it relates to impact on marriage and family. The Baby Boomer generation ushered in greater sexual freedom, pushed the envelope on drugs, and did not always comply with the commitment part of the marriage pact. New freedom sometimes meant exiting out of marriages without making much effort to work through the issues. However, in other cases Baby Boomers did a service to society by making it more feasible for people to end truly bad marriages. In earlier times the fear of being ostracized might have led some people to stay in marriages that had no hope of being rescued. Sometimes, people marry the wrong people and it is better for all concerned to end the marriage. The "staying together for the sake of the kids" mantra of the previous generation, in some cases, did more harm than good.

Baby Boomers gave us some different kinds of families, like step families and blended families, which had positive impact on the children of Generation X, and that has to be noted. But to be fair, a lot of Baby Boomers did not take their marriage as seriously as they should have, and the results speak for themselves. These Baby Boomers did create the high divorce rate; the 50 percent of all marriages failing statistic is a Baby Boomer stat. One has to look back at the times to understand why things happen. The Greatest Generation came home from World War II, started families (Baby Boomers), and that was the action of the times. Baby Boomers grew up, went to college, and rebelled against the status quo. The change component is painted all over the Baby Boomer times of their lives. Suddenly, to some Baby Boomers, marriage and family in its traditional form seemed boring. Remember that Baby Boomers are the generation that thought they could have it all. Well, life does not work that way. Marriage, like any other relationship or enterprise, is not always easy, and to be a success, it takes work and compromise.

Baby Boomers who made that investment have been rewarded. Baby Boomers who found happiness in second marriages were also rewarded because, for the most part, they did find their true love. The Baby Boomer who continuously cheated the system still searches. But credit must go to this new generation who seeks commitment and stable families for their children. In some ways, they better resemble their grandparents then their parents. But there were some single mothers who sacrificed everything for their children and those Baby Boomers should be applauded, not run from, or thought less of by this current generation. Decisions in life have an impact, and marriage and family are at the high end of the stakes game. Most get it right, whether it is to stay in a marriage or divorce, and that should be what gets noticed.

Wednesday, July 6, 2011

Dating and Marriage at this stage of Life

On July 4th in The San Diego Union Tribune a question was posed in the Dear Abby section. It dealt with a topic facing many Baby Boomers today. A woman said that she has been dating a man and they have become engaged. She detailed that they had both been married before and she was struggling with her place in his life, due to his adult children. She was hurt because Eugene, her soon-to-be husband, always makes a point to let her know that his children come first. This is just one of many dynamics facing Baby Boomers as they seek happiness.

Let us first begin with dating. Baby Boomers report the struggle either to meet someone nice that is age appropriate, or the conflict with sharing a life, when they are used to being alone. What does dating mean at this age? Is it companionship, friends to spend time with, or does it still involve courtship? By the way, courtship may be a word outdated to some, but not to Baby Boomers. Because Baby Boomers still have a bit of romance in them, and they believe the right person may be out there even if they are, as they say, of a certain age. Life does not stop, and though some rules have changed from the time you were 19, who amongst us do not get that same thrill from the new encounter with the person who may have potential. However, it is different from your courtship after college, and there are some issues.

Another possible problem is money. If you are lucky to meet someone nice, and in fact, want to spend the rest of your life together, you have a whole lifetime of assets and earnings that are now brought to the table. It is obvious what might occur when one partner is in a different tax bracket than the other. Then, there is what some Baby Boomers call "the elephant in the room," sometimes known as differences in lifestyles. Who pays for what, where do you live, what are the rules, and how do you manage the finances? Some Baby Boomers report on this topic that a separate but equal mindset comes into play. This means that the relationship is on equal footing, but the finances stay separate. This comes into play most often when your partner has his or her Estate planned and the proceeds go to the children.

A couple in Oregon found the nightmare, not the silver lining. Both widowed, they thought that they found their soul mate. They married and moved to Palm Springs. They bought a house, but as it turned out, mostly from the proceeds of the man. After a few years, he changed his will to accommodate his new wife. They, by all accounts, were happy and living out their years on the golf course, going to dinner, and entertaining friends. They were happy until the man died, and his children took the woman to court. In this case, lack of communication regarding what the couple was doing and leaving the children in the dark led to unnecessary discontent. This on the surface is the kind of scare that keeps Baby Boomers from achieving happiness.

It is the pursuit of happiness that leads Baby Boomers to consider marriage. Although becoming a couple at a later stage of life usually requires making some significant adjustments, many Baby Boomers feel this beats the alternative of living life alone. These situations are more common for this generation because many Baby Boomers held off on getting married until later in life. There were career interests and goals of many sorts that took precedence over marriage. Now, those priorities seem a little less important, and for some, are in the rear view mirror.

Baby Boomers report that those in this situation are ready for a meaningful commitment. However, the partner that they choose or have found may have had a different background, and both parties, for the sake of their future, must find common ground. Baby Boomers report that, while these situations are sometimes hard to navigate, the end result is worth the risk and the effort. Baby Boomers have always been different than their predecessor, "The Greatest Generation." That generation, in most cases, had a formula. Marry young, raise children, stay married, and maybe celebrate a golden anniversary. Baby Boomers have had it more complex with changing roles, woman in the work place, and, yes, divorce rates. So the rules are different, and Baby Boomers may be best served by following their heart. Know that once again Baby Boomers are setting new standards, in this case for dating and marriage at this stage of life.

Summary – Chapter 11

Marriage, Family, and Baby Boomers Dating

On a crisp April morning, if San Diego and crisp can ever be used in the same sentence, a Baby Boomer met the love of his life. Sitting on a bench reading the newspaper, with the Pacific Ocean as a back drop, the "one and only" walked into his life. Well, truth be told, she ran into his life. For a time, this Baby Boomer would sit in the idyllic setting, and watch as this pretty distance runner would run by. Finally, with the courage of the patriots of "Bunker Hill," he got off the bench and did what all need to do: he said, "hello." The woman was so very smart, articulate, with a kindness to match the beauty of her facial features. Her blond hair was a companion for her bright expressive eyes. She was a bit shy at first, reserved, but in a polite way, as she answered the Baby Boomer man's inquiry. The ritual of the hello became a staple of these two morning enthusiasts. Soon, that meeting each morning became part of their routine, and something that each of them would look forward to.

As time went on, they would take walks together and later enjoy the scenes and sights of beach front in the beautiful North County of San Diego. As days turned to months, these two professionals, one a Scientist and the other a business professional, found that they had common values on family, like the respect of parents, siblings, and extended family. They found common ground in social relationships, like the kindness, consideration, and care that goes with being a friend. But most importantly, they came to the realization that each was a special person, who could bring joy and happiness, not only to the present, but also to their future.

I am familiar with this Baby Boomer story. As a matter of fact, it could be said that I have firsthand experience. It can be pointed out that all of my reference to the Baby Boomer seeking and finding love, commitment, and "ever after" has data in this story. For it is my story, and Lisa Marie's. You might recognize that name from the dedication at the front of this book. Our relationship is a microcosm for so many Baby Boomers, who worked hard, were absorbed in their career, and never found the person to spend their life with. Baby Boomers in this situation who went to school, worked hard to build a career, and worked long hours to make something of themselves, did often pay the price when it came to relationships. Many Baby Boomers, so intent in climbing the corporate ladder, did leave something behind. Amidst the plane travel, the meetings, and the long hours in the office, time and energy for marriage and family was sacrificed. In another part of this book, a comment was made about a Baby Boomer woman, who I met in my travels interviewing Baby Boomers. She was the woman who was attending the Elder Hostel. What she said always stays with me, for it was the phrase, "Yes, you can have it all, just not all at once."

So, it is with Rick and Lisa, who met and found that luck was on their side to have been able to have found that compatible person, to love "in sickness and in health, to death do us part." They are the kind of couple that when one starts a sentence, the other can finish it, and when one says something, it turns out to be exactly what the other person was thinking. It is the kind of relationship that when you look into the eyes of the other person, you see bliss, support, and a sense of unity that can only be shared with the right person.

Baby Boomers across America are asking themselves, "Am I fulfilled?" Baby Boomers at their current age recognize that they have worked hard and met a lot of their goals. Baby Boomers today are actually focused on doing checks and balances regarding the objectives of their youth. This brings about an examination of how they want to live out the rest of their life. May it be in the past or in the present, Baby Boomers have always found the concept of a life partner to be extremely important. It could be said that Baby Boomers want something beyond a soul mate; what they really desire is a true mate for all things that define the soul. There are Baby Boomers across this country who are searching for and finding the relationship that will make a difference in their life.

So, if Rick and Lisa are emblematic of this Baby Boomer finding love at a later stage in life, how does the story end? And does their story give hope to other Baby Boomers? Read the following, and you be the judge. In October of 2012, Lisa went to Chicago with Rick. Rick's brother and sister-in-law picked them up at the airport, took them to dinner, and welcomed Lisa to the family. Then, as a part of what would be later termed "engagement week," Rick's Uncle Joe and Aunt Fran gave them an engagement party, where the whole family attended. Lisa felt so comfortable, and so much a part of the family she was marrying into. Rick and Lisa then proceeded to Columbus, Ohio, where Lisa's family was so delighted to share in the happiness. Lisa's parents not only approved of this new phase of Lisa's life, but saw a new happiness about her.

On October 23, on the day of Lisa's mother's birthday, Rick proposed. The ring that he slipped on Lisa's finger had been her grandmother's engagement ring. He proposed on a bench, in a beautiful park at sunset, with church bells ringing, and the fall colors lighting up the moment. They met when Rick was sitting on a bench, they courted sitting on a bench looking at the Pacific Ocean, and Lisa accepted engagement, on a bench in her home town of Upper Arlington, Ohio.

Epilogue

On a day with a light gentle breeze, in June of 2009, in Santa Barbara, California, I phoned my best friend, Professor David Mallory Boush. As a respected expert in Marketing, he and his distinguished colleagues had published a book on the subject. He had sent it to me with a kind inscription emblematic of the brotherly relationship that we have had for over forty years. I called him from the outside of a Salvation Army facility on Hollister Street; ironically, it was a quiet spot. I would later think that it was an odd place from which to call. I had read his book, mostly while sitting in the Goleta coffee shop, an eclectic place for reflection. I was doing much of that at the time, wondering about the future. My parents and my oldest brother had passed away. My corporate career was coming to a close, and I had the real sense that I was alone in the world.

I had the blues, as I like to describe it – a nice way of saying things were not quite right. My buddy, true to his word, had stuck by me even though each of our Wednesday calls were getting more mundane. One glimmer of hope was this project that he had helped me define, to chronicle the Baby Boomer generation. Thus, the project that had started as a search for "myself," then evolved to become a search for my generation. Somehow, the idea of traveling the country and speaking to my peers seemed like a novel idea. For in them, perhaps I would discover myself. Both were achieved. In this book, you see commentary on a generation, by the mere formula of taking "planes, trains, and automobiles," as the saying goes, and just simply asking questions of fellow Baby Boomers. It was a discovery process that I will forever cherish. The memories are long, the observation intensive, and the discovery inspiring.

When the travel was complete, I began spending time in one of the most beautiful communities anywhere, Del Mar, California. I decided to communicate what I had learned. I began by writing a blog with my findings and insights about Baby Boomers. Many of those columns of commentary are contained in this book. I also began using Social Media to promote what I was writing and commenting on. I discovered wonderful Baby Boomer groups on Social Media that helped me to better understand the Baby Boomer demographic.

Soon, something else happened. I seemed to get my step back, I was communicating with family again, and that best friend who had helped me articulate my mission, was now saying, in support, that a cottage industry was indeed possible. He agreed that what I had learned, studied, and communicated with and for my generation was now transferable to business. My key goal of making a contribution to society was also now becoming a reality. One further highlight that occurred at this time is that I met a wonderful woman, who later became my wife.

Back in 2007, when I would describe my lack of interest in the business world, people who knew me were puzzled, for I had always seemed to love it. I fed off the experience of interacting with people in the workplace setting. But my drive had been stripped from me slowly, with my elderly parents becoming sick and passing. My older brother, a link to the life of the past, now had passed away. It seemed the only thing that I was now good at was grief.

But the study of Baby Boomers, my generation, was even helped by my loss. I discovered Baby Boomers who had lost a spouse, lost parents, and were also hurting. But something significant took shape, and by seeing and observing the lives of others, I discovered myself again, and found out a great deal as I searched for the Baby Boomer generation.

Ever since I started this journey back in 2009, this has been a labor of love. I started out in Stockton, California, at that time the foreclosure capital of America. I traveled by train across America. I had a stop to honor my late brother in Memphis, Tennessee. He had been active with St. Jude's hospital. They honored him with a wonderful service conducted by a Baby Boomer chaplain. I visited Italy, and saw the town where my father was born. I will always be grateful to the tour guide in Rome, a Baby Boomer, who helped me to see Italy. He also helped send me on my way to see my Dad's town in Calabria.

I remember picking five places for Baby Boomers to retire and not only going and living in each community, but writing about them. I remember picking out the best places for Baby Boomers to vacation, while enjoying and communicating about those communities.

All in all, I went coast to coast, interviewing hundreds of Baby Boomers. While traveling on the train, I engaged many Baby Boomers in in-depth conversations. I spent time talking to Baby Boomers in Starbucks or McDonalds. I spent time talking to Baby Boomers outside of libraries or the inside of Major League baseball stadiums. I watched some Baby Boomers donate their money in Las Vegas, and also watched other Boomers give to more worthy charities. I saw assisted living facilities first-hand, witnessed Baby Boomers as caregivers, and sat with them in bereavement counseling in the Coachella Valley (Palm Springs surrounding area). In a way, the stories that I wrote, over time, wrote themselves due to the many Baby Boomers who had a sharing heart and wanted to communicate about their generation.

I had begun a study of my generation because I had a true interest in where our generation has been, where we our now, and what the future may be like for our always interesting group. I was indeed able to find what I was searching for.

What I have found is that Baby Boomers continue to define themselves. It was the generation that came after what Tom Brokaw titled his book, the "Greatest Generation." It was a generation that ushered in growth in schools, campus unrest, and women's rights and is now changing what the definition "the Golden Years" should be. The generation that gave us the Reagan Revolution, corporate life, and the first Baby Boomer president, Bill Clinton, now asks the question, according to the AARP campaign – "What do I want to be when I grow up?"

Representative of what I am speaking to in this book is a woman I met from Erie, Pennsylvania. She reported that in high school, she was "Hell on Wheels." Then, at 59, she retired as a teacher from that same high school, and now she is delivering "Meals on Wheels." I wanted to tell her story, and the stories of many others like her, in this book about our generation. When I reflect on my own life, it seems, in many ways, to mirror the life of the woman from Erie and the lives of many of the other Baby Boomers that I interviewed. My parents wanted to make sure that I got an education and that I pursued my goals to reach my full career potential and aspirations. Now, like other Baby Boomers, I look for fulfillment in the future. Boomers are thinking about what is next. Does that mean travel, volunteer opportunities, or continued work? As for myself, I can only comment that I want to continue to make a contribution to society. Corporate work is only a memory now, and with this work, as an observer and spokesperson for my generation, passion has now become my vocation.

What you have seen in this book are three things: personal reflection, observation, and some conclusions. As a Baby Boomer, I believe my own life has been emblematic, of my generation, the Baby Boomers. I believe that traveling the country and talking with Baby Boomers has shed some light on the past, present, and future of this generation. The Baby Boomer generation is unique. What makes it unique is its sheer volume of population, the change in society that Baby Boomers have lived through, and their unwillingness to go quietly. They are not a "sit on the sidelines" kind of generation.

It remains a generation with buying power, staying power, and opinion. The Baby Boomer generation has embraced change like no other generation. The Baby Boomers were a group that started as President Truman integrated the armed forces, and they have lived to see the first black man become President. It is a generation, who saw the rise of the New Frontier, under President Kennedy, and also witnessed its darkest moment when he was shot in 1963. It is a generation whose members were school children during the "Cold War," and who suffered mental ice breakers on September 11th, 2001. It is a generation that started their work life when assistants were called secretaries, but that would later learn to use their personal computers to serve their own secretarial needs. It was a generation that protested the war in Vietnam, became disillusioned over Watergate, and then saw a fellow Baby Boomer, Bill Clinton, become President.

I am proud to be a Baby Boomer, I am proud of our generation. Such areas as elderly care for parents, finding marriage late in life, or a second career are every bit as paramount to Baby Boomers today as campus protests, or corporate board meetings were at a different stage of life. We have forever changed the world, for what I would like to think is for the better. Baby Boomers, by my observation, continue to make a difference, and will do so to the end. And along the way, Baby Boomers will still covet their music, remember sports teams, and just maybe continue to grow as people. *In Search of the Baby Boomer Generation* is a continuing journey.

About The Author

Rick Bava was born in Chicago on December 18, 1955, and was raised in the Chicago area. Rick went to the University of Wisconsin, at the age of 16, on a tennis scholarship. While studying at UW, he advanced to play tennis on a professional level and later became successful teaching tennis. Rick also had a radio commentary and newspaper column, both titled "Tennis Tips," and was honored at a very young age to be a member of the PENN Advisory staff.

Rick earned his Bachelor's degree in Communication Arts from UW, Madison studying under Professor Winston Brembeck, a leading authority in the field. He expanded his education further by taking graduate courses at Harvard's Extension Program before beginning his business career. Rick quickly become a business pioneer in the field of Personal Computers, gaining acclaim with Commodore Business Machines. He went on to enjoy a successful 30-year corporate career, working his way up to become the Senior Head of External Affairs for the Computer Services division of the Boeing Company, followed by his role as the Director of World Wide Business Development for Digital Equipment Corporation's Services Division. In 2002, Rick founded and was CEO of his own company, the Bava Group, which became the premier communications consulting firm serving the Fortune 500 community.

After leaving the corporate world, Rick began contemplating what many Baby Boomers refer to as an "encore career." The Baby Boomer generation is enormous in size, experiences, and its impact on society. Rick's communication and marketing skills led him to notice a void in the way the Baby Boomer generation's story was being told. The combination of Rick's personality, educational background, his own life experiences, his natural curiosity about people and his keen observational skills made him uniquely qualified to chronicle the Baby Boomer generation.

To understand the Baby Boomer generation that he has been so much a part of, Rick travelled through the United States for two years, having in-depth conversations with hundreds of Boomers across all socio-economic classes. These interviews became the basis for his popular blog columns "Rick Bava on the Baby Boomer Generation." His blog became very popular among Baby Boomers with personal interest in his columns, and also generated great attention from a vast number of businesses and marketing firms catering to the Baby Boomer generation, who recognized his growing reputation as a Baby Boomer thought leader and influencer. As a result of this prominent, influential blog that addressed the topics most vital to the Baby Boomer generation, Rick was invited to be the keynote speaker at the forum "Baby Boomers in the 21st Century."

But tragedy temporarily turned his life upside-down after he was badly injured in a hit-and-run car accident in May of 2012. Rick emerged from this major setback with more motivation and resilience than ever to represent the Baby Boomers of America.

Today, Rick continues to engage many thousands of Baby Boomers with his insightful commentary about America's 78 million Boomers. He captivates and inspires Baby Boomers nationwide with his monthly column "The Baby Boomer Corner" in Today's Senior Magazine. Rick also continues to keep his eye on the pulse of the Baby Boomer Generation through his association with the Boomer Nation Radio Show. His commentary focuses on the diverse lifestyles and life changes of Baby

Boomers, as well as their goals and thoughts for today and the future. With his magazine and internet columns, radio shows, keynote speeches, and Social Media messages and now this tantalizing new book, *In Search of the Baby Boomer Generation*, Rick is frequently referred to as "a Thought Leader for Baby Boomer Generation."

Rick currently lives in San Diego, California with his wife, Lisa.